MATT AND TOM OLDFIELD

ULTIMATE
FOOTBALL HEROES

SUPERSTARS
KANE · MAGUIRE · TRIPPIER

FROM THE PLAYGROUND
TO THE PITCH

DINO

Published by Dino Books
an imprint of John Blake Publishing
3 Bramber Court, 2 Bramber Road,
London W14 9PB, England

www.johnblakepublishing.co.uk

www.facebook.com/johnblakebooks 🔲
twitter.com/jblakebooks 🔲

Kane first published in 2017
Maguire first published in 2018
Trippier first published in 2018
This collected edition published in 2018

ISBN: 978 1 78946 068 1

British Library Cataloguing-in-Publication Data:

A catalogue record for this book is available from the British Library.

Design by www.envydesign.co.uk

Printed and bound in Great Britain by Clays Ltd, Elcograf S.p.A.

1 3 5 7 9 10 8 6 4 2

Papers used by John Blake Publishing are natural, recyclable products made from
wood grown in sustainable forests. The manufacturing processes conform to the
environmental regulations of the country of origin.

Every attempt has been made to contact the relevant copyright-holders, but some
were unobtainable. We would be grateful if the appropriate people could contact us.

John Blake Publishing is an imprint of Bonnier Book UK
www.bonnierbooks.co.uk

For Noah and Nico,
Southampton's future strikeforce

ULTIMATE
FOOTBALL HEROES

Matt Oldfield is an accomplished writer and the editor-in-chief of football review site *Of Pitch & Page*. Tom Oldfield is a freelance sports writer and the author of biographies on Cristiano Ronaldo, Arsène Wenger and Rafael Nadal.

Cover illustration by Dan Leydon.
To learn more about Dan visit danleydon.com
To purchase his artwork visit etsy.com/shop/footynews
Or just follow him on Twitter @danleydon

KANE

TABLE OF CONTENTS

CHAPTER 1

ENGLAND HERO

Thursday, 5 October 2017

In the Wembley tunnel, Harry closed his eyes and soaked up the amazing atmosphere. He was back at the home of football, the stadium where he had first achieved his childhood dream of playing for England. 19 March 2015, England vs Lithuania – he remembered that game like it was yesterday. He had scored that day and now, with England facing Slovenia, he needed to do it again. As England's captain and Number 9, it was his job to shoot them to the 2018 World Cup.

'Come on, lads!' Harry called out to his teammates behind him: friends like Joe Hart, Kyle Walker and

Eric Dier. It was a real honour to be their leader. With a victory over Slovenia, they would all be on their way to the biggest tournament of their lives in Russia.

Harry looked down at the young mascot by his side and smiled at him. 'Right, let's do this!'

As the two of them led the England team out onto the pitch, the fans clapped and cheered. Harry didn't look up at the thousands of faces and flags; instead, he looked down at the grass in front of him. He was totally focused on his task: scoring goals and beating Slovenia.

'If you get a chance, test the keeper,' Harry said to his partners in attack, Raheem Sterling and Marcus Rashford, before kick-off. 'I'll be there for the rebound!'

Harry's new Premiership season with Tottenham Hotspur had not begun well in August, but by September he was back to his lethal best. That month alone, he scored an incredible thirteen goals, including two goals for England against Malta. He could score every type of goal – tap-ins, headers, one-on-ones, long-range shots, penalties, even free kicks. That's what made him such a dangerous striker.

With Slovenia defending well, Harry didn't get many chances in the first half. He got in good positions but the final ball never arrived.

'There's no need to panic yet,' Harry told his teammates in the dressing room. He really didn't want a repeat of England's terrible performance against Iceland at Euro 2016. That match still haunted him. 'We're good enough to win this by playing our natural game. Be patient!'

As Ryan Bertrand dribbled down the left wing, Harry sprinted towards the six-yard box. Ryan's cross didn't reach him but the ball fell to Raheem instead. His shot was going in until a defender deflected it wide.

'Unlucky!' Harry shouted, putting his hands on his head. 'Keep going, we're going to score!'

Without this kind of strong self-belief, Harry would never have made it to the top of European football. There had been lots of setbacks along the way: rejections, disappointments and bad form. But every time, Harry bounced back with crucial goals at crucial moments. That's what made him such a superstar.

A matter of seconds later, a rebound fell to him on the edge of the penalty area. Surely, this was his moment. He pulled back his left foot and curled a powerful shot towards the bottom corner. The fans were already up on their feet, ready to celebrate. Harry never missed... but this time he did. The ball flew just wide of the post. Harry couldn't believe it. He looked up at the sky and sighed.

On the sideline, England manager Gareth Southgate cheered his team on. 'That's much better – the goal is coming, lads!'

But after ninety minutes, the goal still hadn't come. The fourth official raised his board: eight minutes of injury time.

'It's not over yet, boys!' Harry shouted, to inspire his teammates.

The Slovenian goalkeeper tried to throw the ball out to his left-back but Kyle got there first. Straight away, Harry was on the move from the back post to the front post. After playing together for years at Tottenham, they knew how to score great goals.

As Kyle crossed it in, Harry used his burst of speed to get in front of the centre-back. Again, the England supporters stood and waited anxiously. The ball was perfect and Harry stretched out his long right leg to meet it. The keeper got a touch on his shot but he couldn't keep it out.

Goooooooooooooaaaaaaaaaaaaaaaaaaalllllllllllllllllllllllllllllll!!!!!!!!!!!!!!!!!!!!!!

He had done it! Joy, relief, pride – Harry felt every emotion as he ran towards the fans. This time, he hadn't let them down. He held up the Three Lions on his shirt and screamed until his throat got sore.

'Captain to the rescue!' Kyle laughed as they hugged by the corner flag.

'No, it was all thanks to you!' Harry replied.

At the final whistle, he threw his arms up in the air. It was a phenomenal feeling to qualify for the 2018 World Cup. He couldn't wait to lead England to glory.

'We are off to Russia!' a voice shouted over the loudspeakers and the whole stadium cheered.

It was yet another moment that Harry would never forget. Against the odds, he was making his childhood dreams come true. He was the star striker for Tottenham, the club that he had supported all his life. And now, like his hero David Beckham, he was the captain of England.

Harry had never given up, even when it looked like he wouldn't make it as a professional footballer. With the support of his family and his coaches, and lots of hard work and dedication, he had proved everyone wrong to become a world-class goal machine.

It had been an incredible journey from Walthamstow to Wembley, and Harry was only just getting started.

CHAPTER 2

ALWAYS KICKING

'Mum!' Charlie shouted, stamping his feet.

Kim sighed and put her magazine down. 'What's happened now?'

'I spent ages building a Lego tower and Harry just kicked it over,' her older son answered. 'That was *my* tower!'

'I'm sorry, darling, but I'm sure Harry didn't mean it. Your brother doesn't know what he's doing with his little feet yet.'

Harry was nearly two years old and he was always on the move around their house in Walthamstow, North London. He had a few bumps on his head but it was his legs that caused the most trouble. Everywhere he went, they never stopped kicking.

Kim wasn't surprised, though.

'Do you remember before your brother was born when he was still in my tummy?' she asked Charlie as she lifted Harry up onto the sofa. Charlie didn't reply; he was busy building a new tower. 'He was always kicking, even back then, wasn't he? I didn't get a good night's sleep for months!'

Kim held Harry up in the air to give his legs room to swing. 'No, you don't like letting me sleep, do you?' He smiled and wiggled his hands and feet. 'I knew you'd be a boy; there was no doubt about that. I told your Daddy that you were going to be sporty and do you know what he said? He said, "Great, he'll play for TOTTENHAM!"'

Harry's smile grew wider when he heard the name of their local football club. It was a word that his dad, Pat, said so often that it had become his favourite word. The Kane family lived only five miles away from Tottenham's stadium, White Hart Lane.

'Wow, you really love that idea, don't you!' Kim laughed. 'Well, your Grandad Eric was a good footballer in his day. Maybe you'll get his talent, rather than your Dad's. Bless him, he always says that bad injuries ruined his career but I think it was his bad first touch!'

It was a bright, sunny afternoon and so Kim took her two sons out to the local park. Hopefully, after a few hours of open space and fresh air, Charlie and Harry would sleep well that night, and so would their mum. Once they found a shady spot on the grass, Kim lay down the picnic rug and lifted Harry out of the pushchair.

'Charlie, you've got to stay where I can see you!' she called out as he chased after a squirrel.

After doing a few laps of the rug, Harry sat down and looked around him. He saw leaves and twigs and insects. He saw huge trees above him and patches of blue sky in between. Then his eyes fixed on the exciting scene in front of him. A group of kids were playing football with jumpers for goalposts. That looked like fun. He stood up and went over to explore.

'Harry, stop!' Kim shouted. She chased after her son and scooped him up just before he reached the other kids' football game. In her arms, Harry kept watching and his legs kept moving. He was desperate to kick the ball.

'Not today, darling,' his mum said, giving him a kiss on the cheek. 'But soon, I promise!'

*

'So, how was your day?' Pat asked, as they all ate dinner together. After a long day's work at the garage, he loved to come home to his happy family.

Charlie could now feed himself like a grown-up but Harry still needed a high chair and some help. Even with Pat holding the spoon, Harry got strawberry yoghurt all over his hands and face.

'I built an awesome tower but Harry broke it with his silly little feet,' Charlie told his dad. He was looking for sympathy, but Pat had other ideas.

'Good, your brother's getting ready for his big Tottenham career! Football runs in the family, you know. Just ask your Grandad – I was one of Ireland's best young players but sadly...'

Kim rolled her eyes. Not again! She decided not to mention Harry's kicking in the park. It would only get her husband's hopes up even more.

CHAPTER 3

HEROES AT WHITE HART LANE

'Have you been good boys today?' Pat asked his sons one evening as they all ate dinner together.

Charlie and Harry knew the right answer. 'Yes!'

Their dad smiled and reached into his trouser pocket. He took out three rectangles of white card and placed them down on the table. Then he watched and waited for his sons' reactions.

Harry thought he knew what they were but he didn't want to get his hopes up until he was sure. His dad had promised him that he could go to his first Tottenham game once he turned four. For his birthday, he got a Spurs shirt and a Spurs football, but no Spurs ticket. Charlie had been to White Hart Lane a few times and Harry was desperate to join them. Was his dream finally going to come true? There in the top left corner was the important word, written in navy blue – 'Tottenham'. He was right; they *were* match tickets! Harry jumped for joy.

'Wow, thanks!' he said, running over to give his dad a big hug. 'This is the best gift ever!'

Suddenly, Harry and Charlie weren't interested in eating anymore. Instead, they ran around the living room, waving the tickets in the air and chanting, 'We're going to White Hart Lane! We're going to White Hart Lane!'

Kim laughed. 'You'll need to keep a close eye on them,' she warned her husband. 'This is just the start!'

'Yes, I think I'll look after these,' Pat said, taking the tickets back from his over-excited sons.

It was a three o'clock kick-off on Saturday but Harry and Charlie were sitting in their Tottenham shirts at breakfast. They spent the morning playing football in the garden, pretending to be their heroes.

'David Ginola gets the ball on the left,' Charlie began the commentary, 'he dribbles past one defender and then another. Look at that skill! He's just outside the penalty area now, he looks up and...'

Harry didn't like playing in goal against his brother. He hardly ever made a save because Charlie's shots were too powerful.

...*Gooooooooooooooooooooaaaaaaaaaallllllllllllllllllllll llllllllllllll!!!!!!!!!!!!!!!!!!!!*

Charlie ran towards the corner of the garden and celebrated by pulling his Spurs shirt over his head.

'Right, my turn!' Harry said, picking up the ball.

His number one hero, Teddy Sheringham, had just left Tottenham to sign for Manchester United. But Harry already had his new favourite – German Jürgen Klinsmann. It was a hard name for a four-year-old to say but Harry did his best.

'Kiman runs towards the penalty area...'

He needed to strike the ball perfectly if he wanted to score past his older brother. Harry looked up at the goal and kicked it as hard as he could. The ball bounced and skipped towards the bottom corner...

...*Gooooooooooooooooooooaaaaaaaaaaaaaallllllllllllll llllllllllllll!!!!!!!!!!!!!!!!!!!!*

Normally, Harry celebrated with the Klinsmann dive but his Spurs shirt was white and he couldn't make his White Hart Lane debut wearing a muddy shirt! So instead, he jumped up and pumped his fist. He could tell that it was going to be a very good day.

After lunch, it was finally time for them to leave.

'Have you got your hats?' Kim asked at the front door.

Harry nodded.

'Gloves?'

Harry nodded.

'Good, stay close to your dad and have a great time!'

They were off! Harry couldn't wait to get to White Hart Lane. On the bus, he imagined the people, the noise, the goals. As they crossed through the Walthamstow reservoirs, Charlie had a thought.

'Dad, have you got the tickets?'

There was panic on Pat's face as he checked all of his pockets, once and then twice. 'Oh dear,' he muttered.

Harry's face dropped with disappointment. How had his dad forgotten the tickets? Why hadn't he checked before they left?

Suddenly, a smile spread across Pat's face, and he held up the tickets. 'Just kidding!' he cheered.

'Dad, don't scare us like that!' Harry shouted. He didn't find the joke funny at all.

When they got off the bus, the stadium was right there in front of them. Harry stood there looking up, his mouth wide open. It was even bigger than he'd expected.

'Come on, let's go in and find our seats!' his dad said. 'Don't let go of my hand, okay? If you get lost, Mum won't ever let us come back.'

Harry held on tightly as they moved through the crowds towards the turnstile, on their way to their seats. There were so many people everywhere and so much to see and hear.

'Get today's match programme here!' the sellers shouted.

Some Tottenham fans talked about their players in between bites of burgers and hot dogs. Other

Tottenham fans were already singing songs even before they entered the stadium. It was all so exciting.

Once they were through the turnstile, Harry could see a square of green in the distance. His eyes lit up – the pitch! As they got closer, he couldn't believe the size of it. How did the players keep running from box to box for ninety minutes? It looked impossible.

'Look, there's Ginola!' Charlie shouted, pointing down at the players warming up. 'And there's Klinsmann!'

Harry stood up on his seat to get a better view. He was in the same stadium as his heroes; it didn't get any better than that.

Tottenham, Tottenham!

As the players ran out of the tunnel for the start of the game, the noise grew even louder. Spurs needed a win to stay out of the relegation zone. After a few minutes, Ginola got the ball on the left wing.

'Come on!' the Tottenham fans cheered, rising to their feet.

Ginola curled a brilliant cross into the penalty area. Harry held his breath as Klinsmann stretched to reach it...

Gooooooooooooooooooooooaaaaaaaaaaaaaaaaaaalllll lllllllllllllllllllllll!!!!!!!!!!!!!!!!!!!!!!

What a start! Harry and Charlie jumped up and down together, cheering for their heroes.

The rest of the match was very tense but Tottenham held on for the victory. By the final whistle, Harry was exhausted but very happy. He was already looking forward to his next trip to White Hart Lane.

'So, who was man of the match?' Pat asked his sons on the bus home.

'Ginola!' Charlie replied.

'Klinsmann!' Harry replied.

Their dad shook his head. 'If we ever keep a clean sheet, it's always the goalkeeper!'

CHAPTER 4

RIDGEWAY ROVERS

'Why do we have to leave?' Charlie cried out. 'It's not fair. This is our home!'

Their parents had just given them some terrible news; the family was moving from Walthamstow to Chingford. They had never even heard of Chingford.

'We'll have more space there,' Kim replied. 'You'll have bigger bedrooms and a bigger football pitch in the garden too.'

'Look, we're not talking about Australia!' Pat said. 'Chingford is only a few miles away.'

'But all our friends are *here*,' Charlie argued.

As the conversation carried on, Harry had an important question to ask: 'How far is it from White Hart Lane?'

'It's only five miles away, the same distance as now.'

Kim and Pat finally won the family argument with a killer fact: David Beckham had grown up in Chingford.

'Really?' Harry asked excitedly. After the 1998 World Cup, Beckham was England's most famous footballer. Despite his red card versus Argentina, every kid in the country wanted to look and play like Becks.

His dad nodded. 'He played for a local team called Ridgeway Rovers.'

'Cool, can I play for Ridgeway Rovers too?'

'It's a deal!' Kim said, looking relieved.

Harry was determined to become a star striker for Tottenham and England, especially after visiting White Hart Lane. He practised all the time, with whatever he could find. In the garden and the park, he played with his own real football. It was his pride and joy, and he looked after it carefully. In the street, he played with any can or bottle that he could find. In the house, he swapped his football for rolled-up socks.

'STOP KICKING THINGS!' Charlie shouted angrily from through his bedroom door.

'Sorry!' Harry replied quickly, running downstairs to help with dinner. He had been using his brother's door as a shooting target again. He knew that it wasn't allowed but he just couldn't help himself.

'Can I join Ridgeway Rovers now?' Harry asked his parents as they sat down to eat. He was desperate to test his talent against real opponents on a real pitch.

Pat knew that his son wasn't going to give up until it was sorted. Fifteen minutes later, he returned to the living room with good news. 'The Ridgeway Rovers trials are coming up in a couple of weeks. I'll take you along.'

'Thanks!' Harry cheered. He couldn't wait to follow in Becks' footsteps. But first, he had lots more practice to do.

'It's great to see so many of you down here,' Dave Bricknell, the Ridgeway Rovers coach, told the eager young faces at Loughton Rugby Club. 'Welcome! Today, we're looking for brilliant new players to join our club, but most importantly, we're going to have some fun, yes?'

'YES!' Harry cheered with the other boys.

As they all practised passing in pairs, Dave walked around the pitch. He was looking for a nice touch, as well as accuracy and power in the pass.

'Very good!' he called out to Harry.

Next up was dribbling. It wasn't Harry's favourite skill but he managed to keep the ball under control as he weaved in and out of the cones. He was relieved when it was over and he had only knocked one over.

'Right, it's the moment you've all been waiting for,' Dave said to the group. 'Shooting! Do we have a goalkeeper here?'

Everyone looked around but no-one stepped forward.

The coach looked surprised. 'Really? Not a single keeper?'

Harry was really looking forward to scoring some goals but he also didn't mind playing in goal, especially if it wasn't Charlie who was shooting at him. Slowly, he raised his arm.

'Great! What's your name?' Dave asked.

'Harry.'

'Thanks, Harry! You'll get a chance to shoot later on, I promise.'

He put on a pair of gloves, walked over to the goal and waited. As the first shot came towards him, he didn't even have to move. He caught the ball and rolled it to the side. The next shot was better and he had to throw himself across the goal to tip it round the post.

'What a save, Harry!' Dave clapped. 'I think we've found our new keeper!'

Harry enjoyed diving around but he didn't want to be Ian Walker or David Seaman. He wanted to be Teddy Sheringham or Jürgen Klinsmann.

'Coach,' he called out after the first round of shots, 'I don't really play in goal. I normally play outfield as a striker.'

'Not again!' Dave thought to himself. Young keepers always got bored and asked to move to attack for the glory. Even so, he made a promise to the boy:

'No problem, I'll put you up front for the match at the end. You're a natural in goal, though!'

Harry waited patiently for his chance to shine. It took a little while, even once the match had started. But finally, his teammate kicked a long pass down the pitch and he was off, sprinting as fast as his little legs could go. He wasn't the fastest but he had a head start because of his clever run.

Harry beat the defender to the ball, took one touch to control it and calmly placed his shot in the bottom corner.

Gooooooooooooooooooooaaaaaaaaaaaaaaaaallllllllllllllll llllllllllllllll!!!!!!!!!!!!!!!!!!!

Ten minutes later, Harry had a hat-trick and a place in the Ridgeway Rovers team.

'You're a natural keeper *and* a natural striker,' Dave laughed. 'I guess you're just a natural footballer!'

Harry couldn't wait for the real matches to begin. As he stepped out onto the field for the first time in the blue and white Ridgeway Rovers shirt, he felt unstoppable. This was it. He was ready for the big time, but was the big time ready for him?

When the ball came to him in the penalty area, Harry took a shot and it deflected off a defender and out for a corner.

'I'll take it!' Harry shouted, chasing over to the flag.

It was a long way from the corner to the penalty area, so he kicked it as hard as he could. The ball flew over the heads of everyone, including the goalkeeper. It landed in the back of the net.

Goooooooooooooaaaaaaaaaaaaaaaaaallllllllllllllllllllllll llllllll!!!!!!!!!!!!!!!!!!!!

Harry punched the air with joy – he was off the mark on his debut! It was a lucky strike but that didn't matter. Would he ever get tired of scoring goals? He really didn't think so.

CHAPTER 5

FOOTBALL, FOOTBALL, FOOTBALL

'That's it! Keep your head steady and lean over the ball as you kick it.'

At the weekends, Harry's dad often helped him with extra training in the back garden. There was so much that he wanted to improve, especially his shooting. He couldn't relax if he wanted to keep his place as Ridgeway Rovers' number one striker.

'Right, I think that's enough,' Pat said after an hour. 'You've got a game later today and you'll be too tired to score.'

'Okay, just three more shots,' Harry begged.

If his dad was busy, he went to the park with Charlie. When Harry was younger, his older brother used to make him stand between two trees and try to save his powerful shots for hours. That wasn't much fun but now that he was eight, Charlie let him join in properly. If there were other kids around, they'd play a big match but if it was just the two of them, they had long, competitive one-on-one battles. Harry was a skilful footballer but his older brother had one weapon that could defeat him: strength.

'Come on, that's not fair!' Harry shouted as he picked himself up off the grass. 'You can't just push me off the ball like that.'

Charlie shrugged. 'That was a shoulder-to-shoulder challenge. It's not my fault that I'm bigger than you.'

It was no use complaining; Harry just had to find other ways to beat his brother. Luckily, he was very determined. A few times he stormed off angrily but most of the time, Harry tried and tried until he succeeded.

'You're definitely getting better, bro!' Charlie told him as they walked back home together for lunch.

Harry smiled proudly; that was his aim. He didn't want to just be an average player; he wanted to become a great player like his Tottenham heroes. He didn't care how much time and effort that would take. Harry played football before school, at break-time, at lunchtime, and then after school too.

'See you later, Mum!' he called out as he gulped down a glass of water and threw his bag down.

Kim didn't need to ask where her son was going. She knew exactly where he would be and what he'd be doing. 'Just be careful and make sure you're back for dinner,' was all she said.

In the summer, Harry and his friends played in the park all day. But in the winter, it was too dark so they swapped grass for tarmac. Under the streetlights, their games could go on much longer, although there were more obstacles to deal with.

'Stop!' Harry called out. 'Car coming!'

All shots had to be low and soft. A few broken flowers were fine but broken windows meant game over.

'Kev, don't blast it!'

'Mrs Curtis is watching at the curtain!'

Harry loved their street games because they really

helped him to improve his technique. In the tight space between the pavements, his control had to be excellent and he had to look up quickly to find the pass. His movement had to be good too if he wanted to escape from the defenders and score.

'Yes!' he would scream as he made a sudden run towards goal. If he got it right, his marker wouldn't have time to turn and catch him.

Harry's hero, Teddy Sheringham, was back as Tottenham's Number 10. He watched him carefully in every match and tried to copy his movement. Teddy wasn't the quickest striker in the Premier League but he was always alert and clever around the penalty area.

'Stay tight on Harry,' his opponents would say. 'Don't switch off or he'll score!'

Normally, their street games were friendly and fun, but not always. If the result came down to next goal wins, everyone took it very seriously.

'No way! That went straight over the jumper – that's not a goal.'

'What are you talking about? That was post and in!'

'Stop cheating!'

'You're the one who's cheating!'

Of course, there was no referee, so Harry often had to be the peacemaker. He wanted to win just as much as the other boys, if not more, but he always stayed calm. Getting angry didn't help anyone. If Harry ended up on the losing team one day, he just worked even harder the next day.

Harry's days started and ended with football. It was all he thought about. In bed, he lay there imagining his Tottenham debut:

It was 0–0 with ten minutes to go and he came on to replace Les Ferdinand up front. Darren Anderton got the ball in midfield and played a brilliant through-ball. Harry ran towards goal, and he was one-on-one with the goalkeeper. Could he stay calm and find the net?

Unfortunately, he fell asleep before he found out the answer.

CHAPTER 6

ARSENAL

Harry was used to seeing Premier League scouts at Ridgeway Rovers matches. There was lots of young talent in north east London and no club wanted to miss out on the next David Beckham. If he kept scoring, Harry believed that it could be him.

'Well played, today,' said Ian Marshall, the Chairman of Ridgeway Rovers, as he ruffled the boy's short hair. 'How many is that for the season now?'

Harry pretended to count but he knew the answer. 'Eighteen in fifteen games.'

'You're our little Alan Shearer!'

Harry shook his head. 'I prefer Sheringham.'

Ian laughed. 'Of course, Teddy it is then! Do you mind if I have a quick chat with your dad please?'

While Harry practised his keepie-uppies nearby, the adults chatted.

'We had an Arsenal scout here today,' Ian said. 'He wants your boy to go for a trial there.'

Pat wasn't surprised; he already knew that his son was a very good player. But he wanted to do what was best for him.

'What do you think?' he asked Ian. 'He's still only eight – is he too young to join an academy? I want Harry to keep enjoying his football.'

The Ridgeway Rovers coach nodded. 'I understand. Look, I don't think there's any harm in him trying it out. If he doesn't like it, he can just come back here. We'll always have a place for him.'

Pat thanked Ian. 'Harry loves everything about football but I just don't want to get his hopes up. It can be a very cruel business for youngsters.'

As soon as they were in the car, Harry wanted to know everything. 'What were you and Ian talking about?'

'Wait until we get home. I need to talk to your mum first.'

'Okay, but was it a Tottenham scout?'

'Harry!'

'A West Ham scout?'

'HARRY!'

After a whispered chat with Kim in the kitchen, Pat shared the good news with his son. 'Arsenal want to offer you a trial. What do you think?'

Harry's first thoughts were a mix of pride and disappointment. It was amazing news that a Premier League club wanted him, but why did it have to be Arsenal, Tottenham's biggest rivals?

'But we hate Arsenal, Dad!'

Pat laughed. 'We don't really hate them, son. It's just a football rivalry. They're a great club and they're doing very well at the moment.'

His dad was right; Arsenal were the second-best team in England, just behind Manchester United. They had exciting superstars like Dennis Bergkamp, Patrick Vieira and Thierry Henry. Tottenham, meanwhile, were down in mid-table.

That was enough to make Harry change his mind. 'Okay, so when can I start?'

For the big day, Harry decided not to wear his Tottenham shirt. He was already going to be the new kid at Arsenal and he didn't want to make things even harder.

'How are you feeling?' his mum asked on the journey to London Colney, Arsenal's training ground location.

'Fine,' Harry replied but really, he was getting more and more nervous in the backseat of the car. It was going to be a massive challenge for him, and what if he failed? What if he wasn't good enough and made a fool of himself? This wasn't Ridgeway Rovers anymore.

'You'll be brilliant,' Kim told him, giving his hand a squeeze. 'But maybe don't tell your new coaches that you're a Spurs fan straight away!'

Harry smiled and felt a bit more relaxed. As long as he tried his best, what more could he do?

As they drove into the Arsenal Training Centre, Harry couldn't believe his eyes. Compared to Ridgeway's Peter May Sports Centre, it looked like a whole city. There were ten perfect, full-size pitches, as well as lots of indoor facilities.

'Not bad, is it?' his dad joked.

Once the session began, Harry's nerves turned into adrenaline. 'I can do this!' he told himself. Everything felt better with a football at his feet.

In the drills, he showed off his best touch and passing. Some of the other boys had incredible technique already, but Harry didn't let that get him down. He was waiting for his moment to shine – shooting. When that moment arrived, the Arsenal goalkeepers didn't have a chance. Bottom left, top right, straight down the middle; Harry scored every time.

'Great work!' the coach clapped.

That trial session soon turned into a whole season at Arsenal. At first, it felt strange to play for Tottenham's enemies but Harry soon forgot about that. He was having so much fun. He wasn't as skilful as some of his teammates, but that wasn't really his role – he was the one who scored the goals. He didn't play every minute of every match but he tried to make the most of every opportunity.

At the end of the season, the Arsenal academy had to choose which youngsters to keep and which youngsters to let go. Harry crossed his fingers tightly for weeks but unfortunately, it was bad news. The coaches decided that he was too small for his age.

'I'm so sorry,' his dad said, giving him a hug. 'Be proud and keep going. Once you've had your growth spurt, Arsenal are going to regret it!'

For the next few days, Harry was so angry and upset that he wanted to give up. But luckily, that feeling didn't last long. He realised that he loved football too much to stop. If Arsenal didn't want him, he knew another team that hopefully still did.

'Dad, can I go and play for Ridgeway Rovers again?'

The Peter May Sports Centre would always feel like home.

'Welcome back, kid!' Ian said with a wink. 'What we're looking for is a goalscorer, a fox in the box – do you know of anyone like that?'

Harry grinned. 'Yes – me!'

CHAPTER 7

CHINGFORD FOUNDATION SCHOOL

After playing for Ridgeway Rovers, Harry was soon following in David Beckham's footsteps for a second time when he started at Chingford Foundation School. Becks' signed shirt hung proudly in the entrance lobby at Chingford. Harry looked at it every morning as he arrived at school, hoping that it would bring him luck, but especially on the day of the trial for the Year 7 football team. Chingford had one of the best track records in Greater London and Harry was ready to be their next star.

'I'm the striker that they need and I'll show them at the trial,' he told his brother, Charlie, on the way to school. He wasn't quite as confident as he sounded but he was as determined as ever.

Harry loved scoring goals. It was an amazing feeling when a shot hit the back of the net. But he could do a lot more than just that. During his year at Arsenal, he had improved his all-round game. He was good in possession, and creative too. Setting up chances for his teammates was almost as much fun as scoring.

'Just don't be too selfish,' Charlie warned. 'Mr Leadon hates a show-off!'

Harry didn't forget his brother's advice. After changing into his white Tottenham shirt, he made his way out onto the pitch with the other boys.

'Good luck!' Harry told his mates. They were all competing for places now.

After a warm-up and some passing exercises, Mark Leadon, Chingford's football coach, split the boys up and gave half of them orange bibs.

'I'm looking for team players today,' he told them. 'If you just want to show off how many tricks you can do, go do that in the playground. I want to see how you can work together and help each other to win. Right, let's play!'

Most of Harry's schoolmates knew that he was a good footballer because they had seen him play in the lunchtime games. They knew that he had played for Arsenal, but he was still quite small and he didn't have the flashy skills and speed to dribble past everyone. There were other boys who looked more talented but Harry hadn't played at his best. Yet.

'If we pass the ball around, they'll get tired and the chances will come,' he told his teammates. He had made himself the leader.

Harry was ready to be patient but he didn't need to be. The opposition defenders couldn't cope with his clever runs into space. As the cross came in, he made a late run to beat his marker to the ball.

Goooooooooooooooooaaaaaaaaaaaaaaaaaaaalllllllllllllllll llllllllllllll!!!!!!!!!!!!!!!!!!!!

Harry didn't run off and celebrate on his own; he ran straight to thank the teammate who had set him up. Together, they ran back for the restart. They had more goals to score.

'I like this kid,' Mark thought to himself on the sidelines. 'For an eleven-year-old, he really understands football. He knows where to go and he knows where his teammates are going to go too.'

Harry didn't stop running until Mark blew the whistle to end the game. By then, it had turned into a thrashing. When he found room to shoot, Harry shot and scored. When he could see another player in space, he passed for them to score instead. He was involved in every part of his team's victory.

They walked off the pitch together, with their arms around each other's shoulders. Their man of the match was right at the centre of the gang.

'Well played,' Mark said to them but he was looking straight at Harry.

'Thanks, sir,' he replied politely, but inside, he was buzzing with pride.

Mark was very impressed. Every year, he had excellent young footballers in his school team but this boy seemed special. He had technique, vision, movement *and* work-rate. Mark could tell that it was going to be a good season.

'So, how did it go?' Charlie asked when his brother got home from school that evening.

Harry smiled and shrugged modestly. 'It went okay, I think.'

Harry became the first name on a very successful teamsheet. His goals led Chingford to school cup glory.

'If you keep working hard, your shirt could be hanging up there with Becks one day!' Mark Leadon told him.

CHAPTER 8

HEROES AND DREAMS

'Welcome!' David Beckham announced to a group
of sixteen boys and girls. The England superstar was
in East London to launch his brand-new football
academy. With his white Adidas tracksuit and trendy
haircut, he looked so cool. 'Today, we're going to
practise some of my favourite skills.'

Harry wasn't really listening; he was too busy
staring at his hero. He was one of the Chingford
Foundation School footballers who had been selected
to go to the academy launch. So now, Becks was
right next to him, giving him football tips! Surely,
it was too good to be true? But no, it was really
happening.

Like Becks, Harry wore an Adidas tracksuit, but their hairstyles didn't match. Harry's head was shaved short, like Becks way back in 2000, but Becks had tried five different looks since then! Harry felt very nervous. Not only was Becks watching him but there were also cameras everywhere. Still, he was desperate to impress. Harry dribbled the ball carefully from end to end, and kept his keepie-uppies simple.

'That's it, great work everyone!' Becks called out.

At the end of the day, he shook each of them by the hand and chatted with them. When it was Harry's turn, he was too nervous and shy to speak. Luckily, Becks went first.

'Well done today. Are you one of the lads from Chingford?' he asked.

Harry nodded. 'A-and I play for Ridgeway Rovers too.'

Becks smiled. 'Great club, so what's next? What's your dream?'

Harry didn't need to think about that one. 'I want to play for England at Wembley!'

'Good choice, it's the best feeling in the world. If
you keep working hard, you can do it. Good luck!'

As Harry travelled home with his mum, he could
still hear his hero's inspirational words in his head –
'you can do it'.

*

'Play the pass now!' Harry shouted, as he
sprinted towards goal. It was only one of their street
games, but that didn't matter. Every football match
was important. The pass never arrived, however.

'Car!' one of his mates shouted, picking up the
ball.

As he moved over towards the pavement, Harry
noticed two strange things about this particular
car. Firstly, it wasn't the typical old banger that
usually drove through the area. It was a huge black
Range Rover and it looked brand-new. Secondly, the
car didn't speed off once they were out of the way.
Instead, it stopped and the driver's door opened.

'Hey guys, do you fancy a game?' the man said
with a big smile on his face.

Harry's jaw dropped. Was he dreaming? Was

Jermain Defoe, Spurs' star striker, really standing there asking to play with them?

'Yes, Jermain's on our team!'

'Hey, that's not fair!'

After a few minutes of arguing, the decision was made: Harry and Jermain would play on opposite teams.

'Let's see what you've got!' Jermain told him with a wink.

Harry loved a challenge but this one was impossible. He knew that he couldn't compete with a top Premier League striker yet but he did his best. He chased every pass and got on the ball as often as possible. He wanted to show off all his skills.

When he wasn't racing around the pitch, Harry tried to watch his superstar opponent in action. Jermain scored lots of goals but Harry was more interested in the rest of his play. With a powerful burst of speed, he could escape from any tackle. Jermain was always thinking one step ahead, playing quick passes to get his teammates into really dangerous areas. If there was a loose ball, or a goalmouth scramble, he was always the first to react.

First Becks and now Jermain; Harry was learning from the very best.

After half an hour, Jermain had to leave. 'Thanks for the game, lads!'

The boys all stood and watched as the black Range Rover drove away. Then they looked at each other, their faces full of wonder. It was a night that none of them would ever forget.

'They're not going to believe us at school, are they?' Harry said.

His mates shook their heads. 'Not in a million years.'

CHAPTER 9

TOTTENHAM AT LAST

'I can't believe you're leaving us again,' Ian Marshall said with a wink and a handshake. 'I hope it goes well for you, lad, but if not, just come back home!'

Harry would miss playing for Ridgeway Rovers but Watford had offered him a trial. They weren't as big as Arsenal or Tottenham, but they were a good Championship team. It was the sort of new challenge that he needed.

'Good luck!' Pat called from the car window as he dropped Harry off at the Watford training centre. His son hadn't said much during the journey and he hoped that he wasn't brooding on his experience at

Arsenal. Harry was at a different club now and there was nothing to worry about.

But Harry wasn't worried; he was just focused on doing his best. He might only have a few weeks to impress his new coaches, so he had to get things right. If Harry missed one shot, he had to score the next one.

'How did it go?' Pat asked when he returned to pick him up.

'It was good,' was all Harry said. This time, he was taking it one step at a time. He didn't want to get carried away. It was just nice to be training with a professional team again.

But it turned out that Watford weren't the only ones chasing him. Another club was also interested, the only club in Harry's heart – Tottenham.

Tottenham's youth scout Mark O'Toole had been watching Harry's Ridgeway Rovers performances for nearly a year. Harry was easily the best player in his team. He was a natural finisher and he had good technique. So, what was Mark waiting for?

'He knows exactly where the goal is but most

strikers are either big or quick,' he discussed with the other scouts. 'Harry's neither!'

Mark liked to be 100 per cent certain before he told the Tottenham youth coaches to offer a youngster a trial. But when he heard that Harry was at Watford, he decided to take a risk, and advised the coaches:

'I want you to take a look at a kid who plays for Ridgeway Rovers. He scores lots of goals but he's not a classic striker. I guess he's more like Teddy Sheringham than Alan Shearer.'

'Interesting! What's his name?'

'Harry Kane.'

'Well, tell him to come down for a trial.'

When his dad told him the news, Harry thought his family were playing a prank on him. How could they be so mean? Surely, they knew how much he wanted to play for his local club.

'No, I'm serious!' Pat told him. He tried to look serious but he couldn't stop smiling. 'I got a call from a Tottenham youth scout. They want you to go down to the training centre next week.'

After checking a few times, Harry celebrated with a lap of the living room.

'I'm going to play for Tottenham! I'm going to play for Tottenham!'

He had only been training with Watford for about a month, but there was no way that he could say no to Spurs. His dream team was calling him.

Harry waited and worried but finally the big day arrived.

'How are you feeling?' Pat asked as they drove to Spurs Lodge in Epping Forest.

Harry nodded. His heart was beating so fast that he thought it might jump out of his mouth if he tried to speak.

'Just remember to enjoy it, son,' his dad told him. 'It's a big opportunity but you've got to have fun, okay?'

Harry nodded again. Nothing was as fun as scoring goals.

As they parked their car, Harry could see the other boys warming up on the pitch. In their matching club tracksuits, they seemed to be having a great time together. This was the Under-13s but they all looked at least fifteen. Harry was still waiting for his growth spurt. What if they didn't want a little kid to join their group? What if he made a fool of himself? No, he couldn't think like that. He had to keep believing in himself.

Mark O'Toole was there at the entrance to greet them. 'Welcome to Tottenham! Are you ready for this, kid?'

This time, Harry had to speak. 'Yes, thanks.'

After a deep breath, he walked out onto the pitch in his lucky Tottenham shirt. He had nothing to lose.

Two hours later, Harry was on his way back home, sweaty and buzzing.

'They scored first but I knew we would win it. We had all the best players. George is really good in midfield and Danny can dribble past anyone. I reckon he can kick it even harder than Charlie! The other team didn't stand a chance, really. We had to work hard but–'

'Whoa, slow down, kiddo!' his dad laughed. 'So, you had a good time out there?'

'It was so much fun! I scored the winning goal!'

'I know – it was a great strike too.'

Harry frowned. 'How do you know that?'

His dad laughed. 'I watched from the car! I didn't want to put extra pressure on you by standing there on the sidelines but I wasn't going to miss your first session. Well done, you played really well tonight.'

After six weeks on trial, Harry became a proper Spurs youth team player. It was the proudest moment of his life but he had lots of hard work ahead of him. He had been the best player at Ridgeway Rovers, but he was now just average at Tottenham. It was like starting school all over again.

Luckily, Harry was a quick and willing learner. If it meant he got to play for Spurs, he would do anything the coaches asked him to do.

'Excellent effort, Harry!' John Moncur, the head of youth development, shouted.

Harry was enjoying himself but as summer approached, he began to worry. Soon, it would be time for the end-of-season letters again. Would Spurs decide to keep him for another year? After his experience at Arsenal, he couldn't bear another rejection. The day the post arrived, Harry's hands were shaking.

'Open it!' his brother Charlie demanded impatiently.

When he tore open the envelope, Harry read the dreaded word and his heart sank: '*Unfortunately...*'. It was the release letter. He tried to hold back the tears but he couldn't. 'I don't understand – I had a good season!'

The phone rang and Pat went to answer it. Within seconds, the sadness was gone from his voice. Instead, he sounded relieved. 'Don't worry, these things happen...Yes, I'll tell him right now.'

'Panic over!' Pat called out as he returned to the living room. Harry looked up and saw a big smile on his dad's face. What was going on? 'They sent you the wrong letter by mistake. Spurs want you to stay!'

CHAPTER 10

ONE MORE YEAR

Alex Inglethorpe was Tottenham's Under-18s coach
but once a week, he helped out with the Under-14s
training. He liked to keep an eye on the younger age
groups because the most talented boys would soon
move up into his team. Ryan Mason and Andros
Townsend were already making the step-up. Who
would be next?

During the session, Alex offered lots of advice,
especially to the team's best players. There were a
couple of speedy full-backs, plus a tall centre-back
and a classy playmaker in central midfield. And then
there was Harry.

Harry didn't really stand out as an amazing young

footballer, but Alex loved the boy's attitude. He
played with so much desire and all he wanted to do
was score goals for his team. Harry understood that
he wasn't as strong or quick as the other strikers, but
he didn't let that stop him. He loved a challenge, and
competing with Tottenham's best young players was
certainly a challenge. With the pressure on, he never
panicked. He just made the most of his technique
and worked hard on his weaknesses.

'That's it, Harry! Shield the ball from the defender
and wait until the pass is on. Lovely!'

Harry was the perfect student. After most sessions,
he would stay behind for extra shooting practice. For
a youth coach, that desire was a very good sign.

'Let's wait and see what happens when he grows
a bit,' Alex kept telling everyone at the Tottenham
academy. But they couldn't wait forever. Next year,
Harry would be moving up to the Under-16s. Before
then, they had to make a big decision about his future.

'Thanks for coming,' the Under-14s coach said,
shaking hands with Harry's parents. 'I wanted to
talk to you about your son's progress. As you know,

everyone loves Harry here at Spurs. He works so hard and he's a pleasure to work with.'

Pat and Kim could tell that there was a 'But' coming.

'But we're worried. He's still small for his age and he's not a speedy little striker like Jermain Defoe. Don't get me wrong, Harry's got a very good understanding of the game but he needs more than just that if he wants to play up front for Spurs.'

'Okay, so how long does he have to get better?' Pat asked. Once they knew the timeframe, they could make a plan.

The Under-14s coach frowned. 'Every age group is a big new challenge and unless we see real improvement, we don't think that Harry will make it in the Under-16s next year.'

So, one more year. When they got home, Pat sat Harry down in the living room and told him the news. He could see the tears building in his son's eyes. First Arsenal and now Tottenham...

'Don't worry, this isn't over,' Pat said, putting an arm around Harry's shoulder. 'We just have to work even harder to prove them wrong. We believe in you. Do you want to give up?'

Harry shook his head firmly. 'No.'

His dad smiled. 'Good, that's my boy! We'll make a plan tomorrow.'

For the next twelve months, Harry trained with Tottenham as normal, but he also did extra sessions away from the club.

'I want to help but me and you kicking a ball around in the garden won't cut it anymore,' his dad joked. 'It's time to get serious!'

At first, 'serious' just meant lots of boring running and not much actual football. Harry did short sprints until he could barely lift his legs. 'What's the point of this?' he thought to himself as he stood there panting in the rain. This wasn't the beautiful game that he loved.

'Let's have a chat,' his coach said. He could tell that Harry was hating every second of it. 'Look kid, you're never going to be a 100-metre champion but a short burst of pace can make a huge difference for a striker.'

Harry thought back to Jermain Defoe during that

street game a few years earlier. He was really good at making space for the shot and his reaction speed was amazing. That was what Harry needed. If the ball dropped in the penalty area, he had to get there first. If a goalkeeper made a save, he had to win the race to the rebound.

'Brilliant, Harry!' his coach cried out a few minutes later. 'That's your best time yet!'

Soon, they moved on to ball work. Harry practised his hold-up play, his heading and, of course, his shooting. He could feel the improvement and so could Tottenham. After a few months, Harry was looking fitter and much more confident on the pitch. Most importantly, he was a better striker and he was scoring more goals.

'Congratulations, kid!' Alex told him after another brilliant performance. 'I knew you'd prove them wrong. And you're getting taller every time I see you.'

Yes, Harry was finally growing! Everything was falling into place at just the right time. Thanks to lots of extra effort, Spurs wanted him to stay. Now, Harry just needed to grow into his tall new body.

CHAPTER 11

MEXICO AND SWITZERLAND

By the time he turned fifteen, Harry had become one of Tottenham's hottest prospects. He still played a lot of games for the Under-16s but he was also getting experience at higher levels. No matter who he played against, Harry kept scoring goals.

'That kid is one of the best natural finishers I've ever seen,' Spurs coach Tim Sherwood told Alex Inglethorpe. 'Why have I never heard of him?'

The Under-18s coach laughed. 'He's a late developer!'

'Okay, well look after him carefully – he could be our next goal machine.'

At the start of the 2008–09 season, Jonathan

Obika had been Alex's number one striker in
the Spurs academy side but the team played lots
of matches and it was good to have competition
for places.

'Welcome to the squad!' Alex said as he gave
Harry the good news. 'At first, you'll be on the
bench but if you keep making the most of your
opportunities, you'll force your way into the starting
line-up. You deserve this.'

Harry was delighted. Not only was he moving
up but he was joining a very good side. There was
Steven Caulker at the back, Ryan Mason in the
middle and Andros Townsend on the wing. With
teammates like that, he was going to get plenty of
chances to score. Harry couldn't wait.

'If I grab a few goals, I could be playing for the first
team soon!' he told Charlie excitedly.

It was his older brother's job to keep his feet on
the ground. 'And if you miss a few sitters, you
could be playing for the Under-16s again!' Charlie
teased.

Luckily, that didn't happen. Harry kept on scoring

and soon he was off on an exciting international adventure.

'I'm going to Mexico!' he told his family in December. 'I made the Spurs team for the Copa Chivas.'

'Never heard of it!' Charlie replied with a smile. He was very proud of his younger brother, but it wasn't very cool to show it.

Kim was more concerned about Christmas. 'When do you leave?' she asked.

Harry shrugged; he wasn't bothered about the details. He was playing football for Tottenham; that was all he needed to know. 'In January, I think.'

It was going to be the trip of a lifetime. He couldn't wait to have lots of fun with Ryan, Steven and Andros and win the tournament. What an experience it would be!

'Just you behave yourself,' his mum told him at the airport. 'Don't let the older boys get you into trouble!'

After a long flight, the squad arrived in Guadalajara and found the familiar Tottenham cockerel on the side of a big coach.

'We're famous!' Ryan joked.

In the Copa Chivas, Tottenham faced teams from Spain, Costa Rica, Brazil, Paraguay, Norway and, of course, Mexico.

'Come on boys, we're representing England here!' Harry said, looking down at their white Spurs shirts.

It was hard work in the heat but Tottenham did well. In eight matches, Harry managed to score three goals.

'Only Ryan got more than me!' he told his parents proudly when he returned to Chingford. It had been the best trip ever, but he was glad to get back to his own bedroom and home cooking.

A few months later, Harry was off again. Tottenham were playing in the *Torneo Bellinzona* in Switzerland against big clubs like Sporting Lisbon and Barcelona.

'Barca who?' Steven joked. They weren't scared of anyone.

Harry started two of their five matches and, although he didn't score, he played a big role in helping his team to win the tournament.

'I like setting up goals too, you know!' he reminded Ryan after their final win. It was a great feeling but nothing beat scoring goals.

Harry had really enjoyed his travels and he had learnt a lot from playing against teams from other countries. But back in England, it was time to think about his Spurs future. With his sixteenth birthday coming up, would Tottenham offer him a scholarship contract? He felt like he was improving all the time but he didn't want to get his hopes up. As time went by, his fears grew.

'Harry, have you got any plans for Tuesday?' John McDermott, the head of the academy, asked him casually.

He quickly worked out the date in his head. 'That's my birthday! Why?'

John smiled. 'Do you think you'll have time to come in and sign your contract?

Harry had never felt so relieved. He couldn't wait to tell his family and friends. After all his hard work, he was finally getting his reward. Signing with Spurs would be the best birthday present ever.

CHAPTER 12

GETTING CLOSER

Ahead of the 2009–10 season, the Tottenham Under-18s lined up for their squad photo. Harry had grown so much that the cameraman placed him on the back row next to the goalkeepers. He wasn't yet important enough to sit in the front row, but that was where he aimed to be next year.

Once everyone was in position, the cameraman counted down. '3, 2, 1... Click!'

Most of his teammates looked very serious in the photos but Harry couldn't help smiling. Why shouldn't he be happy? He was playing football for his favourite club in the world!

Harry's season started in Belgium at Eurofoot.

Ryan, Andros and Steven had all gone out on loan, so he was suddenly a senior member of the youth squad.

'A lot of excellent players have played in this tournament,' coach Alex Inglethorpe told them. 'This is going to be a great experience for all of you. We will be playing a lot of games while we're out here, so get ready to test your fitness!'

After his successful trips to Mexico and Switzerland, Harry couldn't wait for his next international adventure. He was a year older now and a much better striker. The tournament schedule was really tiring but Harry scored three goals in his first four games.

'You're on fire!' his strike partner Kudus Oyenuga cheered as they celebrated their win over Dutch team Willem II.

In the end, Tottenham didn't reach the semi-finals but Harry had his shooting boots on, ready for the Premier Academy League to begin. Or so he thought, anyway. But after four matches, he still hadn't scored.

'Just be patient,' Kudus kept telling him.

It was easy for Kudus to say; he had already found the net three times. 'But scoring goals is what I do best!' Harry argued.

'I think you're just trying too hard,' Tom Carroll, their tiny midfield playmaker, suggested. 'Just relax and I bet the goals will come.'

Harry was grateful for his teammates' support and advice. He scored in his next match against Fulham and once he started, he didn't stop. After two free-kick strikes against Watford, first-team coach Harry Redknapp picked him as a sub for the League Cup match against Everton.

'No way! This is too good to be true,' Harry said when he saw the squad list. His name was there next to top professionals like Jermaine Jenas and Vedran Ćorluka.

Alex laughed. 'No, it's for real! Just don't get your hopes up; you probably won't get off the bench.'

Harry didn't come on, but he got to train with his heroes and share a dressing room with them. The experience inspired him to keep working hard. He could feel himself getting closer and closer to his Tottenham dream.

By Christmas, Harry was the Under-18s top scorer with nine goals, and the new academy captain.

'Alex always had a good feeling about you,' John McDermott said as he congratulated Harry. 'You're certainly proving him right these days! If you keep it up, the future is yours.'

Harry celebrated by scoring his first hat-trick of the season against Coventry City. And the great news just kept coming. In January 2010, he was called up to the England Under-17s for the Algarve Tournament in Portugal.

'Welcome!' the coach John Peacock said at his first squad meeting. 'I guess you must know a lot of these guys from the Premier Academy League?'

'Yes,' Harry replied, trying to hide his nerves. He had played against Benik Afobe, Ross Barkley and Nathaniel Chalobah before but they probably didn't even remember him. He was the new kid and he suddenly felt very shy. Luckily, his new teammates were very friendly.

'Nice to meet you, we needed a new striker,' Nathaniel grinned. 'Benik already thinks he's Thierry Henry!'

Harry soon felt like one of the gang. Off the pitch, they had lots of fun together but on the pitch, they were a focused team. The Under-17 European Championships were only a few months away, and so the Algarve Tournament was a chance for players to secure their places.

As he walked onto the pitch wearing the Three Lions on his shirt for the first time, Harry had to pinch himself to check that he wasn't dreaming. A few years earlier, Spurs had been close to letting him go – but now look at him! It was hard to believe. Harry didn't score against France or Ukraine but he would never forget those matches. He was an England youth international now.

Harry knew that if he played well until May, he had a chance of going to the Euros in Liechtenstein. That's what he wanted more than anything. He kept scoring goals for the Tottenham Under-18s and the Reserves, and crossed his fingers. He finished with eighteen goals in only twenty-two Premier Academy League games. Surely that would be enough to make the England squad?

In the end, Harry never found out because he was too ill to go to the tournament. Instead of representing his country at the Euros, he had to sit at home and watch Nathaniel, Ross and Benik winning without him. When England beat Spain in the final, Harry was both delighted and devastated.

'Congratulations, guys!' he texted his teammates but inside, he was very jealous. He should have been there with them, lifting the trophy.

'You'll get more chances,' his mum told him as he lay on the sofa feeling sorry for himself.

It didn't seem that way at the time, but Harry always bounced back from disappointments. There was a new season to prepare for, and a first professional Tottenham contract to sign. That was more than enough to lift him out of his bad mood. It was the best feeling in the world as he signed his name on the papers.

'Thanks for always believing in me,' Harry told

Alex as they chatted afterwards. 'I couldn't have done this without you.'

His Under-18s coach shook his head. 'You did it all yourself but you haven't achieved anything yet, kid. The next step is the hardest but you've got what it takes.'

Harry smiled. It was true; he wouldn't give up until he made it into the Spurs first team.

CHAPTER 13

EXPERIENCE NEEDED

At seventeen, Harry was on his way to becoming a Spurs superstar but he still had a lot to learn. Luckily, there were plenty of teachers around him at Tottenham. In the Reserves, he often played alongside first team stars who were recovering from injuries, like David Bentley and Robbie Keane. Harry loved those matches. He was always watching and listening for new tips.

'If you need to, take a touch but if you hit it early, you might catch the keeper out.'

'Don't just assume that he's going to catch it. Get there in case he drops it!'

By 2010, Harry was also training regularly with

Harry Redknapp's squad. It was hard to believe that he was sharing a pitch with world-class players like Gareth Bale, Luka Modrić and Rafael van der Vaart. But best of all, Harry was working with his hero, Jermain Defoe. Eventually, he plucked up the courage to talk about that street game.

'Oh yeah, I remember that!' Jermain laughed. 'That was you? Wow, I feel *really* old now!'

Jermain became Harry's mentor and invited him to his extra shooting sessions.

'You're a natural goalscorer, H, but it takes more than instinct to become a top striker. You need to practise, practise, practise! What are you aiming for when you shoot?'

It seemed like a really stupid question. 'The goal,' he replied.

'Okay, but what part of the goal? Top corner, bottom corner?'

'Err, I don't know, I guess I–'

Jermain interrupted Harry. 'No, no, no! You've got to know exactly what you're aiming at, H. Before you hit this one, I want you to picture the goal in

79

your head and then aim for the top right corner.'

Harry took his time and placed the ball carefully into the top right corner.

'Good, but you won't get that long to think in a real match.'

Jermain called a young defender over: 'As soon as I play the pass to Harry, close him down.'

Under pressure, Harry hit the target again but his shot went straight down the middle of the goal. 'No, the keeper would have saved that,' Jermain said. So Harry tried again and again until he hit that top right corner.

'Nice! Now let's work on making that space to shoot. Let's hope you're quicker than you look!' Jermain teased.

He was very impressed by Harry's attitude. Not only did he love scoring goals but he also loved improving his game. That was a winning combination. Jermain kept telling the Spurs coaches, 'If you give him a chance, I promise you he'll score!'

But for now, Redknapp already had Jermain, Roman Pavlyuchenko and Peter Crouch in his squad.

Harry would have to wait for his chance. He was doing well for the Reserves but was that the best place for him to develop? Spurs' youth coaches didn't think so.

'He's a great kid and a talented player but what's his best position?' Les Ferdinand asked Tim Sherwood.

That was a difficult question. Harry was a natural finisher but he was also good on the ball. He could read the game well as a second striker, linking the midfield and attack.

Sherwood's silence proved Ferdinand's point. 'That's the big issue. He's a goalscorer but he's not strong enough to battle against big centre-backs.'

'Not yet, no.'

'Plus, he's not quick enough to get in behind the defence.'

This time, Sherwood disagreed. 'He's quicker than he looks and he's lethal in the box.'

After a long discussion, the Spurs coaches agreed on an action plan – Harry would go out on loan in January 2011 to a lower league club.

'We've spoken to Leyton Orient and they want to take you for the rest of the season,' Sherwood told him in a meeting.

At first, Harry was surprised and upset. He didn't want to leave Tottenham, even if it was only for a few months.

'Look, kid, a spell in League One will be good for you,' Sherwood explained. 'You need first-team experience and you're not going to get that here at the moment, I'm afraid. We also need to toughen you up a bit, put some muscle on that skinny frame. Don't worry – we're not going to forget about you!'

Harry spoke to his parents and he spoke to his teammates. They all agreed that it was a good idea.

'Everyone goes out on loan at some point,' Ryan told him. 'It's better than being stuck in the Reserves, trust me!'

'I was at Orient last season,' Andros told him. 'It's a good club and they'll look after you. At least, Spurs aren't asking you to go miles from home. Leyton is just up the road!'

They were right, of course. If a loan move to

Leyton Orient would help him to improve and get into the Tottenham first team, Harry would go. It really helped that he wouldn't be going alone.

'Let's do this!' Tom cheered as they travelled to their first training session together.

CHAPTER 14

LEYTON ORIENT

Rochdale's pitch looked bad even before the match kicked off. Where had all the grass gone? As the Leyton Orient squad warmed up, they kept away from the boggy penalty areas and corners. They didn't want to make things worse. When Harry tried a short sprint, his boots sank into the squelch and it was difficult to lift them out. How was he supposed to make runs into the box?

Orient's striker Scott McGleish watched and laughed. 'Welcome to League One, kid!'

The Spotland Stadium was certainly no White Hart Lane. After seventy minutes of football and heavy rain, it looked more like a mud bath than a pitch. On the bench, Harry sat with his hood up, shaking his legs to keep warm. The score was 1–1, perfect for a super sub...

'Harry, you're coming on!' the assistant manager Kevin Nugent turned and shouted.

This was it – his Leyton Orient debut. Harry jumped to his feet and took off his tracksuit. As he waited on the touchline, he didn't even notice the rain falling. He was so focused on making a good first impression for his new club.

'It's fun out there today!' Scott joked, high-fiving Harry as he left the field.

Harry grinned and ran on. He was desperate to make a difference, either by scoring or creating the winning goal. He chased after every ball but before he knew it, the final whistle went.

'Well done, lad,' his manager Russell Slade said, slapping his wet, muddy back.

Harry had enjoyed his first short battle against the big League One centre-backs. They wanted to teach the Premier League youngster about 'real football', and he wanted to show them that this Premier

League youngster could cope with 'real football'.
Scott was right; it *was* fun!

'So, how did you find it?' Kevin asked back in
the dressing room. Alex Inglethorpe had left him in
charge of Harry and Tom during their loan spell at
the club.

'It's different, that's for sure!' Harry replied after a
nice hot shower. 'I need to get stronger but I'm ready
for the challenge.'

Orient's assistant manager was impressed. The kid
had a great attitude and that was very important
in professional football. He could see the hunger in
his eyes.

Harry was picked to start the next home game
against Sheffield Wednesday. It was a big responsibility
for a seventeen-year-old. He fought hard up front but
it wasn't easy against really experienced defenders. At
half-time, it was still 0–0.

'You're causing them lots of problems,' Kevin
reassured him. 'Keep doing what you're doing and
be patient.'

Harry felt more confident as he ran out for the

second half. He had fifteen, or maybe twenty, minutes to grab a goal before the manager took him off. 'I can do this,' he told himself.

When Orient took the lead, the whole team breathed a sigh of relief. They started passing the ball around nicely and creating more chances. Harry only needed one. When it arrived, he steadied himself and placed his shot carefully.

Goooooooooooooooaaaaaaaaaaaaaaaaaalllllllllllllllllll llllll!!!!!!!!!!!!!!!!!!!!

He had scored on his full debut! Harry ran towards the Orient fans to celebrate. It felt like the start of big things.

'You're one of us now!' Scott cheered as they high-fived on the touchline.

*

'So, how is Harry getting on?' Alex asked Kevin when they met up a few months later.

The Orient assistant manager chuckled. 'That boy's a real fighter, isn't he? His legs are no bigger than matchsticks but he's fearless. He's good in front of goal, too.'

'What about that red card against Huddersfield?'

Kevin shook his head. 'The second yellow was very harsh,' he explained. 'I'm not sure he even touched the guy! You know that's not Harry's way. He's one of the good guys.'

Tottenham's youth coach nodded. He knew all about Harry's character. Some youngsters really struggled to adapt to new environments, but clearly not him. Alex never had any doubt that Harry would make the most of his first-team experience.

With Orient chasing a playoff spot, Harry was back on the bench for the last few matches of the season. It wasn't where he wanted to be but he was pretty pleased with his record of five goals in eighteen games. It was a decent start to his professional career.

'Welcome back, stranger!' Ryan joked when Harry returned to Tottenham in May.

Despite going out on loan, he had never really left his beloved club. After training with Orient, Harry often went back to do extra sessions with the Spurs Under-21s. They couldn't get rid of him that easily.

Over the summer of 2011, Redknapp sold Peter

Crouch and Robbie Keane, and replaced them with Emmanuel Adebayor. Harry was feeling positive about his sums.

'Two strikers left and only one came in,' he thought to himself. 'That means one spare spot for me!'

It looked that way at the start of the 2011–12 season. In August, Harry made his Tottenham debut at White Hart Lane, against Hearts in the UEFA Europa League. They were already 5–0 up from the first leg, so Redknapp threw him straight into the starting line-up, with Andros and Tom. Harry had never been so excited.

'I'm keeping Jermain out of the team!' he joked with his brother.

'What shirt number did they give you?' Charlie asked.

'37.'

'And what number is Jermain?'

'18.'

'Well, you're not the star striker yet then, bro!'

But Harry wasn't giving up until he *was* Tottenham's star striker. In the twenty-eighth minute, he chased after Tom's brilliant through-ball. It was a move that they had practised so many times in the Spurs youth teams. Harry got there first, just ahead of the Hearts keeper, who tripped him. Penalty!

Harry picked himself up and walked over to get the ball. This was *his* penalty, a great opportunity to score on his Spurs debut. He placed it down on the spot and took a few steps back. He tried to ignore the goalkeeper bouncing on his line. He pictured the goal in his head, just like Jermain had taught him.

After a deep breath, he ran towards the ball but suddenly, doubts crept into his head. Was it a bad idea to shoot bottom left like he usually did? He paused just before he kicked it and that gave the keeper time to make the save. Harry ran in for the rebound but it was no use; he had missed the penalty.

Harry was devastated but he didn't stand there with his head in his hands. The nightmares could wait until after the match. For now, he kept hunting for his next chance to become a Tottenham hero…

CHAPTER 15

MILLWALL

'Go out there and score!' Jermain shouted as Harry ran on to replace him.

Tottenham were already 3–0 up against Shamrock Rovers. There was still time for him to grab a fourth.

Danny Rose's cross flew over Harry's head but Andros was there at the back post. As he knocked it down, Harry reacted first and shot past the defender on the line.

Goooooooooooooooooaaaaaaaaaaaaaaaaalllllllllllllllll lllllllll!!!!!!!!!!!!!!!!!!!!!!

Harry turned away to celebrate with Andros. What a feeling! He roared up at the sky. He was a Tottenham goalscorer now, and he could put that awful penalty miss behind him.

Unfortunately, however, that was the end of Tottenham's Europa League campaign. It was a real blow for their young players because the tournament was their big chance to shine. What would happen now? There wasn't space for them in Spurs' Premier League squad, so they would either have to go back to the Reserves or out on loan again.

'Right now, I just want to play week in week out,' Harry told his dad. 'I don't care where!'

Pat smiled. 'Be careful what you wish for. You wouldn't like the cold winters in Russia!'

In the end, Harry and Ryan were sent on loan to Millwall in January 2012. The Lions were fighting to stay in the Championship and they needed goals.

'We only scored one goal in the whole of December,' Harry's new manager Kenny Jackett moaned. 'We played five matches, that's over 450 minutes of football!'

Harry's job was clear and he couldn't wait to help his new team. In his Millwall debut against Bristol City, he had a few chances to score but he couldn't get past former England goalkeeper David James.

When City won the match with a last-minute goal, Harry couldn't believe it. He trudged off the pitch with tears in his eyes.

'Hard luck, kid,' Jackett said, putting an arm around his shoulder. 'You played well. The goals will come.'

His new strike partner, Andy Keogh, gave him similar advice. 'Just forget about the misses. If you keep thinking about them, you'll never score!'

The Millwall players and coaches liked Harry and they wanted him to do well. Despite his talent, he wasn't an arrogant wonderkid who thought he was way too good for them. He was a friendly guy, who worked hard for the team and always wanted to improve.

But six weeks later, Harry was still waiting for his first league goal for Millwall. It was the longest drought of his whole life. What was going wrong? Why couldn't he just put the ball in the net? Eventually, he did it away at Burnley.

He made the perfect run and James Henry played the perfect pass. Harry was through on goal. Surely,

he couldn't miss this one! The goalkeeper rushed out
to stop him but he stayed calm and used his side foot
to guide the ball into the bottom corner.

*Goooooooooooooooaaaaaaaaaaaaaaaaalllllllllllllllll
llllllllllll!!!!!!!!!!!!!!!!!!!!*

Harry pumped his fists and jumped into the air. It
was finally over! James threw himself into Harry's
arms.

'Thanks mate!' Millwall's new goalscorer shouted
above the noise of the fans. 'There's no stopping me
now!'

With his confidence back, Harry became a goal
machine once more. The Championship defenders
just couldn't handle his movement. He was deadly
in the penalty area, hitting the target with every shot
and header. But he was also brilliant when he played
behind the striker. In a deeper role, he had the
technique and vision to set up goals.

'Cheers!' Andy shouted after scoring from his
perfect pass.

Harry also loved to hit a long-range rocket. Against
Peterborough, he spun away from his marker and

chased after the ball. It was bouncing high and he was on his weaker left foot, but Harry was feeling bold. Why not? Jermain and Robbie had taught him a very important lesson at Tottenham – if you shoot early, the keeper won't be ready. Harry struck his shot powerfully and accurately into the far corner.

Gooooooooooooooooooooooaaaaaaaaaaaaaaaaaalllllll lllllllllllllllllllll!!!!!!!!!!!!!!

Harry ran towards the fans and slid across the grass on his knees.

'You're on fire!' Andy cheered as they celebrated together.

With his nine goals, Harry won Millwall's Young Player of the Season award. It was a proud moment for him and a nice way to say goodbye to the club.

'We're going to miss you!' Jackett told him after his last training session. 'It's been a pleasure working with you. Good luck back at Spurs – you're going to be great.'

Harry was sad to leave Millwall but he was also excited about returning to Tottenham. He had learnt a lot from his loan experience. He was now a stronger player, both physically and mentally. It was much harder to push him off the ball, and much harder to stop him scoring.

'2012–13 is going to be my season!' Harry told his family confidently.

But first, he was off to play for England at the UEFA European Under-19 Championships in Estonia. Nathaniel, Benik and Ross were in the squad too, along with some exciting new players: Eric Dier was a tough defender and Nathan Redmond was a tricky winger.

'There's no reason why we can't win this!' their manager Noel Blake told them.

Although he wore the Number 10 shirt, Harry played in midfield behind Benik and Nathan. He enjoyed his playmaker role but it made it harder for him to do his favourite thing – scoring goals. After a draw against Croatia and a win over Serbia, England needed to beat France to reach the semi-finals.

As the corner came in, most of the England attackers charged towards the goal. But not Harry. He waited around the penalty spot because he had noticed that the French goalkeeper wasn't very good at catching crosses. When he fumbled the ball, it fell straight to Harry, who was totally unmarked. He calmly volleyed it into the net.

Goooooooooooooooooooooaaaaaaaaaaaaaaaalllllllllllll llllllllllllllll!!!!!!!!!!!!!!!!!!!!

2–1 to England! Harry pumped his fists and pointed up at the sky. He was delighted to score such an important goal for his country.

'You're a genius!' Eric cheered as the whole team celebrated.

Unfortunately, Harry wasn't there to be England's hero in the semi-final against Greece. He had to watch from the bench as his teammates lost in extra-time. It was such a horrible way to crash out of the tournament.

'At least we've got the Under-20 World Cup next summer!' Harry said, trying to make everyone feel a little bit better.

He focused once again on his top target – breaking into the Tottenham first team.

CHAPTER 16

TOUGH TIMES

On the opening day of the 2013–14 season, Harry travelled up to Newcastle with the Tottenham squad. New manager André Villas-Boas wanted to give his young players a chance. Jake Livermore started the match, and Harry and Andros waited impatiently on the subs bench. Would this be the day when they made their Premier League debuts?

'Is it bad to hope that someone gets injured?' Andros joked.

With ten minutes to go, Newcastle scored a penalty to make it 2–1. Harry's heart was racing; surely, this was going to be his moment. Tottenham needed to score again and he was the only striker on the bench.

'Harry, you're coming on!'

He quickly took off his yellow bib, and then his grey tracksuit. He pulled up his socks and re-laced his boots. He tucked his navy-blue Spurs shirt into his white shorts.'37 KANE' was ready for action.

'Good luck!' Andros said as Harry walked down to the touchline.

'Get a goal!' Villas-Boas said as Harry waited to come on.

'Let's do this!' Jermain cheered as Harry ran on to join him up front.

Harry had less than ten minutes to score and become an instant Spurs hero. Anything was possible but Newcastle were in control of the game. Harry's Premier League debut was over before he'd really touched the ball.

'Don't worry, that was just a first taste of the action,' Jermain promised him.

Harry hoped that his mentor was right. He shook hands with his opponents and the match officials. Then he walked over to clap the Tottenham fans in the away stand. He had done his best to save the day for his club.

He couldn't wait for his next chance to play but he wasn't even a substitute for their next match against West Brom. With Emmanuel Adebayor back in the team, he was back in the Reserves. Harry was disappointed but he didn't give up.

'I'm still only nineteen,' he told himself. 'I've got plenty of time to shine.'

A few days later, he joined Norwich City on loan for the rest of the season. The Canaries were in the Premier League, so this was a great opportunity to show Spurs that he was good enough to play at the top level.

'Bring it on!' he told his new manager Chris Hughton.

Against West Ham, Harry came on with twenty minutes to go. That gave him plenty of time to score. He dribbled forward, cut inside and curled the ball just wide of the post.

'So close!' Harry groaned, putting his hands on his head.

Minutes later, he beat the West Ham right-back and pulled the ball back to Robert Snodgrass... but his shot was blocked on the line! Somehow, the match finished 0–0 but Harry was happy with his debut.

Afterwards, Hughton told the media, 'I think Kane will be a super player'.

Harry was delighted with the praise. His first start for Norwich soon arrived against Doncaster in the League Cup. He couldn't wait.

'I'm definitely going to score!' he told his teammates.

Sadly, Harry didn't score and he only lasted fifty minutes. He tried to carry on but he couldn't; his foot was way too painful. He winced and limped off the pitch.

'What happened?' his brother asked as he rested on the sofa back at home.

'I've fractured a metatarsal,' Harry explained.

'Isn't that what Becks did before the 2002 World Cup?' Charlie joked, trying to cheer his brother up. 'You've got to stop copying him!'

Harry smiled, but he was dreading the surgery and then the months without football. It would drive him crazy.

'You're a strong character,' Alex Inglethorpe told him when he returned to Tottenham, 'and you're going to come back even stronger!'

Harry's new girlfriend helped to take his mind off his injury. He and Katie had gone to the same primary and secondary schools but it was only later that they started dating. They got on really well and made each other laugh, even during the tough times.

Harry spent October and November in the gym, slowly getting his foot ready to play football again. It was long, boring work but he had to do it if he wanted to be playing again before the new year. That was his big aim. In December, Harry started training with the first team again, and starring for the Reserves.

'I'm feeling good!' Harry told his manager Chris Hughton with a big smile on his face. It was great to be playing football again. He had missed it so much.

On 29 December 2012, he was a sub for the

Manchester City match. By half-time, Norwich were losing 2–1.

'They're down to ten men, so let's get forward and attack,' Hughton told his players in the dressing room. 'We can win this! Harry, you're coming on to replace Steve.'

Harry's eyes lit up. He had been hoping for ten, maybe fifteen, minutes at the end but instead he was going to play the whole second half.

This was his biggest challenge yet. Harry was up against City's captain Vincent Kompany, one of the best centre-backs in the world. These were the big battles that he dreamed about. Harry held the ball up well and made clever runs into space. He didn't score but he was back in business.

'Boss, that was just the start!' he promised Hughton.

Before long, however, Harry was told that he had to return to Tottenham. Villas-Boas wanted a third striker as back-up for Jermain and Emmanuel. Harry was happy to help his club but he wanted to play regular football. What was the point of him being there if he wasn't even getting on the bench? A few weeks later, Villas-Boas sent him back out on loan to Leicester City.

'This is all so confusing!' Harry moaned to Katie. It had turned into a very topsy-turvy season. 'Do Spurs want me or not?'

It was a question that no-one could answer. Harry tried his best to adapt to another new club but soon after scoring on his home debut against Blackburn, he was dropped from the Leicester starting line-up. It was a massive disappointment. It felt like his career was going backwards.

'If I'm only a sub in the Championship, how am I ever going to make it at Spurs?' he complained to his dad on the phone. Leicester felt like a very long way away from Chingford.

Pat had seen his son looking this sad before. 'Remember when you were fourteen and Tottenham told you that you weren't good enough?' he reminded him. 'You didn't give up back then and you're not going to give up now!'

Harry nodded. He *was* good enough! All he

needed was a run of games and a chance to get back into goalscoring form. He just had to believe that the breakthrough would come.

CHAPTER 17

BREAKTHROUGH

'I'm not going anywhere this season,' Harry told
Tottenham firmly. After four loan spells, he was
determined to stay at the club. 'I'm going to prove
that I should be playing here week in, week out!'

Harry wasn't a raw, skinny teenager anymore.
He was now twenty years old and he looked like a
fit, powerful striker at last. That was thanks to his
Football League experience and lots of hard work in
the gym to build up his strength. He now had even
more power in his shot.

'Looking good, H!' Jermain said in pre-season
training. His encouragement was working. Harry was
getting better and better.

The 2013 U-20 World Cup in Turkey had been a very disappointing tournament for England, but not for Harry. He set up their first goal against Iraq with a brilliant header, and a few days later scored a great equaliser against Chile from outside the penalty area. He hit the ball perfectly into the bottom corner, just like he did again and again on the training ground.

'What a strike!' England teammate Ross Barkley said to Harry as they high-fived.

When he returned to England in July, Harry felt ready to become a Premier League star but again, Spurs had signed a new striker. Roberto Soldado cost £26 million after scoring lots of goals for Valencia in La Liga. Watching his rival in action, Harry didn't give up. He believed in himself more than ever.

For now, cup matches were Harry's chance to shine. In the fourth round of the League Cup, Spurs were heading for a disastrous defeat as opponents Hull took the lead in extra-time. Could Harry save the day?

When Jermain passed the ball to him, he had his back to goal, and needed to turn as quickly as possible. Harry used his strength and speed to spin cleverly past his marker. With a second touch, he dribbled towards the penalty area. He was in shooting range now. There were defenders right in front of him, blocking the goal, but he knew exactly where the bottom corner was. Harry could picture it in his head.

Goooooooooooooooooooooaaaaaaaaaaaaaaaaalllllllllll llllllllllllllllll!!!!!!!!!!!!!!!

Yes! Harry pumped his fists and ran towards the fans. The job wasn't done yet but his strike had put Spurs back in the game. When the tie went to penalties, he was one of the first to volunteer.

'I've got this,' he told Spurs manager André Villas-Boas. It was time to make up for that miss in the Europa League.

Harry was Spurs' fifth penalty taker. The pressure was on – he had to score, otherwise they were out of the competition. This time, he felt confident. He had a plan and he was going to stick to it, no matter what. As the goalkeeper dived to the right, Harry slammed his shot straight down the middle. The net bulged – what a relief!

'Well done, you showed a lot of guts there,' Tim Sherwood told him afterwards, giving him a hug. 'Your time is coming!'

In December 2013, Sherwood took over as Tottenham manager for the rest of the season, after the sacking of Villas-Boas. Harry didn't want to get his hopes up but he knew that his former Under-21 coach believed in his talent. Hopefully, Sherwood would give him more opportunities now. By February, he was coming off the bench more regularly but only because Jermain had signed for Toronto FC in Canada.

'I can't believe you're leaving!' Harry told him as they said goodbye. It was one of his saddest days at White Hart Lane. 'It won't be the same around here without you.'

Jermain smiled. 'It's time for me to move on and it's time for you to step up. I want you to wear this next season.'

It was Jermain's Number 18 shirt. Harry couldn't believe it.

'Wow, are you sure?' he asked. It would be such an honour to follow in his hero's footsteps. 'I promise to do you proud!'

Harry did just that when he finally got his first Premier League start for Tottenham against Sunderland in April. After years of waiting, Harry's time had come. He had never been so nervous in his life.

'Relax, just do what you do best,' Sherwood told him before kick-off. He was showing lots of faith in his young striker. 'Score!'

In the second half, Christian Eriksen curled a beautiful cross into the six-yard box. As the ball bounced, Harry made a late run and snuck in ahead of the centre-back to steer the ball into the bottom corner.

Goooooooooooooooooooooaaaaaaaaaaaaaalllllllllllllllll llllllllllll!!!!!!!!!!!!!!!!!!

Harry was buzzing. With his arms out wide like an aeroplane, he ran towards the Spurs fans near the corner flag. He had scored his first Premier League goal for Tottenham. It was time to celebrate in style.

Aaron Lennon chased after him and jumped up on his back. 'Yes, mate, what a goal!' he cheered.

Harry was soon in the middle of a big player hug. He was part of the team now and that was the greatest feeling ever.

There were six more league matches in the season and Harry started all of them. He was full of confidence and full of goals. Against West Bromwich, Aaron dribbled down the right wing and crossed into the six-yard box. Harry jumped highest and headed the ball past the defender on the line.

Goooooooooooooooooooooaaaaaaaaaaaaaaaaalllllllllllllll lllllllllllllllll!!!!!!!!!!!!!!!!!

A week later, they did it again. Aaron crossed the ball and Harry flicked it in. 2–1 to Tottenham!

'You've scored in three games in a row,' Emmanuel Adebayor shouted over the White Hart Lane noise. 'You're a goal machine!'

Harry had also already become a favourite with

the fans. They loved nothing more than cheering for
their local hero.

He's one of our own,
He's one of our own,
Harry Kane – he's one of our own!

Even an own goal against West Ham didn't stop
Harry's rise. In only six weeks, he had gone from sub
to England's hottest new striker.

'What an end to the season!' Tim Sherwood said
as they walked off the pitch together. 'You'll be
playing for a different manager next season, but don't
worry. If you keep banging in the goals, you're going
to be a Tottenham hero, no matter what!'

CHAPTER 18

EXCITING TIMES AT TOTTENHAM

'Do you think he'll bring in a big new striker?' Harry asked Andros during preseason.

His friend and teammate just shrugged. They would have to wait and see what the new Tottenham manager, Mauricio Pochettino, would do.

As the 2014–15 season kicked off, Spurs had signed a new goalkeeper, some new defenders and a new midfielder. But no new striker! That left only Emmanuel, Roberto and Harry. Harry was feeling really good about his chances. He worked extra hard to impress Pochettino.

'Great work, you've certainly got the desire that I'm looking for in my players,' his manager told him.

'This could be a huge season for you!'

Emmanuel started up front against West Ham in the Premier League but it was Harry, not Roberto, who came on for the last ten minutes. That was a good sign. If he kept scoring goals in other competitions, surely Pochettino would have no choice but to let him play. Harry got five goals in the Europa League and three in the League Cup.

'Kane needs to start in the Premier League!' the fans shouted in the stands.

Harry was making a name for himself with the England Under-21s too. He loved representing his country, especially in the big games. Against France, he positioned himself between the two centre-backs and waited like a predator. When Tom Ince played the through-ball, Harry was already on the move, chasing after it. He was too smart for the French defenders and he chipped his shot over the diving goalkeeper.

Goooooooooooooooooooooaaaaaaaaaaaaaaaaaaaallllllllll lllllllllllllll!!!!!!!!!!!!!!!

Two minutes later, Tom crossed from the right and

Harry was there in the six-yard box to tap the ball into the net.

'That's a proper striker's goal!' his teammate told him as they celebrated together.

Tom was right. Harry was a real goalscorer now, always in the right place at the right time. 'That's thirteen goals in twelve games!' he replied proudly.

By November 2014, there was lots of pressure on Pochettino to give Harry more game-time in the Premier League. Away at Aston Villa, he came on for Emmanuel with half an hour to go.

'Come on, we can still win this match!' his old friend Ryan Mason told him. Soon, Andros was on the pitch too. They were all living their Spurs dreams together.

In injury time, Tottenham won a free kick just outside the penalty area. It was Harry's last chance to save the day for Spurs. Érik Lamela wanted to take it but Harry wasn't letting his big opportunity go. He took a long, deep breath to calm his beating heart. He looked down at the ball and then up at the goal. 'This is going in!' he told himself.

He pumped his legs hard as he ran towards the ball. He needed as much power as possible. But rather than kicking it with the top of his boot, he kicked it with the side. As the ball swerved through the air, it deflected off the head of a Villa defender and past their scrambling keeper.

Goooooooooooooooaaaaaaaaaaaaaaaaaalllllllllllllllll lllllllllll!!!!!!!!!!!!!!!!!!!

It was the biggest goal that Harry had ever scored. He ran screaming towards the corner flag with all of his teammates behind him. In all the excitement, Harry threw himself down onto the grass for his favourite childhood celebration – the Klinsmann dive. Soon, he was at the bottom of a pile of happy players.

'What a beauty!' Danny Rose cheered in his face.

After scoring the match-winner, Harry was the talk of Tottenham. The fans had a new local hero and they wanted him to play every minute of every game. Against Hull City, Christian Eriksen's free kick hit the post but who was there to score the rebound? Harry!

Even when he didn't score for a few matches, Pochettino stuck with Harry. As a young player, he was still learning about playing at the top level.

'I believe in you,' his manager told him. 'You've got lots of potential and you've got the hunger to improve.'

With Pochettino's support, Harry bounced back against Swansea City. As Christian whipped in the corner kick, Harry made a late run into the box. He leapt high above his marker and powered his header down into the bottom corner.

Goooooooooooooooooooooaaaaaaaaaaaaalllllllllllllllll llllllllll!!!!!!!!!!!!!!!!!

Once he started scoring, Harry couldn't stop. He was such a natural finisher. On Boxing Day, Harry even scored against one of his old teams. Only eighteen months earlier, he had been sitting on the Leicester City bench. Now, he was causing them all kinds of problems as Tottenham's star striker. With hard work and great support, he was proving everyone wrong yet again.

Pochettino was delighted with his young striker's

form but he didn't want him to burn out. 'Get some rest because we've got big games coming up.'

Harry was so excited about the 2015 fixture list ahead – Chelsea on New Year's Day and then a few weeks later, the biggest game of them all: The North London Derby – Tottenham vs Arsenal.

'Don't worry, boss,' he said with a big smile. 'I'll be ready to score some more!'

CHAPTER 19

GOALS, GOALS AND MORE GOALS

As the Tottenham team walked out of the tunnel at White Hart Lane, Harry was second in line, right behind their goalkeeper and captain, Hugo Lloris. He had come so far in the last eighteen months – it was still hard to believe. There were thousands of fans in the stadium, cheering loudly for their team, and cheering loudly for him.

He's one of our own,
He's one of our own,
Harry Kane – he's one of our own!

Harry looked down at the young mascot who was

holding his hand. Ten years before, that had been one of his biggest dreams – to walk out on to the pitch with his Spurs heroes. Now, he was the Spurs hero, so what was his new dream? Goals, goals and more goals, starting against their London rivals Chelsea.

'Come on, we can't let them beat us again!' Harry shouted to Ryan and Andros. They were all fired up and ready to win.

Chelsea took the lead, but Harry didn't let his head drop. It just made him even more determined to score. He got the ball on the left wing and dribbled infield. He beat one player and then shrugged off another. He only had one thing on his mind – goals. When he was just outside the penalty area, he looked up.

He was still a long way out and there were lots of Chelsea players in his way, but Harry could shoot from anywhere. The Premier League would soon know just how lethal he was. For now, however, the defenders gave him just enough space. His low, powerful strike skidded across the wet grass, past the keeper and right into the bottom corner.

Goooooooooooooooaaaaaaaaaaaaaaaaaallllllllllllllllllll llllll!!!!!!!!!!!!!!!!!!!!!!!!

Game on! Harry ran towards the Tottenham fans and jumped into the air. He was used to scoring goals now, but this was one of his best and most important.

'You could outshoot a cowboy!' Kyle Walker joked as he climbed up on Harry's back.

At half-time, Spurs were winning 3–1 but Harry wanted more. 'We're not safe yet,' he warned his teammates. 'We've got to keep going!'

As the pass came towards him, Harry was just inside the Chelsea box with his back to goal. It didn't look dangerous at first but one lovely touch and spin later, it was very dangerous indeed. Harry stayed calm and placed his shot past the goalkeeper. It was like he'd been scoring top goals for years.

'Kane, that's gorgeous!' the TV commentator shouted. 'How good is *he*?'

The answer was: unstoppable. Even one of the best defences in the world couldn't handle him.

The match finished 5–3. It was a famous victory for Tottenham and Harry was their hero. After shaking hands with the Chelsea players, he walked around the pitch, clapping the supporters. Harry loved making them happy.

'If we play like that against Arsenal, we'll win that too!' he told Andros.

Harry got ready for the big North London Derby by scoring goals, goals and more goals. The timing was perfect; he was in the best form of his life just as Arsenal were coming to White Hart Lane. Revenge would be so sweet for Harry. Arsenal would soon realise their big mistake in letting him go.

After five minutes, Harry cut in from the left and curled a brilliant shot towards goal. He got ready to celebrate because the ball was heading for the bottom corner yet again. But the Arsenal keeper made a great save to tip it just round the post. So close! Harry put his hands to his head for a second but then kept going. If at first you don't score, shoot, shoot again.

At half-time, Tottenham were losing 1–0. 'We're

still in this game,' Pochettino told his players in the dressing room. 'If we keep creating chances, we'll score!'

When Érik took the corner, Harry stood lurking near the back post. He was waiting for the rebound. The keeper saved Mousa Dembélé's header but the ball bounced down in the box. Before the Arsenal defenders could react, Harry pounced to sweep it into the net.

Goooooooooooooooooaaaaaaaaaaaaaaaalllllllllllllllll llllllllll!!!!!!!!!!!!!!!!!!!!!

Harry roared and pumped his fists. Scoring for Spurs against Arsenal meant the world to him. He had dreamed about it ever since his first trip to White Hart Lane.

'Right, let's go and win this now!' Harry told his teammates.

With five minutes to go, it looked like it was going to be a draw. As Nabil Benteleb's cross drifted into the box, Harry's eyes never left the ball. He took a couple of steps backwards and then leapt high above Laurent Koscielny. It was a very difficult chance. To

score, his header would have to be really powerful
and really accurate.

As soon as the ball left his head, Harry knew that
he had got the angle right. It was looping towards
the corner but would the keeper have time to stop
it? No, Harry's perfect technique gave David Ospina
no chance.

*Goooooooooooooooaaaaaaaaaaaaaaaalllllllllllllllll
llllll!!!!!!!!!!!!!!!!!!!*

As the ball landed in the net, Harry turned away
to celebrate. What a moment! With the adrenaline
flooding through his veins, he slid across the grass,
screaming. As he looked up, he could see the Spurs
fans going crazy in the crowd. All that joy was
because of him!

The final minutes felt like hours but eventually, the
referee blew the final whistle. Tottenham 2, Arsenal
1! The party went on and on, both down on the
pitch and up in the stands.

'I might as well retire now!' Harry joked with
Ryan. 'Nothing will ever beat scoring the winner in
the North London Derby.'

'Not even playing for England?' his teammate asked him. 'Mate, Roy Hodgson would be a fool not to call you up to the squad!'

Harry was desperate to play for his country. Like his hero Becks, he wanted to be the national captain one day. After doing well for the Under-21s, he was now ready to step up into the senior team. He had won both the January and February Premier League Player of the Month awards. Then, in March, Harry got the call he had been waiting for.

'I'm in!' he told his partner Katie excitedly. He wanted to tell the whole world.

'In what?' she asked. 'What are you talking about?'

'The England squad!'

The amazing news spread throughout his family. Everyone wanted a ticket to watch his international debut.

'I might not even play!' Harry warned them, but they didn't care.

He was glad to see that lots of his Tottenham teammates were in the England team too. Training with superstars like Wayne Rooney and Gary Cahill

would be a lot less scary with Kyle, Andros and
Danny by his side. A week later, Ryan also joined the
Spurs gang.

'Thank goodness Fabian Delph got injured!' he
laughed. 'I was gutted to be the only one left behind.'

They were all named as substitutes for the Euro
2016 qualifier against Lithuania at Wembley. But
would any of them get to come on and play? They all
sat there on the England bench, crossing their fingers
and shaking with nerves.

With seventy minutes gone, England were
winning 3–0. It was time for Roy Hodgson to give
his young players a chance. Harry's England youth
teammate Ross Barkley was the first substitute and
Harry himself was the second. He was replacing
Wayne Rooney.

'Good luck!' Ryan and Andros said, patting him on
the back.

Harry tried to forget that he was making his
England debut at Wembley. That was something he
could enjoy later when the match was over. For now,
he just wanted to score.

As Raheem Sterling dribbled down the left wing, Harry took up his favourite striking position near the back post. Raheem's cross came straight towards him; he couldn't miss. Harry had all the time in the world to place his header past the keeper.

Gooooooooooooooooooaaaaaaaaaaaaaaallllllllllllllllll llllllllllll!!!!!!!!!!!!!!!

In his excitement, Harry bumped straight into the assistant referee. 'Sorry!' he called over his shoulder as he ran towards the corner flag.

'Was that your first touch?' Danny Welbeck asked as they celebrated.

'No, it was my third or fourth,' Harry replied with a cheeky grin. 'But I've only been on the field for about a minute!'

There had been so many highlights for Harry during the 2014–15 season already, but this was the best of all. He had scored for England on his debut. All of his dedication had paid off and he felt so proud of his achievements. Harry's childhood dream had come true.

CHAPTER 20

HARRY AND DELE

'So, do you think you can score as many this season?'
Charlie asked his brother.

Lots of people thought Harry's twenty-one Premier
League goals were a one-off, a fluke. They argued
that the PFA Young Player of the Year wouldn't be as
good in 2015–16 because defenders would know all
about him now. They would mark him out of
the game.

But Harry knew that wasn't true. 'Of course I can.
In fact, I'm aiming for even more this time!'

Charlie smiled. 'Good, because when you scored
those goals against Arsenal, the guys in the pub

bought me drinks all night. Sometimes, it's fun being your brother!'

Harry was still getting used to his fame. It was crazy! Every time he took his Labradors Brady and Wilson out for a walk, there were cameras waiting for him. They even took photos of Katie when she went out shopping.

'Our normal life is over!' she complained as she flicked through the newspapers.

After a very disappointing Euro 2015 with the England Under-21s, Harry was really looking forward to the new season. It would be his first as Tottenham's top striker. With Emmanuel gone, Harry now wore the famous Number 10 shirt. He was following in the footsteps of Spurs legends Jimmy Greaves, Gary Lineker and Harry's own hero, Teddy Sheringham.

Pochettino had strengthened the Spurs squad over the summer. They had signed Son Heung-min, a goal-scoring winger, and Dele Alli, a young attacking midfielder.

Harry and Dele clicked straight away. After a few

training sessions, Dele knew where Harry would run, and Harry knew where to make space for Dele. It was like they had been playing together for years. Soon, they were making up cool goal celebrations.

'It's like you guys are back in the school playground!' captain Hugo Lloris teased, but it was great to see them getting along so well.

Despite all of his excitement, Harry didn't score a single goal in August 2015. The newspapers kept calling him a 'one-season wonder' but that only made him more determined to prove them wrong.

'You're playing well and working hard for the team,' Pochettino reassured him. 'As soon as you get one goal, you'll get your confidence back.'

Against Manchester City, Christian's brilliant free kick bounced back off the post and landed right at Harry's feet. He was in lots of space and the goalkeeper was lying on the ground. Surely he couldn't miss an open goal? Some strikers might have passed the ball carefully into the net to make sure but instead, Harry curled it into the top corner.

Goooooooooooooooooaaaaaaaaaaaaaaaaalllllllllllllllll lllllllll!!!!!!!!!!!!!!!!!!!

Harry was delighted to score but most of all, he was relieved. His goal drought was over. Now, his season could really get started.

'Phew, I thought you were going to blaze that one over the bar!' Dele joked.

After that, Harry and Dele became the Premier League's deadliest double act. Between them, they had power, skill, pace and incredible shooting. By the end of February 2016, Tottenham were only two points behind Leicester City at the top of the table.

'If we keep playing like this, we'll be champions!' Pochettino told his players.

Every single one of them believed it. Spurs had the best defence in the league and were also one of the best attacking sides. Dele, Érik and Christian created lots of chances, and Harry scored lots of goals. It was one big, happy team effort. The pranks and teasing never stopped.

'How long do you have to wear that thing for?'

Dele asked during training one day. 'Halloween was months ago, you know!'

'Very funny,' Harry replied, giving his teammate a friendly punch. He was wearing a plastic face mask to protect his broken nose. 'Who knows, maybe it will bring me luck and I'll wear it forever!'

'Let's hope not!' Christian laughed.

Next up was the game that Harry had been waiting months for – the North London Derby. Could they win it again? Arsenal were only three points behind Spurs, so the match was even more important than usual.

'Come on lads, we've got to win this!' Harry shouted in the dressing room before kick-off, and all of his teammates cheered.

The atmosphere at White Hart Lane was incredible. The fans never stopped singing, even when Tottenham went 1–0 down. They believed that their team would bounce back, especially with Harry up front.

Early in the second half, Harry thought he had scored the equaliser. The goalkeeper saved his vicious shot, but surely he was behind the goal-line?

'That's in!' Harry screamed to the referee. But the technology showed that a tiny part of the ball hadn't crossed the line.

It was very frustrating but there was no point in complaining. Harry would just have to keep shooting until he got the whole ball into the net.

In the end, it was Toby Alderweireld who made it 1–1. Tottenham were playing well, but they needed a second goal to take the lead.

The ball was heading out for an Arsenal goal-kick but Dele managed to reach it and flick it back to his best friend, Harry. It looked like an impossible angle but with the supporters cheering him on, anything seemed possible. In a flash, Harry curled the ball up over the keeper and into the far corner.

Goooooooooooooooooooooaaaaaaaaaaaaaaaaaaaaaallll lllllllllllllllllll!!!!!!!!!!!!!

It was one of the best goals Harry had ever scored. He felt on top of the world. He took off his mask as he ran and slid across the grass. Dele was right behind him and gave him a big hug.

'Maybe you *should* keep wearing that!' he joked.

Tottenham couldn't quite hold on for another big victory. A draw wasn't the result that Spurs wanted, but Harry would never forget his incredible goal.

'We're still in this title race,' Pochettino urged his disappointed players. 'We just have to win every match until the end of the season.'

Harry and Dele did their best to make their Premier League dream come true. Dele set up both of Harry's goals against Aston Villa and they scored two each against Stoke City. But with three games of the season to go, Tottenham were seven points behind Leicester.

'If we don't beat Chelsea, our season's over,' Harry warned his teammates.

At half-time, it was all going according to plan. Harry scored the first goal and Son made it 2–0. They were cruising to victory but in the second half, they fell apart. All season, the Spurs players had stayed cool and focused but suddenly, they got angry and made silly mistakes. It finished 2–2.

'We threw it away!' Harry groaned as he walked

off the pitch. He was absolutely devastated. They had worked so hard all season. And for what?

'We've learnt a lot this year,' Pochettino told his players once everyone had calmed down. 'I know you feel awful right now but you should be so proud of yourselves. Next season, we'll come back stronger and win the league!'

There was one bit of good news that made Harry feel a little better. With twenty-five goals, he had won the Premier League Golden Boot, beating Sergio Agüero and Jamie Vardy.

'And they said I was a one-season wonder!' Harry told his brother Charlie as they played golf together. A smile spread slowly across his face. He loved proving people wrong.

CHAPTER 21

ENGLAND

When Harry first joined the England squad back in 2015, he was really nervous. It was a massive honour to represent his country but there was a lot of pressure too. If he didn't play well, there were lots of other great players that could take his place. Plus, it was scary being the new kid.

'You'll get used to this,' Wayne Rooney reassured him. 'I remember when I first got the call-up. I was only seventeen and it was terrifying! Just try to ignore the talk and enjoy yourself.'

Wayne helped Harry to feel more relaxed around the other senior players. They had fun playing golf and table tennis together. They were nice guys and Harry soon felt like one of the lads.

'France, here we come!' he cheered happily.

England qualified for Euro 2016 with ten wins out of ten. Harry added to his debut goal with a cheeky chip against San Marino and a low strike against Switzerland.

'At this rate, you're going to take my place in the team!' Wayne told him.

Harry shook his head. 'No, we'll play together up front!'

When Roy Hodgson announced his England squad for Euro 2016, Harry's name was there. He was delighted. There were four other strikers – Wayne, Jamie Vardy, Daniel Sturridge and Marcus Rashford – but none of them were scoring as many goals as him.

'You'll definitely play,' his brother Charlie told him.

Harry couldn't wait for his first major international tournament. His body felt pretty tired after a long Premier League season with Tottenham, but nothing was going to stop him.

'I really think we've got a good chance of winning it,' he told Dele, who was in the squad for France too.

His friend was feeling just as confident. 'If we play like we do for Spurs, we can definitely go all the way!'

Harry and Dele were both in the starting line-up for England's first group match against Russia. With Wayne now playing in midfield, Harry was England's number-one striker. He carried the country's great expectations in his shooting boots.

'I *have* to score!' he told himself as the match kicked off in Marseille.

England dominated the game but after seventy minutes, it was still 0–0. Harry got more and more frustrated. He was struggling to find the burst of pace that got him past Premier League defences. What was going wrong? His legs felt heavy and clumsy.

'Just be patient,' Wayne told him. 'If you keep getting into the right areas, the goal will come.'

When they won a free kick on the edge of the Russia box, Harry stood over the ball with Wayne and his Tottenham teammate Eric Dier. Everyone expected Harry to take it but as he ran up, he dummied the ball. Eric stepped up instead and curled the ball into the top corner. 1–0!

'Thanks for letting me take it,' he said to Harry as they celebrated the goal.

'No problem!' he replied. England had the lead and that was all that mattered.

But just as they were heading for a winning start to the tournament, Russia scored a late header. As he watched the ball flying towards the top corner, Harry's heart sank. He was very disappointed with the result and with his own performance in particular. It wasn't good enough. If he didn't improve, he would lose his place to Jamie or Daniel or Marcus.

'I believe in you, we all believe in you,' Hodgson told him after the game. 'So, believe in *yourself* !'

Harry tried not to read the player ratings in the English newspapers. Instead, he focused on bouncing back. If he could score a goal against Wales in the next game that would make everything better again.

But at half-time, it was looking like another bad day for Harry and England. He worked hard for the team but his goal-scoring touch was gone. The ball just wouldn't go in. When Gareth Bale scored a free kick to put Wales 1–0 up, Harry feared the worst.

'We need a quick goal in the second half,'
Hodgson told the team in the dressing room. 'Jamie
and Daniel, you'll be coming on to replace Harry and
Raheem.'

Harry stared down at the floor. Was that the end
of his tournament? He was really upset but he had to
accept the manager's decision.

Harry watched the second half from the bench
and cheered on his teammates. He was a good team
player. When Jamie scored the equaliser, he joined in
the celebrations. When Daniel scored the winner in
injury time, he sprinted to the corner flag to jump
on him.

'Get in!' he screamed.

It was only after the final whistle that Harry started
worrying again. Had he lost his place in the team, or
would he get another chance against Slovakia?

'I'm sorry but I've got to start Daniel and Jamie in
the next match,' Hodgson told him. 'Rest up and get
ready for the next round. We need you back, firing!'

Without Harry, England couldn't find a goal, but
0–0 was enough to take them through to the Round

of 16. He would get one more opportunity to score against Iceland, and he was pumped up for the biggest game of his international career.

It started brilliantly. Raheem was fouled in the box and Wayne scored the penalty. 1–0! It was a huge relief to get an early goal but two minutes later, it was 1–1.

'Come on, focus!' Joe Hart shouted at his teammates.

Harry and Dele both hit powerful long-range strikes that fizzed just over the crossbar. England looked in control of the game, but then Iceland scored again.

'No!' Harry shouted. His dream tournament was turning into an absolute nightmare.

England needed a hero, and quickly. Daniel crossed the ball to Harry in his favourite position near the back post. It was too low for a header so he went for the volley. Harry watched the ball carefully onto his foot and struck it beautifully. Unfortunately, it just wasn't his day, or his tournament. The goalkeeper jumped up high to make a good save. So close! Harry put his hands to his face – he was so desperate to score.

As the minutes ticked by, England started panicking. Harry's free kick flew miles wide. What a disaster! The boos from the fans grew louder.

'Stay calm, we've got plenty of time!' Hodgson called out from the touchline.

That time, however, ran out. At the final whistle, the Iceland players celebrated and the England players sank to their knees. They were out of the Euros after a terrible, embarrassing defeat.

As he trudged off the pitch, Harry was in shock. It was the worst feeling ever. He felt like he had really let his country down. Would they ever forgive him?

To take his mind off the disappointment, Harry watched American Football and focused on his future goals. With Tottenham, he would be playing in the Champions League for the first time, and trying to win the Premier League title. With England, he would be playing in the qualifiers for World Cup 2018. There were lots of exciting challenges ahead.

'I need to make things right!' Harry told himself.

CHAPTER 22

TOTTENHAM FOR THE TITLE?

'Argggghhhhhhhhhhhhhhhhhh!' Harry screamed as he lay down on the turf. He tried to stay calm but it felt like really bad news. As he waved for the physio, the pain got worse and worse. White Hart Lane went quiet. The Spurs fans waited nervously to see whether their star striker could carry on.

'You're not singing anymore!' the opposing Sunderland fans cheered bitterly.

If only Harry hadn't slid in for the tackle. Tottenham were already winning 1–0 thanks to his goal. That was his job: scoring goals, not making tackles. But Harry always worked hard for the team. As he went to block the Sunderland centre-back, his right ankle twisted awkwardly in the grass. If the injury wasn't too serious, Harry promised himself that he would never defend again.

Unfortunately, it *was* serious. Harry tried to get up and play on but that wasn't possible. He hobbled over to the touchline and sat down again. The Spurs fans cheered and clapped their hero but Harry's match was over. He was carried down the tunnel on a stretcher.

'There's good news and there's bad news,' the doctor told him after the X-rays. 'The good news is that there's no fracture. The bad news is that there's ligament damage.'

Harry wasn't a medical expert but he knew that 'ligament damage' meant no football for a while. 'How long will I be out of action?' he asked, fearing a big number.

'It's too early to say but you should prepare yourself for eight weeks out. Hopefully, it won't be that long.'

Eight weeks! If everything went well, Harry would be back before December but it was still a big blow. His 2016–17 season had only just started. He had only played in one Champions League match. Tottenham needed him.

'Who's going to get all our goals now?' he asked.

'Without you hogging all the chances, I'll score loads more!' Dele replied.

It was good to have Katie and his teammates around to cheer Harry up. It was going to be a boring, difficult couple of months for him. He would just have to recover as quickly as possible. To keep himself going, Harry picked out a key date in the calendar: 6 November. The North London Derby – that was what he was aiming for.

'I always score against Arsenal!' Harry reminded everyone.

Thanks to lots of hard work in the gym, he made it just in time. Harry was delighted to be back on the pitch, even if he wasn't at his best. Early in the second half, Tottenham won a penalty and Harry quickly grabbed the ball. It was the perfect chance to get a comeback goal.

He took a long, deep breath and waited for the

referee's whistle. As the Arsenal keeper dived to his left, Harry placed it down the middle.

Goooooooooooooooooaaaaaaaaaaaaaaaaallllllllllllllll lllllll!!!!!!!!!!!!!!!!!!!!

He was back! Harry pumped his fists at the crowd as his teammates jumped on him.

'What a cool finish!' Son cheered.

Harry didn't last the full match, but he was pleased with his return. 'If I want to win the Golden Boot again, I've got some catching up to do!' he told Pochettino.

Tottenham got knocked out in the Champions League Group Stage, but Harry still had time to grab his first goals in the competition.

'Never mind, we've just got to focus on the Premier League title now,' he told Dele. 'We'll conquer Europe next year!'

After all his goals, Harry became a transfer target for Real Madrid and Manchester United. Tottenham wanted to keep their local hero for as long as possible, so they offered Harry a big new contract until 2020. Saying no didn't even cross his mind.

'I can't leave!' Harry said happily. 'This is my home and we've got trophies to win.'

To celebrate, he went on another scoring spree. Two against Watford, three against West Brom, three against Stoke, two against Everton. By March, he was up to nineteen goals and at the top of the goal-scoring charts again.

'Congratulations, you're back where you belong,' Katie told him.

Harry was pleased but the Premier League title was his number one aim. Spurs were in second place behind Chelsea. Harry would give his all to catch them.

For Harry, winning the 2017 FA Cup was aim number two. In the quarter-finals, Tottenham faced his old club Millwall. So much had changed in the five years since his loan spell there. He would always be grateful to the Lions for their support but that didn't mean he would take it easy on them. Trophies always came first.

As soon as the ball came to him, Harry shot at goal. The Millwall keeper saved it but Harry didn't even notice. He was lying on the grass in agony.

'Is it your right ankle again?' the physio asked after rushing over to him.

Harry just nodded. Was it the same injury all over again? He couldn't bear to think about another eight weeks on the sidelines. He managed to limp off the pitch and down the tunnel. He didn't need to use the stretcher this time and that was a good sign.

'There is ligament damage,' the doctors confirmed, 'but it's not as serious as before. We'll do our best to get you back for the semi-final.'

With a target to aim for, Harry was determined to recover in time. He was back in action two weeks before their big cup match against Chelsea. There was even time for him to score a goal.

'See, I'm feeling sharp!' he promised Pochettino. There was no way that he could miss playing in the FA Cup semi-final. He was a big game player and his team needed him.

The atmosphere at Wembley was electric. As usual, Harry was the second Spurs player out of the tunnel. As he looked up, he could see big blocks of white in the crowd.

'Tottenham! Tottenham! Tottenham!'

If the stadium was this loud for the semi-final, what would the final be like? But Harry couldn't get ahead of himself. He had to focus on beating Chelsea first.

The Blues took the lead but with Harry on the pitch, Spurs were always in the game. He stayed onside at the front post to flick on Christian's low cross. Thanks to his clever touch, the ball flew right into the bottom corner.

Goooooooooooooooooooaaaaaaaaaaaaaaaaaaaallllllllllll llllllllllllllllll!!!!!!!!!!!!

'It's like you've got eyes in the back of your head!' Christian cheered as they hugged.

'Why would I need that?' Harry asked. 'The goal doesn't move – it's always in the same place!'

Despite his best efforts, Chelsea scored two late goals to win 4–2. It was very disappointing but Tottenham's season wasn't over yet.

'We've got five Premier League matches left,' Harry told Dele. 'If we can get all fifteen points, the pressure is on Chelsea.'

The first three points came at White Hart Lane in

the North London Derby against Arsenal. Dele got the first goal and Harry scored the second from the penalty spot. The dream was still alive! But at West Ham a week later, Spurs fell apart again. Harry, Dele and Christian tried and tried but they couldn't get the goal they needed. In the second half, Tottenham panicked and conceded a silly goal. The 1-0 defeat left them seven points behind Chelsea.

'No, the title race isn't over yet,' Pochettino told his players. 'Come on, let's finish on a high!'

There was no chance of Harry relaxing. Even if he didn't win the Premier League, he could still win the Golden Boot. He was only three goals behind Everton's Romelu Lukaku with three games to go. Harry closed the gap to two with a neat flick against Manchester United.

'Three goals against Leicester and Hull? I can do that!' he told Dele.

'But what if Lukaku scores again?'

Dele was right; Harry needed to aim even higher. Against Leicester, his first goal was a tap-in, his second was a header and the third was a rocket from the edge of the penalty area. Harry had another amazing hat-trick but he wasn't finished yet. In injury time, he got the ball in the same position and scored again!

Harry was pleased with his four goals but he couldn't help asking himself, 'Why couldn't I do that against West Ham?' He was never satisfied.

Harry would have to think about that later, though. With one game to go, he was on 26 goals and Lukaku was on 24. At the final whistle in the Arsenal vs Everton game, Lukaku was up to 25 goals for Everton thanks to a penalty, but meanwhile Harry was way ahead on 29! With two fantastic finishes and a tap-in, he had grabbed yet another hat-trick against Hull.

'Wow, you were only two goals off the Premier League record,' his proud dad told him. 'And you missed eight games through injury!'

Harry was delighted with his second Golden Boot in a row but it didn't make up for another season without a trophy. Tottenham kept getting so close to glory but would they ever be crowned champions? Harry, the local hero, never stopped believing.

CHAPTER 23

ONE OF EUROPE'S FINEST

Harry jumped up in the England wall but the free kick flew past him and into the top corner. As he watched, his heart sank. Scotland were winning 2–1 at Hampden Park with a few minutes to go.

'Come on, we can't lose this!' Harry shouted to his teammates.

England were unbeaten in qualification for the 2018 World Cup and this, in June 2017, was a key match against their British rivals. It was also Harry's first match as the national captain. For all of these reasons, he refused to let it end in an embarrassing defeat.

With seconds to go, Kyle Walker passed to Raheem Sterling on the left wing. Harry was surrounded by Scottish defenders but he was clever enough to escape. The centre-backs watched Raheem's high cross sail over their heads and thought they were safe. But they weren't. They had missed Harry's brilliant run to the back post.

There wasn't enough time or space to take a touch, so Harry went for a side-foot volley. With incredible technique and composure, he guided his shot past the keeper.

Goooooooooooooooooooooaaaaaaaaaaaalllllllllllllllll llllll!!!!!!!!!!!!!!

It was another big goal in a big game. Under pressure, Harry hardly ever failed.

'You're a born leader,' England manager Gareth Southgate told him after the match. 'That's why I gave you the captain's armband.'

At twenty-four, Harry wasn't a bright young talent anymore. After three excellent seasons, he was now an experienced player with lots of responsibility for club and country. Now he felt ready to take the next step and become one of Europe's finest.

'I might not have as much skill as Cristiano

Ronaldo and Lionel Messi but I can score as many goals,' he told Dele.

Harry was full of ambition ahead of the 2017–18 season. It was time to shine in the Champions League as well as the Premier League. But first, he had to get August out of the way.

'Maybe I should just take the month off!' Harry joked at home with Katie.

No matter how hard he tried and how many shots he took, he just couldn't score. He was trying to ignore all the talk about his August goal curse. Their beautiful baby daughter was certainly helping to take his mind off things.

'Yes, you could stay home and change Ivy's nappies with me!' Katie replied with a smile. She knew that Harry could never stay away from football. He loved it so much.

On 1 September, he travelled with England to play against Malta. 'Don't worry, I've got this,' he told his teammates. 'August is over!'

As Dele twisted and turned in the penalty area, Harry got into space and called for the pass. The goalkeeper rushed out but he calmly slotted the ball into the net.

Goooooooooooooooooooaaaaaaaaaaaaaaalllllllllllllll lllllllll!!!!!!!!!!!!!!!!!!

On the touchline, Southgate pumped his fists. Tottenham fans all over the world did the same. Their goal machine was back.

'Finally!' Dele teased him. 'What would you do without me?'

Harry was too relieved to fight back. 'Thanks, you're the best!' he replied.

Once he scored one, Harry usually scored two. He did it against Malta and then he did it against Everton in the Premier League. As always, Harry's timing was perfect. Tottenham were about to start their Champions League campaign against German giants Borussia Dortmund.

'They picked the wrong time to face me!' he said confidently.

Harry won the ball on the halfway line, headed it forward and chased after it. He wasn't letting anyone get in his way. As he entered the Dortmund penalty

area, the defender tried to push him wide. Harry
didn't mind; he could score from any angle! Before the
keeper could react, the ball flew past him.

The Tottenham fans went wild.

He's one of our own,
He's one of our own,
Harry Kane – he's one of our own!

Harry went hunting for another goal and he got it.

'He just gets better and better!' the commentator
marvelled.

It was Harry's first Champions League double, but
he wanted a third. He was always hungry for more
goals. With a few minutes to go, Pochettino took
him off.

'The hat-trick will have to wait until next week!' he
told his star striker, patting him on the back.

The APOEL Nicosia defence was prepared for
Harry's arrival but there was nothing that they could
do to stop him. He made it look so easy. He scored
his first goal with his left foot and the second with his

right. There was half an hour left to get his third but he only needed five minutes.

Kieran Trippier curled the ball in from the right and Harry ran from the edge of the box to glance it down into the bottom corner. All that heading practice had been worth it.

Goooooooooooooooooooooooaaaaaaaaaaaaaaaalllllllll llllllllllllllll!!!!!!!!!!!!!!

Harry ran towards Kieran and gave him a big hug. He was always grateful for the assists but this one was particularly special. Harry had his first ever Champions League hat-trick.

'That was perfect!' he told Son afterwards, clutching the match ball tightly.

'Yeah, it was a good win,' his teammate replied.

'No, I mean it was a perfect hat-trick,' Harry explained. 'One with my right foot, one with my left, and one with my head. That's the first time I've ever done that!'

Son laughed. 'You score so many goals. How can you remember them all?'

Every single goal was important to Harry and he

often watched videos of his matches to help him improve. He never stopped working on his game.

'Is Kane the best striker in Europe right now?' the newspapers asked. Harry had already scored thirty-six goals by September and he still had three months of the year to go!

To keep his feet on the ground, Harry thought back to his early football days. Arsenal had rejected him and Tottenham had nearly done the same. As an eleven-year-old boy, he had told his hero David Beckham that he wanted to play at Wembley for England. Thanks to lots of practice and determination, Harry had achieved that dream and so much more.

His shirt now hung next to Becks' shirt in the hallway at Chingford Foundation School. Harry had the future at his goalscoring feet. He would do everything possible to lead England to World Cup glory in Russia. But before that, Harry was still determined to win trophies with his boyhood club, Tottenham.

Turn the page for a sneak preview of
another brilliant football story by
Matt and Tom Oldfield. . .

STERLING

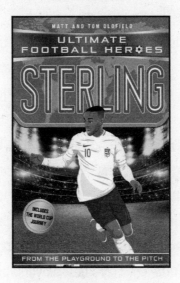

Available now!

CHAPTER 1

A DREAM COME TRUE

It was 14 November 2012. This was the biggest day of Raheem's life so far – after all, you only made your England debut once. Two months earlier, he had been called up for the World Cup 2014 qualifier against Ukraine and named as a substitute. He didn't get to come on but he still learned a lot from training with the country's best players. It was hard watching from the bench, especially when the team was losing with ten minutes to go. With his pace and skill, Raheem knew he could have made a difference on the wing against a tired defence but in the end, England managed to get a draw without him.

This time, though, in Sweden, not only was

Raheem playing but he was starting. 'I'll be testing some of the younger players in tomorrow's friendly,' Roy Hodgson, the England manager, had told him as they walked off the training pitch the day before. 'You'll be starting, Raheem – we believe you're ready for this.' Roy had always had great faith in him; at Liverpool, he had given him his debut at the age of just fifteen. Raheem could only nod and flash his trademark big smile. It was the news he'd been waiting for.

In the tunnel before the match in Stockholm, he took a deep breath and let the noise of the 50,000 fans in the stadium fire him up. This was what he was born to do. Moments later, he walked out onto the pitch, holding the hand of a Swedish mascot. Just like for Liverpool, Steven Gerrard was there with him as captain and mentor. In the dressing room before the game, Stevie could see that Raheem was nervous.

'There's nothing to worry about, kid. It's no different to playing in front of the Kop at Liverpool. Don't rush things today – just do your thing and enjoy it. Something tells me this won't be your only England cap!'

Stevie patted him on the back and left him to his pre-match stretches. It was a real comfort to have such experienced teammates alongside him – these big games could be pretty scary for a seventeen-year-old.

As the national anthem played, Raheem looked down proudly at the famous three lions on his white tracksuit top. He still couldn't quite believe that he was wearing the England shirt so soon into his career. What a year 2012 had been and there was still a month of it to go. Despite being born in Jamaica, England was certainly Raheem's footballing home. His homeland would always have a special place in his heart but it was in London and Liverpool that he had developed as both a player and a person.

Just before kick-off, another Liverpool teammate, Glen Johnson, came over to give him some words of advice: 'Raheem, stay focused today. You're on the right wing and I'm at right back so we'll be working together a lot. Make those amazing attacking runs when you can but don't forget to defend too. I don't want to spend the whole game clearing up your mess!' Glen gave him a friendly slap on the back and they took up their positions ready for the start.

Raheem knew it wouldn't be an easy game; the Sweden team included experienced Premier-League players like Jonas Olsson and Seb Larsson, plus one of his favourite players in the world, the amazing striker Zlatan Ibrahimović. Raheem was really looking forward to playing against Zlatan and seeing his tricks and flicks up close. Zlatan did not disappoint, scoring the first goal after 20 minutes.

Five minutes later, Raheem found space for the first time in the match and he ran at the Swedish defence before passing to Danny Welbeck, who nearly set up a goal. Raheem could sense the Sweden fans holding their breath when he had the ball at his feet. They knew he was a threat and that gave him confidence.

Raheem was involved again as England made it 1-1. Stevie passed to him deep inside his own half and this time, rather than dribbling, he did what coaches had always told him to do – 'get your head up and look up for the pass'. He could see Ashley Young making a great run over on the left and he played a great ball out to him. Ashley did brilliantly and crossed for Danny to score.

England took the lead before half-time but the second half was all about Zlatan. His second goal was a volley, his third was a powerful free-kick and his fourth was one of the best goals Raheem had ever seen, an impossible overhead kick from thirty yards out. Watching such an amazing performance, Raheem was sure that he had the desire and the talent to be that good. He just needed to keep working hard.

With five minutes to go, Raheem was substituted. 'Well done, lad,' Roy said as he made his way off the pitch. As he took his seat on the bench, Raheem felt really tired but pleased with the way he had played. It hadn't been the dream debut he had hoped for but it had been an amazing experience to represent his country. He couldn't wait to do it again, especially back at Wembley. As a kid, he had lived around the corner from the new stadium, playing football in the streets as it was being built. To play on that pitch in front of all those fans would be unbelievable.

On the flight back to England, Raheem thought back on how far he'd come. There were times when his future had looked bleak. But thanks to football, he stayed out of trouble and learnt respect, hard work and self-esteem. He owed a lot of people for the support they had given him over the years – his mum Nadine, his teachers, his coaches. They had all believed in his talent.

Most of all, he thought about what Chris, his teacher at Vernon House, had once said to him. 'If you carry on the way you're going, by the time you're seventeen you'll either be in prison or playing for England.' Raheem smiled to himself; thankfully, he had achieved the second option. But he promised himself that this was just the beginning.

HARRY KANE HONOURS

Individual

🏆 PFA Young Player of the Year: 2014–15

🏆 Premier League PFA Team of the Year: 2014–15, 2015–16, 2016–17

🏆 Premier League Golden Boot: 2015–16, 2016–17

KANE

⑩ THE FACTS

NAME: HARRY EDWARD KANE

DATE OF BIRTH: 28 July 1993

AGE: 24

PLACE OF BIRTH: Walthamstow, London

NATIONALITY: England

BEST FRIEND: Dele Alli

CURRENT CLUB: Tottenham

POSITION: ST

THE STATS

Height (cm):	188
Club appearances:	239
Club goals:	126
Club trophies:	0
International appearances:	23
International goals:	12
International trophies:	0
Ballon d'Ors:	0

★ ★ ★ **HERO RATING: 88** ★ ★ ★

GREATEST MOMENTS

Type and search the web links to see the magic for yourself!

 **7 APRIL 2014,
TOTTENHAM 5-1 SUNDERLAND**

https://www.youtube.com/watch?v=3XnvmoUOAXk

Harry's first Premier League goal was a long time coming. After four loan spells, he finally got his chance at Tottenham under Tim Sherwood. Against Sunderland, Christian Eriksen curled a brilliant ball into the six-yard box and Harry beat his marker to score. It was a real striker's finish and a sign of the great things to come.

2 NOVEMBER 2014, ASTON VILLA 1-2 TOTTENHAM

https://www.youtube.com/watch?v=VYIDn3ohqo8

This was the goal that changed Harry's career at White Hart Lane. He has definitely scored better goals but this last-minute free kick won the match for Tottenham. Before this, Harry was a substitute. After this, he became the star striker we know and love.

7 FEBRUARY 2015, TOTTENHAM 2-1 ARSENAL

https://www.youtube.com/watch?v=y62kN8PGHFo

This was the day that Harry became a true Tottenham hero. In the big North London Derby, he scored two goals to secure a famous victory. Harry's first goal was a tap-in but the second was a world-class header. He used his power and technique to direct the ball right into the corner of the Arsenal goal.

19 MARCH 2015, ENGLAND 4-0 LITHUANIA

https://www.youtube.com/watch?v=OPBjwNKhoKc
It was Harry's international debut at Wembley and he had only been on the pitch for 80 seconds. Raheem Sterling crossed from the left and, as usual, Harry was in the right place at the right time. He scored with a simple header at the back post and then bumped into the match official!

6 OCTOBER 2017, ENGLAND 1-0 SLOVENIA

https://www.youtube.com/watch?v=yMloUtQRHos
On a tense night at Wembley, the new England captain led his country to the 2018 World Cup in Russia. In the last minute, Kyle Walker crossed from the right and Harry stretched out his lethal right leg to poke the ball past the keeper.

MATT AND TOM OLDFIELD

PLAY LIKE YOUR HEROES
THE HARRY KANE FINISH

SEE IT HERE ▶ YouTube

https://www.youtube.com watch?v=EAWRV0GThIs&t=314s

STEP 1: Make a clever forward run between the defenders.

STEP 2: When you get the ball, control it perfectly. That first touch is really important!

STEP 3: Use your skill and strength to escape your marker and open up a bit of space to shoot.

STEP 4: Don't wait! Strike the ball as early as possible to surprise the keeper.

STEP 5: Keep it low! When the ball zips across the grass, it's harder for the keeper to save.

STEP 6: Aim for the corner! Picture the goal in your head and pick your spot. Go for the right or the left but never go down the middle.

STEP 7: As the ball hits the back of the net, run towards the fans in the corner with your arms out wide and a big grin on your face.

TEST YOUR KNOWLEDGE

QUESTIONS

1. Who was Harry's first Tottenham hero?

2. What position did Harry first play at Ridgeway Rovers?

3. Which other England legend also played for Ridgeway Rovers?

4. Which three clubs did Harry have trials with when he was a youngster?

5. Name three of Harry's teammates in the Tottenham youth team.

6. How many loan spells did Harry have before settling at Spurs?

7. Who was the Spurs manager when Harry made his first Premier League start?

8. Who gave Harry his Number 18 shirt when he left Tottenham?

9. Harry scored on his England debut – True or False?

10. How many goals did Harry score for England at Euro 2016?

11. How many Premier League Golden Boots has Harry won so far?

Answers below. . . No cheating!

1. *Teddy Sheringham* 2. *Goalkeeper* 3. *David Beckham* 4. *Arsenal, Watford and Tottenham* 5. *Any of Tom Carroll, Jonathan Obika, Kudus Oyenuga, Ryan Mason, Andros Townsend and Steven Caulker* 6. *Four – Leyton Orient, Millwall, Norwich City and Leicester City* 7. *Tim Sherwood* 8. *Jermain Defoe* 9. *True – Harry scored after only 80 seconds against Lithuania!* 10. *0* 11. *2*

MAGUIRE

TABLE OF CONTENTS

CHAPTER 1

"SLABHEAD" SAVES THE DAY!

Cosmos Arena, Samara, 7 July 2018

What a massive moment it was for Gareth
Southgate's young England team – they were about
to play in the 2018 World Cup quarter-finals! As
the players arrived at the Cosmos Arena, however,
they looked happy and relaxed. Harry Maguire had a
particularly big smile on his face. Why not? He was
in fantasy land!

In Summer 2014, Harry had just finished seventh
in League One with his hometown club, Sheffield
United.

In Summer 2015, he had just been relegated from
the Championship, while on loan at Wigan Athletic.

In Summer 2017, he had just been relegated from the Premier League with Hull City.

But now, in Summer 2018, Harry was an international footballer, starring for England at the World Cup!

The tournament had already been a big success for the team. They had beaten Tunisia, they had thrashed Panama and best of all, they had finally won a World Cup penalty shoot-out, against Colombia. Could they now go all the way and win the trophy? The players believed, and the fans believed too. England had gone football crazy once again!

It's coming home, it's coming home,
It's coming, FOOTBALL'S COMING HOME!

Every player was now a national hero, from goalkeeper Jordan Pickford all the way through to goal machine Harry Kane.

But perhaps the biggest heroes of all were Southgate's all-Yorkshire back three. Harry Maguire and Kyle Walker were both from Sheffield, while John Stones was born nearby in Barnsley. Kyle brought the speed, John brought the brains, and Harry brought the strength.

Each of them brought their own skill. Together, they formed a deadly defensive team. They were brilliant at the back, but also awesome in attack!

Harry was absolutely buzzing by the time the players arrived in the dressing room. After all, it wasn't every day that he got to play in a World Cup quarter-final! Sweden would be tough opponents but the new England were fearless. If they played well, they could beat anyone.

But wait, there was a problem! As Harry pulled on his red '6 MAGUIRE' shirt, it didn't fit. At six feet four, he was a big guy who needed a big shirt.

'Especially with that Slabhead of yours!' his England and Leicester teammate, Jamie Vardy, was always joking.

'Cheers, Vards!' Unfortunately for Harry, that nickname stuck. Now, lots of his teammates called him 'Slabhead' too.

With minutes to go before kick-off, the England's kit man, Pat, rushed off to print his name and number on a bigger shirt.

Some players might have panicked in that nerve-wracking situation, but not Harry. That wasn't his style. He was a laid-back lad, both on and off the pitch. He could handle the big-game pressure. In fact, he loved it. It was what being a professional footballer was all about.

'Thanks, Pat!' Harry shouted, quickly pulling on his new shirt. 'Right, let's win this, lads!'

It was still only his tenth cap but he was already one of the team leaders.

As usual, Harry started calmly, passing the ball around the defence, to Kyle and John, and to his left wing-back, Ashley. Southgate wanted his team to play out confidently from the back – that's why Harry was in the team!

For a big man, Harry was so comfortable on the ball. Whenever he spotted some space in front of him, he dribbled forward on the attack. With his skill and strength, it was so hard to stop him.

In the thirtieth minute, England won a corner-kick.

'Come on!' their fans cheered loudly in the stands. 'This is it!'

After lots of work in training, Southgate's side were now set-piece specialists. Every time the ball came into the box, they looked like they were going to score.

The deliveries were always dangerous, from Ashley on the left and Kieran Trippier on the right.

And the headers were always heroic, from John and from the two Harrys.

Earlier in the World Cup, in the last minute against Tunisia, Maguire had won the first header and Kane had scored the second. What could they do now against Sweden in the quarter-final?

As Ashley crossed from the left, Harry Maguire made his move towards the penalty spot. This ball was his, and no-one was going to stop him! He muscled his way past the Sweden defenders and powered a thumping header into the bottom corner.

Goooooooooooooooooooaaaaaaaaaaaaaaaallllllllllll llllllllllll!!!!!!!!!!!!!!!!!!!

What a time to score his first-ever international goal! Harry raced towards the fans, pumping his fists and roaring like a lion. Playing for his country meant so much to him. Since his childhood, he had always been England's biggest fan. Now, he was England's goalscoring hero.

Down by the corner flag, Harry slid across the grass on his knees and his teammates piled on top of him.

'Yes, Slabhead!' John cheered.

'Slabhead, you beauty!' Kieran screamed.

As he got back to his feet, Harry looked up and listened. The delighted England fans were singing his song:

Harry Maguire, your defence is terrified!
Harry Maguire, na na na na na na na na na na!

What a feeling! Harry knew that his family would be singing along proudly. They were all there in Russia to cheer him on – his parents, Alan and Zoe, his brothers, Joe and Laurence, his sister Daisy, and his girlfriend, Fern. Without them, Harry's journey might never have happened.

And what a journey it had been! Harry had travelled with Joe and Laurence to watch England at Euro 2016. Just two years later, he was scoring in a World Cup quarter-final.

Harry couldn't get carried away, though.

'Focus!' Southgate shouted from the sidelines.

England had defending to do. Harry won header after header, and tackle after tackle. He certainly wasn't going to ruin his big match by making a big mistake.

In the second half, Jesse Lingard crossed to Dele Alli – 2–0 to England!

When the referee blew the final whistle, John jumped up into Harry's arms.

'We did it, Big Man – we're in the World Cup semi-finals!'

The England celebrations went on and on at the Cosmos Arena. The players partied on the pitch, right in front of their loyal fans. They were all staying in Russia, but as for football itself:

It's coming home, it's coming home,
It's coming, FOOTBALL'S COMING HOME!

'Slabhead saves the day!' Jamie cheered, giving Harry a big hug. He was so pleased for his friend and teammate.

'Cheers, Vards. I wouldn't be here if it wasn't for your annoying banter!'

It took a little while for the importance of their victory to sink in. England hadn't reached the World Cup semi-finals since 1990. That was twenty-eight years ago!

It wasn't just that, though. With their spirit and style, the players had made their country so proud. Back at the base camp, Harry watched all the amazing videos of the celebrations at home in England.

'Wow, look how happy we've made everyone!' he thought to himself.

Harry's face was all over the Internet, and it was even tattooed on a fan's chest!

At the age of twenty-five, Harry had already

achieved his childhood dreams and more. Not only had he become a top Premier League player, but now he was also an England World Cup hero. 'England World Cup hero' – would he ever get used to the sound of those words?

It hadn't been an easy road to glory, however. Harry had worked his way up, step by step, level by level, game after game.

It had taken years of dedication, determination, and brotherly battles.

It had taken years of support from family, friends and coaches.

But boy, had it all been worth it!

CHAPTER 2

BROTHERLY BATTLES

Growing up, Joe and Harry were as inseparable as
brothers can be. Where one young Maguire went,
the other one almost always followed. Joe was older
by eighteen months but that never stopped Harry.
Anything his brother could do, he could do too –
walking, reading, riding a bike and, of course, playing
football.

Their dad, Alan, had been a good player when he
was younger. He was now a coach at the local club
in Sheffield, Brunsmeer Athletic, and he got his sons
kicking as soon as he could.

'That's it!' Alan shouted as Joe booted the ball
towards goal. With a dramatic dive, he let his son's

shot roll right past him and into the net. *GOAL!*

'Yes!' Joe cheered, lifting his shirt over his head just like he'd seen the superstars do on TV.

'Right, your turn, Harry.'

Anything his brother could do, he could do too, only better! Harry was so determined. As he stood there between the goalposts, Alan could see a very serious look on his younger son's little face.

Harry took a really long run-up, swung his right leg back as far as it would go, and then *Bang!* He booted the ball into the air and it landed perfectly in the bottom corner. *GOAL!*

'What a strike!' his dad cried out with a shocked look on his face. He hadn't even bothered with his usual dramatic dive. How had Harry done that? He was still only four years old!

'Yes!' Harry cheered, sliding across the mud on his knees.

Joe watched on with a sulky frown. He wasn't going to let his younger brother take all the glory. 'Right, it's my turn again!' he said sternly.

Hours later, Alan was still standing there between

the goalposts as his sons took shots at goal, over and over again.

As they got older, the Maguire brothers became more and more competitive. They battled over school reports, pocket money, TV shows and, of course, football.

'Boys, that's enough!' their mum, Zoe, would shout whenever they dared to play one vs one in the living room. 'You know the rules – go outside if you want to do that!'

In their back garden, Joe and Harry didn't have to worry about breaking vases, or tripping over table legs. They were free to play, and play hard.

'Let the battle begin!' Joe said, grinning like an evil villain.

He was bigger and stronger than Harry, and he often used that to his advantage. Fouls? In their back-garden games, there was no such thing! They could do as many pushes, pulls, shoulder barges and sliding tackles as they liked.

After all, there were no referees in their brotherly battles – just parents ready to step in if they really started fighting.

'Play nicely out there, okay?'

'Yes, Mum!'

Harry loved every minute of it. Yes, he was smaller, but he was more skilful than his brother. He was a natural with the ball at his feet. He knew that he could dribble past Joe, and if only he could dodge his angry arms and long legs, then… *GOAL!*

Harry was also braver. He hated losing, and especially losing to his elder brother. That was the worst thing in the world! Joe would boast about it for days. So, Harry always did everything he could to make sure that didn't happen.

He chased, he challenged,

He barged, he blocked.

Their battles were always close and always fierce. They couldn't help it; they were competitive kids who loved football.

'Sorry!' they called out when they smashed a kitchen window.

'Sorry!' they called out when they turned the garden into a mud-bath and their dad had to lay down new grass.

Sometimes, their battles went on all day long and then carried on the next morning too. However long it took, they always ended with red faces, red knees and sweaty shirts.

'Well played,' Harry said, shaking Joe's hand. He was tired but happy because he had another victory to add to his list. 'Another battle tomorrow?'

'Of course,' his brother replied immediately. 'I want revenge!'

Harry and Joe's one vs one battles later turned into two vs two. Laurence wanted to do everything his older brothers did, and so did their sister, Daisy. With double the players, there was double the trouble.

It was total mayhem in the Maguire back garden, with tackles flying in everywhere. Their dad's freshly-laid grass didn't stand a chance.

'Why are our kids so competitive?' Zoe asked, as she kept watch from the window. 'I don't know where they get it from!'

Alan smiled fondly. 'Oh, I think I know. Sorry!'

CHAPTER 3

BRUNSMEER ATHLETIC

As much as Harry loved his brotherly battles with Joe, they did get a little boring after a while. It was the same challenge, every time! There were so many other opponents out there for Harry to compete with. Plus, how fun would it be to finally play *with* Joe, rather than against him?

'Dad, when can I come and play for Brunsmeer?' Harry begged. 'Please!'

When he was younger, Alan had been Brunsmeer Athletic's big, powerful centre-back, but now he was their Under-11s coach. Joe was already in the team and when Harry turned eight years old, he was finally allowed to join him. He was at least a year younger than everyone else, but that never stopped Harry. Anything his brother could do, he could do too.

Joe was a strong defender, just like his dad. Harry, however, was a different type of player. He wasn't as big as the rest of his family and he was more comfortable on the ball. He loved dribbling and passing his way towards goal.

'Right, we'll play you in centre midfield,' Alan decided before he had even trained with the team.

Harry would have played anywhere, but centre midfield was the best position on the pitch. He still got to battle bravely for the ball, just like he did in the back garden at home. But on top of that, he also got to rush forward and use his skills to attack.

'It's the best of both worlds!' he told Joe happily.

Harry loved wearing Brunsmeer's red and black stripes. Every Sunday morning, he woke up bright and early, buzzing for the match ahead. The weather, the pitch, the opponents – none of that really mattered to him. Harry just wanted to play and have fun. When it came to football, he was totally fearless.

'Bring it on!' he shouted in wind, rain or sunshine.

Harry was like a busy bee, buzzing all over the pitch. He treated every match like a brotherly battle that he could not lose. *Tackle! Block! Header! Interception!*

'Great work, bro!' Joe called out again and again.

But once Harry was on the ball, everything slowed down. Now that he had it, he didn't want to waste it. If he could see a teammate in space, he played the simple pass, but if not, he held on to it and dribbled forward. He made it look so easy. He wasn't the quickest player around but it was so hard to get the ball off him.

'The Maguire Boys' were soon the talk of the Sheffield youth leagues. With Joe controlling the back and Harry bossing the midfield, Brunsmeer were unbeatable.

Harry and Joe were the deadliest duo around. When they played together for their primary school team, the game was over before it even started. Their opponents didn't stand a chance!

Parents would ask:

'How did you get on?'

'We lost 12–0!'

'12–0? Who were we playing against?'

'Immaculate Conception.'

'Were the Maguire Boys playing?'

'Yes, both of them.'

'That explains it then!'

Alan was very proud of his sons but he never gave them special star treatment. In fact, quite the opposite – as they got older, he expected more from them than from anyone else in the team.

'You're a lot better than that,' he would tell Harry whenever he had a poor game. 'Your passing was sloppy today and you were totally off the pace!'

At first, the criticism hurt but Harry knew that his dad was just trying to help him improve as a footballer. Everyone made mistakes; everyone had a bad day every now and again. He just had to believe in himself and keep getting better.

'If you keep learning and working hard, you could all be professional footballers one day,' Alan said to his three sons. The youngest, Laurence, was now

following in his brothers' footsteps. He believed
in them.

'A professional footballer!' Harry repeated to
himself excitedly. That was his dream, but could it
really be more than just a dream? With lots of hard
work, he hoped so.

CHAPTER 4

WORLD CUP 2002

'Morning, Harry!' Mrs Emmot, the Immaculate Conception Primary Headmistress called out as she walked past the assembly hall.

Harry tore his eyes away from the big screen for long enough to turn and reply politely, 'Morning, Miss!'

'So, are England finally going to win the World Cup again?' she asked.

'Of course, Miss!' he nodded eagerly.

Harry had only been five years old for the 1998 tournament, so 2002 was his first proper World Cup, and he was loving it! Every day, there were more exciting international football matches to watch –

France vs Senegal, Brazil vs China, Cameroon vs Germany, Mexico vs Italy...

'This is the best thing ever!' Harry cheered. It was a non-stop football fiesta.

The 2002 World Cup was taking place in Japan and South Korea. They were eight hours ahead of English time, which meant that the 3.30pm kick-offs were shown at 7.30am for Harry in Chesterfield. Perfect – he could watch the matches on a big screen in the assembly hall before the school day started!

Harry watched, Harry learned and Harry dreamed. How amazing would it be to become one of the best players on the planet! 'The Maguire Boys' were the stars of the local school tournaments but one day, they could be World Cup stars. Anything was possible!

Although Harry watched as many World Cup matches as he could, the team he was really supporting was England. The nation had high hopes for Sven-Göran Eriksson's team. With Michael Owen up front, David Beckham in midfield, and Sol Campbell in defence, why couldn't the Three Lions go all the way?

Harry was still playing in central midfield for his club and for his school, but his favourite England player was the young centre-back, Rio Ferdinand.

Ferdinand was a cool new kind of defender. He was still awesome at tackling, heading and marking strikers, but he was also awesome at passing. When he got the ball in defence, he didn't panic and hoof the ball up the pitch like some centre-backs. Instead, Ferdinand was calm, classy and confident.

'Apparently, he was an attacker when he was younger,' Harry's dad told him.

Of course! That made total sense to Harry. Hopefully, if he grew big and tall, he could be the next Rio Ferdinand...

Against England's old rivals Argentina, it was Beckham who stepped up and scored a penalty under so much pressure. 1–0!

In the second half, however, it was Ferdinand's turn to be the hero. As hard as Argentina's star striker Gabriel Batistuta tried, he just couldn't get through! In the Immaculate Conception assembly hall, Harry cheered every block and every clearance.

When the final whistle blew, he punched the air.

'What a win!'

Harry got even more excited during England's Round of 16 match against Denmark. In the fifth minute, Beckham curled a corner to the back-post and Ferdinand headed the ball over the goal line. 1–0! While Rio danced on the pitch in Japan, Harry danced at his school in Chesterfield.

'England! England!' he chanted with his friends.

Owen made it 2–0 and Emile Heskey made it 3–0. The Three Lions were through to the World Cup quarter-finals!

At 7.30am on Friday, 21 June, the Immaculate Conception assembly hall was packed for the massive match against Brazil. Harry was England's biggest fan and he wanted them to win so badly. He was too nervous to even eat.

'You do know you're not playing in the game, right?' Joe joked.

Very funny! Harry rolled his eyes at his brother but in his head, he was thinking, 'How amazing would it be if I *was* playing in a World Cup quarter-final?'

That dream would have to wait. For now, he was cheering on Ferdinand, Beckham and co. When Owen scored, Harry jumped for joy. 1–0 – England were beating Brazil!

Sadly, it couldn't last. Just before half-time, Ronaldinho dribbled through the defence and passed to Rivaldo. 1–1!

'Come on, England!' Harry shouted up at the screen.

Early in the second half, Brazil won a free kick way out on the right wing. Ronaldinho placed the ball down and looked up at the England goal.

'No way, he can't shoot from there!' Harry said to his friends. 'He's going to cross it.'

But the ball sailed over David Seaman's arm and into the top corner. 2–1!

Harry's young heart sank. What a disaster! The England players kept going but they couldn't grab a second goal. Their World Cup was over.

'What a fluke!' Harry muttered moodily. 'There's no way Ronaldinho meant to do that.'

After a few days of disappointment, Harry went

back to watching the semi-finals on the big screen at school. Even though his favourite player and favourite team were out, he could still learn lots from players like Ronaldo and Germany's Michael Ballack.

Harry would never forget the 2002 World Cup. By the end of that special month, he knew what his life-long dream would be – to one day play for England at a major international tournament.

CHAPTER 5

THE BOY'S A BLADE!

In Sheffield, there are two big football teams:
Sheffield Wednesday and Sheffield United. The clubs
are fierce rivals, so it's important to choose your
colours carefully – blue and white for Wednesday, or
red and white for United.

Harry had a very difficult decision to make. His
dad was a Wednesday fan but his mum supported
United! Which team would Harry pick? Would he
become an Owl or a Blade?

Alan did his best to persuade his son. He took
Harry to matches at Wednesday's big Hillsborough
stadium.

'See?' his dad turned to him as the crowd clapped

and cheered loudly. 'This is the team to support, son!'

Harry loved the loud atmosphere at Hillsborough but the football was hard to watch. Wednesday seemed to lose every single match they played! When Harry was ten years old, in 2003, they got relegated from the First Division to the Second Division.

'You should have seen us back in 1997,' his dad said, trying to stay positive. 'Wednesday finished seventh in the Premier League! We'll be back there soon, I'm sure.'

United, meanwhile, were flying high. With Rob Page in defence, Michael Brown in midfield and Carl Asaba and Paul Peschisolido in attack, the Blades finished third in the First Division. That was a massive nineteen places higher than Wednesday! United were even one match away from promotion to the Premier League but they sadly they lost to Wolves in the play-off final.

'Never mind,' his mum sighed. 'There's always next year!'

Despite that disappointment, Harry decided that supporting United looked a lot more fun than supporting Wednesday. Plus, by the age of eleven, he had another very special reason for wearing red and white. After a year at Barnsley, Harry had been scouted by the Sheffield United youth academy.

'Sorry, Dad, I'm a Blade now!' he announced proudly. He had the club kit to prove it.

It didn't take long for Alan to also become a Blades fan. If he wanted to support his son, what else could he do?

Life at Sheffield United was a dream come true for Harry. It was exactly the kind of challenge he had been looking for. He loved competing with top players and training under top coaches.

'I'm learning so much!' Harry told his dad happily at dinner.

'Hey, what are you saying about my sessions at Brunsmeer?' Alan joked.

Wearing his team tracksuit, Harry couldn't help dreaming of the future. In five years' time, he could be playing for the Under-18s, then the reserves, then the Sheffield United first team. In ten years' time, he could be a Bramall Lane hero!

'One step at a time,' he had to keep reminding himself.

Unfortunately, Harry's next step wasn't becoming Sheffield United's first-ever twelve-year-old wonderkid. Instead, he became one of the club's ball boys at Bramall Lane.

'Ball boy? What a boring job!' his younger brother, Laurence, argued but Harry loved it, even on the wettest, coldest winter nights.

At every Sheffield United home game, Harry got to watch the senior players in action, right from the side of the pitch. They were so close that he could reach out and touch them! Sometimes, he *did* touch them when he handed them the ball for a throw-in.

'Keith Gillespie smiled at me,' Harry told Laurence, 'and he even said thanks!'

Suddenly, ball boy sounded like a pretty awesome job, in fact.

Harry's stool next to the pitch was one of the best seats in the whole Bramall Lane stadium, especially during the 2006–07 season, because The Blades were playing in the Premier League!

So, Harry could not only watch Sheffield United stars Phil Jagielka and Rob Hulse, but also:

Chelsea's John Terry and Didier Drogba…

…Manchester United's Rio Ferdinand and Cristiano Ronaldo…

…Liverpool's Xabi Alonso and Steven Gerrard…

…and Arsenal's Cesc Fàbregas and Thierry Henry.

Harry was in fantasy land! It was an amazing opportunity to study superstar footballers up close. Their decision-making, their movement, their vision, their teamwork. Harry tried to take in as much as he could. He wanted every game to go on forever.

Even after Sheffield United were relegated back to the First Division, Harry carried on being a ball boy in the Championship. There was still plenty for him to watch and learn from players like Ryan Shawcross at Stoke City and Kevin Phillips at West Brom.

It was those Premier League glory days, however, that made Harry more determined than ever. He had a new target to aim for. With hard work and self-belief, Harry would lead The Blades back to the big-time.

CHAPTER 6

MR SPORTY

Although football was Harry's favourite thing in the world, he loved playing all sports. Anything that involved running and competing, he would say 'I'm in!' immediately. He always wanted to win, even if there was no trophy.

When he enrolled at St Mary's Roman Catholic High School, he had a wide range of options. Harry quickly showed his new PE teacher, Mr McKee, that he was an excellent all-round sportsman.

Harry ran the 800 metres,

he threw the heavy discus,

he joined the school's successful cross-country team,

he played golf,

he played tennis,

he played badminton,

he played rugby,

he played hockey...

The list went on and on and on.

'Is there any sport that you're not good at?' Mr McKee joked.

Harry smiled cheekily. 'I'm not much of a gymnast, Sir. I can barely do a forward roll!'

'Well, we'll see about that, Maguire!'

When Harry decided that he wanted to achieve something, he worked really, really hard until he achieved it. He took that same can-do attitude with his school subjects too.

'Your determination will get you far in life!' his deputy headteacher told him when he got his GCSE results aged sixteen. He had got 3 A*s, 4 As and a B. His parents were delighted and so were his brothers, although they didn't always show it.

'What happened with that B, clever clogs?' Joe teased.

'Shhh you!' their mum laughed. 'We're so proud of you, son! What's next – college?'

Harry's parents had always let him play as much sport as he wanted, just as long as it didn't get in the way of his schoolwork. Education was very important for them, and for Harry's future.

'You've got to keep concentrating on your studies,' his mum told him when he was fourteen. 'There are hundreds of young players there at the academy, and most of them are not going to make it as professional footballers. You're a bright boy, so make sure you've got a Plan B!'

Harry had listened to his parents. He had the good grades he needed to go to college, but he was still playing for the Sheffield United youth team and hoping to have a long career at the club. He liked Maths but he *loved* football!

In between all the other sports, Harry had still found time to shine for the St Mary's football team. He was their midfield maestro, controlling games with his passing and dribbling. Once the battle started, no opponent could stop him.

'Once you get out on the pitch, it's like you double in size or something,' his best friend Danny joked. 'Maybe you're a superhero!'

Harry had proved that he was an excellent all-round sportsman, but football was his natural talent. With his perfect mix of passion and technique, he made the beautiful game look so easy.

'You've got what it takes to get to the top,' his PE teacher Mr McKee told him again and again. 'Whatever you do, don't give up on your dream!'

Mr McKee didn't really need to tell him, though. No-one was more determined than Harry. It was time to focus fully on football. Some of his friends thought he should have done that a lot earlier, but Harry disagreed. Over time, he had learned different skills from each of his different sports:

Cross-country gave him the stamina to run for even longer on the football pitch.

Rugby improved his bravery, and his dribbling skills too. If he could weave through tackles with a ball in his hand, he could do it with a ball at his feet too!

Hockey helped to develop his passing abilities and his vision on the ball. That was really important in football as well.

'See? It's all part of my training!' Harry argued.

Now, though, it was time for Mr Sporty to become Mr Football.

CHAPTER 7

THE PERFECT POSITION

By the time he turned sixteen, Harry knew that
he was going to become a professional footballer.
His family knew it, his friends knew it – even the
Sheffield United youth coaches knew it. There
were two important questions, however, that still
needed to be answered:

1) Was Harry good enough to play for Sheffield
   United? And…

2) What position would Harry play?

The first question could wait but the second
couldn't because all of a sudden, Harry was growing
taller and taller each day. He shot up into the sky –

six feet tall, six feet one, six feet two. . . all the way up to six feet four!

'Blimey, kid, what have you been eating lately?' the Sheffield United youth coaches asked in awe as they looked up at him.

Since his very first game for Brunsmeer, Harry had been a busy central midfielder, full of energy and skill. But now that he was a giant, could he still play that role? He wasn't so quick and nimble anymore. With longer legs, he felt so clumsy on the ball.

'Where do you want to be in three years' time?' the academy manager, John Pemberton, asked him during an important meeting in his office.

Harry knew the answer to that one. 'I want to be playing for the first team,' he replied confidently.

'Well, I'm sorry but I don't think you'll make it in midfield,' Pemberton told him. He had a plan, though: 'Let's see what you can do in defence instead.'

If it would help the team, Harry was happy to try anything. Just as long as he played professional football, he didn't mind *where* he played on the pitch.

'Welcome to the family position!' Joe chuckled. He

was a centre-back, their dad was a centre-back, their brother Laurence was a centre-back, and now Harry was too.

'Thanks,' Harry replied. 'I think I'm going to need your help!'

Zonal marking, offside traps, clever strikers – it was a whole new world for Harry to get used to. Fortunately, he was a fast learner and he had great teammates and coaches to help him.

'That's it – show them who's boss!' the academy manager shouted as Harry jumped highest to win a header. He was so competitive that he hated losing a single battle.

The ball flew through the air, over the halfway line, and landed at the feet of United's striker.

'Blimey, that big head of yours is more powerful than your boot!' Harry's centre-back partner, Terry Kennedy, laughed.

Pemberton was delighted with the youngster's progress. Harry could read the game so well for a young player and get himself into the right positions to deal with any danger. He was starting to look like he'd been a defender all his life. It was time for Stage Two of the master plan.

'Maguire, go short for the pass!' Pemberton called out as the goalkeeper got ready to kick the ball downfield.

Harry had the height and strength of a centre-back but he could pass and dribble like a midfielder. That made him a very rare talent and Pemberton wanted to make the most of him.

When the goalkeeper rolled it to him, Harry just hoofed the ball long straight away. He couldn't take risks so close to his own goal. He was a defender now! His coach, however, had other ideas.

'Take your time on the ball,' Pemberton urged. 'Play like you used to play in midfield. Don't worry if you make a few mistakes.'

At first, Harry made lots of mistakes.

Sometimes, when the strikers pressed him, he panicked and played a bad pass, either too short or too heavy. *GOAL!*

'Sorry!'

Sometimes, he tried to dribble past one opponent too many and got tackled. *GOAL!*

'Sorry!'

Whatever the reason, Pemberton always said the same thing. 'Head up, keep going!'

Harry hated giving away goals. It left a horrible sinking feeling in his stomach. His teammates didn't say anything but they didn't have to. Harry knew that it was all his fault. He was letting his team down badly.

'But I'm just doing what I'm told!' he argued with himself. His manager had told him to be bold on the ball.

Harry had to persevere and he had to improve. Thanks to lots of hard work in training, he soon looked his usual, comfortable self again. And Harry's skills became Sheffield United's secret weapon.

Under pressure in their own half? No problem! Harry would bring the ball out of defence, weaving his way up the pitch and then picking out a pass.

1–0 down, with a few minutes to go? No problem! Harry moved forward confidently, looking for the chance to shoot.

'Congratulations, kid,' Pemberton smiled. 'You've found your perfect position!'

CHAPTER 8

FA YOUTH CUP

There was no stopping Harry, now that he had found his perfect position. He couldn't wait to test himself against England's best young strikers in the 2011 FA Youth Cup.

'Let the battles begin!' Harry and Terry cheered together.

Could anyone defeat Yorkshire's deadliest defensive duo? It didn't seem so:

Cheltenham Town 1–4 Sheffield United
Sheffield United 3–0 Millwall
Sheffield United 3–1 Blackpool
Leicester City 1–2 Sheffield United

With four wins in a row, the young Blades were
through to the semi-finals.

'Great work, lads,' Pemberton cheered proudly.
'Two more performances like that and we'll be in the
final!'

Sheffield United had never got that far in the sixty
years of the FA Youth Cup. Could these kids make
history? The club's fans were delighted to have
something to cheer about. Their senior team was
struggling down at the bottom of the First Division.

United! United! United!

Mark Smith, the Reserves coach, gave Harry some
very good news. 'Speedo is really impressed with
you. Keep it up, kid!'

Gary Speed, the Sheffield United manager, had
watched him play? Wow, Harry was now even more
determined to dazzle in defence!

A few days after his eighteenth birthday, he
travelled to Villa Park to take on Aston Villa. Ahead
of the biggest game of his football career, Harry felt
more excited than nervous. Harry believed in himself
and he believed in all of his brilliant teammates.

Together, they could handle the pressure and win yet another battle.

'Let's keep it tight tonight,' Pemberton told them in the dressing room before kick-off. 'Remember, we've got the home leg back at Bramall Lane still to come.'

The young Blades wanted to win both games, though. Harry and Terry at the back were stopping every Villa attack. What could Sheffield United do on the counter-attack? Just before half-time, Jordan Slew dribbled into the Villa box and cut the ball back for Joe Ironside to score. 1–0!

Watching from the halfway line, Harry punched the air with joy. Now, he had more defending to do.

A long ball over the top... no problem! Harry calmly let it run through to his goalkeeper.

A cross into the box... no problem! With his big head, Harry cleared the danger.

A long-range shot... no problem! Harry bravely blocked it with his body.

When the final whistle blew, he punched the air again, this time with both fists. A win *and* a cleansheet – what a perfect late birthday present!

'We're halfway there, lads,' Pemberton said, patting them all on the back.

In the second leg, Sheffield United scored, again just before half-time. This time, though, the goal was created by their dazzling defenders. Harry crossed from the left to Terry at the back post. He headed it down for Elliott Whitehouse to tap in. 2–0 on aggregate!

Harry joined in the team celebrations and then ran back to his own half. He had more defending to do.

A Villa shot from the edge of the area... no problem! Harry blocked it with his long legs.

Another long-range Villa shot... no problem! Harry headed the ball away.

What a hero! At the final whistle, he threw his arms up above his head and hugged Terry. Two big games, two big clean sheets.

'We did it!' Harry shouted. 'We're in the final!'

It was already one of Sheffield United's greatest ever achievements, but could the young Blades go all the way and win the trophy? It wasn't going to be easy. Their final opponents would be Premier League giants, Manchester United. The club had already won the FA Youth Cup nine times, most famously with their Class of 1992, featuring David Beckham, Ryan Giggs, Paul Scholes, Gary Neville, Phil Neville and Nicky Butt.

Nineteen years on, their Class of 2011 was packed with future superstars too, including a young midfield maestro called Paul Pogba.

'We've got nothing to be scared of tonight,' Pemberton told his players before the first leg at Bramall Lane. 'We deserve to be here, so let's show them what we can do!'

It was going to be Harry's biggest test yet. Jesse Lingard, Ravel Morrison and Will Keane were all excellent and promising young attackers at Manchester United with lots of speed, skill and clever movement.

'Come on, this is going to have to be our best game ever!' Harry told Terry as they took up their positions on the pitch.

Unfortunately, with 30,000 fans watching, Harry's night quickly became a nightmare.

As Pogba crossed from the right wing, Lingard slipped away from Harry and got to the ball first. His shot deflected up off the goalkeeper and struck the crossbar. As it bounced down, Harry tried to clear it but instead, he could only head the ball into his own net. 1–0 to Manchester United!

What a disaster! Harry had that horrible sinking feeling in his stomach again. He had let his team down. He wanted to hide away but he couldn't.

'Head up, keep going!' – that's what his coach always told him. Harry stayed strong and fought until the final whistle.

'Well done, kid,' Pemberton said, putting an arm around Harry's broad shoulders. With a 2–2 draw, Sheffield United's FA Youth Cup dream was still alive. 'You showed real guts out there.'

In the second leg at Old Trafford, the young Blades did their best, but ultimately Manchester United were just too good. Morrison and Keane scored two goals each in a 4–1 thrashing.

No, Sheffield United hadn't won, but Harry was still really proud of his runners-up medal. The FA Youth Cup final had taught him some tough lessons about football at the highest level. Harry still had a long way to go and lots to learn, but he was on the right track.

CHAPTER 9

FIRST GAME FOR THE FIRST TEAM

By April 2011, the Sheffield United manager, Micky Adams, was under real pressure. The Blades were about to get relegated down to League One, and the fans were furious. They booed the team's most experienced players, shouting,

'Get them off, they don't deserve to wear the shirt!'

What did the fans want Adams to do instead?

'Give the kids a chance!' they demanded.

The juniors had just reached the FA Youth Cup final, after all. They couldn't do any worse than the seniors.

Who should Adams choose? Elliott? Joe? Jordan?

Terry? No, Harry was the team's stand-out player and not just because of his height. He also had that amazing mix of passion and talent. It was time to see if he was ready for the Championship challenge.

When Harry first started training with the first team, some of the senior players were shocked. They took one look at him and thought, 'No way, that kid's too big to be a good footballer!'

That all changed, though, when Harry got the ball. With a neat first touch, he dribbled forward from the back, gliding past one player and then another. With great composure, he looked up and played a clever pass through to the striker. Wow! Sheffield United's senior players were *really* shocked now!

'Ok, that kid can *play*!' they said, having all changed their minds.

Harry didn't play in the home game against Leeds United but he was there on the subs bench just in case. It was like the good old days of being a ball boy at Bramall Lane. From up close, he could watch Sheffield United's centre-back Nyron Nosworthy really carefully.

How tightly did he mark the Leeds strikers? How often did he talk to the other defenders?

Harry was always looking to learn. He had come a long way since those ball boy days and he was now so close to achieving his childhood dream. So close that he could almost reach out and touch it.

Harry's whole family was there at the stadium, hoping to see him make his debut.

'You'll get your chance soon,' his mum reassured him after the match.

She was right. Harry was back on the bench for the home game against Cardiff City and this time, he didn't stay there.

Sheffield United were heading towards another disastrous defeat. They were losing 1–0 early in the second half, when not one but two defenders got injured! First Nyron hobbled off, and then Joe Mattock. Nick Montgomery came on for Nyron, but who would Adams bring on to replace Joe? Harry's heart was beating extra fast on the bench.

'Maguire, you ready?' one of the coaches called out.

Harry nodded eagerly. Of course, he was ready!
He jumped up out of his seat and tucked in his red
and white shirt on the touchline. '40 MAGUIRE,'
the back of it read. This was it – his first game for the
Sheffield United first team.

'Just take your time and keep it simple,' his
manager Micky Adams told him. 'Good luck!'

The Sheffield United fans clapped and cheered as
Harry ran onto the field. Finally, Adams was listening
to them, and giving the kids a chance. The mood
lifted around Bramall Lane.

'They reckon this guy's going to be the next John
Terry!'

'He's a future England captain, I heard, and he's a
local lad too.'

Harry was determined to make a good first
impression and live up to those great expectations.
He was playing against Craig Bellamy, one of the best
and smartest strikers in the league. The Welshman
had scored eighty-one Premier League goals for clubs
like Manchester City and Liverpool.

What a big first test for Harry! As he took a deep

breath, the words of his youth coach flashed through his head – 'Show them who's boss!'

He was ready for battle. When the first pass arrived at Bellamy's feet, BOOM! Harry won the ball with a tough tackle that sent Bellamy flying through the air.

'That's more like it!' The Sheffield United supporters rose to their feet to clap and cheer their new young star. 'I love him already!'

Slowly, Bellamy got back to his feet. He accepted Harry's handshake and smiled. 'Boy, you're a big lad! Is that why they brought you on?'

After that very strong start, however, Harry nearly went from hero to villain. United passed the ball across the defence, just like Pemberton had always encouraged the youth team to do. That style was perfect for Harry but just as it came to him, he slipped and fell. *GASP!* The fans feared the worst but fortunately, Cardiff didn't score a second goal.

Phew! Harry breathed a sigh of relief.

'Forget that, keep going!' Neill Collins, his centre-back partner, told him.

Harry focused on his task and fought hard until the final whistle. The match ended in another defeat for Sheffield United but at least the game had brought one bright light at the end of the dark tunnel: Harry.

He walked all the way around the stadium, thanking the fans for their amazing support. He wanted to stay on the pitch and keep playing.

'Great performance, kid,' Adams said as Harry finally made his way down the tunnel to the dressing room.

Upstairs in the players' lounge, his family was waiting to congratulate him too.

'Well done, I'm so proud of you!' his mum said, hugging him tightly.

'Yes but we lost,' Harry reminded her. 'Again.'

'You played so brilliantly, though. Could you hear everyone cheering when you made that big tackle?'

'Could you hear everyone groaning when you nearly gave away that goal?' his brother Laurence added cheekily.

Sheffield United only had five games left in the Championship season. Harry started four of them

and even won the man of the match award against
Preston. He would have started the other game too,
if he hadn't been suspended.

The suspension happened in a game against Bristol
City, Nick tried to pass the ball back to Harry but
instead, it fell to the striker. Harry panicked and
brought him down. *Foul!* The referee gave Bristol
City a penalty and sent Harry off.

'Nooooo! Why did I dive in like that?' he groaned
as he slowly jogged off the pitch. The horrible sinking
feeling was back.

That red card helped to keep Harry's feet firmly
on the ground. He couldn't get too big for his big
boots. Yes, he was now a Sheffield United first-team
star and a fans' favourite, but he still had lots more to
learn.

CHAPTER 10

LIFE IN LEAGUE ONE

And what better place to learn than in League One? That's where Sheffield United would be playing for the 2011–12 season. During the summer, Harry's centre-back partner, Neill, passed on some helpful advice.

'Look, I know you like to get the ball down and pass it around, but you're playing a different kind of football now. In League One, it's much more physical. Teams are going to hoof long balls up to their big, strong strikers, who will to try to push you around. Just be ready for that.'

'Thanks, I will be!'

Harry didn't mind playing dirty if he had to. He was six feet four, after all!

On the opening day of the season, Sheffield United

travelled to Oldham Athletic. Their striker, Matt Smith, was even taller than Harry – he was six feet six!

'See!' Neill said with a smile. 'Welcome to League One!'

Luckily, Harry loved nothing more than a challenge. He didn't win every header but he did keep Smith quiet.

Early in the second half, Harry went forward for a corner-kick. The penalty area was like a wrestling ring, with lots of pushing and shoving everywhere. But when the cross came in, Harry outmuscled and then outjumped his marker to power a header into the top corner.

Gooooooooooooooooooooaaaaaaaaaaaaaaaaalllllllllllll lllllllllllllll!!!!!!!!!!!!!!!!!!!!!

It was the moment Harry had dreamt about since he was eleven years old – his first goal for Sheffield United! He watched the ball land in the back of the net and then ran over to the away fans to celebrate. He lept high into the air and then dropped to his knees. It was the greatest feeling ever.

Neill was one of the first teammates to hug Harry.

'Ok fine, you're ready for League One!' he joked.

Sheffield United started the season well with four wins out of five, and three clean sheets. Thanks to Harry, they had the best defence in the division.

The team's new manager, Danny Wilson, was delighted. Young players usually made a few mistakes, especially centre-backs. But at the age of eighteen, Harry already looked just as calm and consistent as an experienced pro like Neill.

But would Sheffield United be able to hold on to their star centre-back for long? Hopefully, for as long as the club got promoted back up to the Championship.

The Blades spent the whole season in the top six but in the end, they finished third, three points behind their bitter rivals, Sheffield Wednesday.

'Hey, it's not over yet,' Wilson told his disappointed players. 'We just have to win the play-offs now!'

There was good news to help cheer Harry up. He was one of three United players named in the League One Team of the Year. Not bad for a nineteen-year-old playing in League One for the first time! It was a very proud moment but Harry kept his eyes on the prize – promotion through the play-offs.

With a tense 1–0 win over Stevenage, Sheffield United were through to the final. As a local lad, Harry was especially excited. Two years earlier, he had been a youth player and a ball boy. Now, he was about to play in a final at Wembley Stadium. Everything was happening so fast but somehow, Harry stayed as calm as ever.

'We know Huddersfield will be a tough team,' he told the media, 'but we have always believed that we will be in the Championship next season.'

As Harry walked out onto the pitch, he looked up at the 52,000 cheering fans. The atmosphere was amazing and the game hadn't even kicked off yet.

'I could get used to playing in front of a crowd like this!' he chuckled to himself.

Pressure? Harry loved pressure! It was what being a top professional footballer was all about. He couldn't wait for the biggest battle of his life to begin.

'Come on, let's do this!' he cheered.

Sadly, it wasn't the fun final that both sets of fans

were hoping for. Instead, it was tight and tense. Neither team was brave enough to take a risk, in case they made a mistake. After 120 minutes without a goal, the match went all the way to penalties.

'At least that's another clean sheet for us!' Harry joked, trying to lighten the mood. Neill was taking one of Sheffield's five penalties and he looked nervous.

Both teams hugged their goalkeepers and wished them luck. Who would be the hero? United's Steve Simonsen, or Huddersfield's Alex Smithies?

After ten penalties, the score was 2–2. The shoot-out went to sudden death, and even Harry was starting to feel a little anxious. One miss and it would be all over.

3–2 to Huddersfield, 3–3, 4–3 to Huddersfield...

It was Harry's turn to take a penalty. 'You've got this!' Neill shouted to him as he made the long walk from the halfway line to the penalty area. So many of Harry's friends and family were there at Wembley to watch him win. He couldn't let them down.

Harry placed the ball down on the spot and took a few steps backwards. He looked down at the ball and then up at the target. 'You've got this!' he told himself as he started his run-up. The keeper dived to his left and Harry smashed his shot straight down the middle.

Gooooooooooooooooooooaaaaaaaaaaaaaaaalllllllllllll llllllllllllll!!!!!!!!!!!!!!!!!!!

Harry didn't show any emotion. He just picked the ball out of the net, put it back on the spot, and walked back to his teammates.

The penalty shoot-out went all the way to the eleventh men. It was goalkeeper vs goalkeeper! Smithies went first… and scored.

It was all down to Simonsen now. He stepped up… and blasted the ball over the bar!

Sheffield United would not be playing in the Championship next season. As the Huddersfield players celebrated, Harry stood there, frozen in a daze of despair. It was the most painful moment he had ever experienced. That horrible sinking feeling was nothing compared to this.

'Head up, kid,' Wilson said as he walked over to give Harry a reassuring hug. 'You should be so proud of what you've achieved this season. Unbelievable! You'll be back – *we'll* be back.'

CHAPTER 11

GAME AFTER GAME

After Harry's fantastic breakthrough season in 2011–12, lots of clubs wanted to sign him. The list even included Premier League teams like Newcastle United. Was it time to move on to bigger things?

A few Sheffield United players did move on. Right-back Matthew Lowton joined Aston Villa, and midfielder Stephen Quinn joined Hull City. Harry, however, chose to stay at the club.

'I don't want to go somewhere else and sit on the bench,' he decided. 'I want to keep playing game after game!'

Week in week out, Harry was the star of the Blades' defence. He was already the Bramall Lane hero that he had hoped to be. During the 2011–12 season, he had played in fifty-six matches. That was a massive number for a teenager!

'At a Premier League club, I might not even play ten proper matches,' Harry argued. 'No thanks!'

First-team experience was so important, no matter which division it was in. Harry needed to be playing under pressure, in matches that really mattered. How else was he going to learn and improve as a centre-back? With Neill by his side, Harry was getting a great football education at Sheffield United.

'If you can defend well in League One, you can defend well in the Premier League,' his manager Danny Wilson assured him. 'Trust me, you've got what it takes!'

Plus, Harry couldn't walk away from his local club without having another go at achieving his number one aim – promotion to the Championship.

In the 2012–13 season, Harry's consistency continued. He wore the Number 5 shirt now and he only missed two of United's forty-six league matches.

Game after game, he battled bravely against big, strong strikers.

'No-one's getting past Maguire today!'

Game after game, he used his body to block powerful shots.

'That's heroic defending there from Maguire!'

Game after game, he jumped highest to win headers.

'A towering leap from Maguire!'

Game after game, he stopped goals with his crunching, sliding tackles.

'Maguire with a crucial challenge!'

Game after game, he brought the ball forward out of defence to set up attacks.

'What a run this is from Maguire. Will he go all the way?'

Not only was Harry becoming a brilliant centre-back, but he was also a local lad. The Sheffield United fans loved him even more for that.

Harry, Harry Harry, Harry, Harry, Harry Harry, HARRY MAGUIRE!!

One day, they knew, he would move on to bigger and better things, but they wanted to keep him for as long as possible.

Don't leave us, Harry, we love you!

In February 2013, he made his 100th senior start for Sheffield United, and he was still not quite twenty years old. He felt like an experienced professional now, even if he didn't look like one.

'Sometimes, I forget how young you are,' Neill joked, 'but then I look at your awful clothes and your scruffy haircut, and I remember!'

What did Harry wish for on his twentieth birthday? Promotion to the Championship, of course.

'Come on, we can do it!' he told his teammates.

Again, Sheffield United were in the top six all season but again, they finished in the play-off places. Last year's Wembley defeat to Huddersfield still haunted them but Harry stayed positive. He was desperate to play at a higher level.

'This is our year, lads!'

The Blades beat Yeovil Town 1–0 in the first leg at Bramall Lane and the team travelled to Huish Park feeling confident. The sun was shining and United were wearing their black and red away kit, the colours of Harry's childhood club, Brunsmeer Athletic. It was going to be a good day.

In the first few minutes, however, Yeovil scored. It was now 1–1 on aggregate. Harry kicked the air in frustration. What a terrible start!

Sheffield United didn't give up, though. They fought back and nearly grabbed the goal they needed. Jamie Murphy's curling shot crashed against the crossbar. So close!

'Unlucky, keep going!' Harry called out.

In the last few minutes, Yeovil crossed a hopeful ball into the box. It flew over Harry's head and fell to their striker, Ed Upson. Harry watched in horror as Upson's header whizzed towards the top corner.

No, no, NO! Harry turned away in disgust. He couldn't bear to see the ball land in the back of the net. There would be no return trip to Wembley Stadium. Their season was over.

Nothing could ease Harry's pain – not even another Sheffield United Player of the Year award, and not even a spot in the League One Team of the Year for the second year in a row.

Yes, he was Mr Consistent, but would Harry ever be able to lift his team out of the lower leagues?

CHAPTER 12

ENGLAND CALLING — PART ONE

The older Harry got, the more he thought back to his childhood dreams. He had achieved so many of them already. He was a professional footballer, and a very successful one too. He was playing for his favourite club, Sheffield United, and the fans loved him. He had scored goals at Bramall Lane and he had even played at Wembley. What else was left?

International football! Ever since World Cup 2002, Harry had been England's biggest fan. For the most important matches, the Maguire family liked to throw massive parties at their house. Wearing his white England shirt, Harry watched and hoped.

His heroes were the two centre-backs: Rio

Ferdinand and John Terry. They were the best in the business – calm, quick, strong, and classy on the ball.

'With those guys at the back, we can't lose!' Harry thought, but sadly, he thought wrong.

He was miserable when England lost on penalties to Portugal at Euro 2004.

'We were robbed!'

He was devastated when the same thing happened again at the 2006 World Cup.

'How could Cristiano Ronaldo get Wayne Rooney sent off like that? They play together at Manchester United!'

He was heartbroken when England didn't even qualify for Euro 2008.

'Who am I going to support now?'

England fared a little better in the 2010 World Cup but Harry was still disappointed when they got thrashed by their old rivals Germany. Then at Euro 2012, they lost on penalties... AGAIN!

'We're cursed!' Harry told his best friend, Danny.

For years, Harry only thought about supporting England – on TV and at Wembley. The idea of actually *playing* for England seemed impossible!

Once he became a Sheffield United's best centre-back, however, people started talking about a call-up to the Under-21s. He didn't want to get his hopes up, though.

'They hardly ever give League One players a chance,' he reminded his brothers.

In November 2012, that all changed. The England Under-21s were about to play a friendly match against Northern Ireland but they were struggling for numbers. Jason Lowe and Sammy Ameobi were both injured and Wilfried Zaha had been called up to the senior squad.

'Is it too late to call up a few extras?' the Under-21s manager Stuart Pearce asked his coaches.

No, it wasn't, because the match was nearby – at Blackpool's Bloomfield Road stadium. The first player they asked was Leicester City striker Martyn Waghorn. And the second? Harry, of course!

At first, he didn't believe it. Was it Danny playing a prank on him? No, it really was Stuart Pearce on the phone, calling him up to the England Under-21s.

'Wow, thanks, it's a real honour!' Harry replied, trying not to sound too much like a star-struck kid.

But that was exactly how he felt at first. He was the only League One player in the squad and many of his new teammates were already Premier League stars. Harry watched them on *Match of the Day* every Saturday night.

Connor Wickham played for Sunderland, Andros Townsend played for Tottenham, and Nick Powell played for Manchester United. Captain Jordan Henderson had signed for Liverpool for nearly £20million!

'Welcome to the team!' Jordan said with a smile.

Harry had no idea if he would get to play in the match but it was a great experience to train with such brilliant players and coaches. Was he good enough to compete at this level? Of course, he was. He just had to believe in himself.

'Blimey, you're a beast!' Connor told him after receiving one of his trademark tackles.

At Bloomfield Road, Harry watched the first half from the subs bench. The England Under-21s had

won all of their matches in 2012 and Northern
Ireland were no match for them. Harry was
impressed by his team's flowing, passing football. He
couldn't wait to join in if he got the opportunity...

Jordan and Josh McEachran created chance after
chance and eventually, Connor headed home. 1–0!

England were winning but Pearce wanted more.
After sixty minutes, he made a triple substitution.
Benik Afobe came on for Andros in attack, Nathaniel
Clyne came on for Adam Smith at right-back, and
Harry came on for Andre Wisdom at centre-back.

Wearing the white Number 15 shirt, Harry jogged
out onto the pitch. The 9,000 supporters in the
stadium clapped quietly. It was a cold Tuesday night
in Blackpool, rather than a sell-out at Wembley, but
Harry didn't care about that. He was an England
international now! The last of his childhood dreams
was coming true.

'Right, focus!' Harry told himself.

He could enjoy his proud moment with his family.
For now, he had some defending to do. If he played
well, maybe Pearce would call him up again.

The last thirty minutes flew by in a flash. What could Harry do to leave his mark on the match? He did his best to show off his heading and his passing, as the Three Lions cruised to victory. There were no goals or heroic blocks, but he was pleased with his debut, and so was his manager.

'Well done, you looked really comfortable out there!' Pearce said at the final whistle, shaking his hand.

Harry was still buzzing when he returned to Sheffield United.

'Oh, here comes our England star,' his teammates teased. 'We better roll out the red carpet!'

Harry laughed along but that taste of international football had made him more focused than ever. Now, he knew that he could do it – he was good enough to reach the highest level. With hard work and determination, he could one day play in the Premier League, and perhaps even play for his country at a major tournament.

Although that turned out to be Harry's one and only appearance for the Under-21s, his England days were far from over.

CHAPTER 13

GOAL MACHINE!

Neill and the new Sheffield United manager Chris
Morgan were always reminding Harry about the
rules of being a centre-back:

'Defend first, and attack second.'

'If in doubt, get it out!'

'Safety first!'

Harry knew the rules but every now and then, he
couldn't help breaking them.

'If I see space ahead of me, why shouldn't I dribble
forward?' he thought. That was his old mid-fielder
brain talking. Sometimes it was a little risky but most
of the time, it really helped the team to attack.

Harry could weave his way through tackles, he

could play perfect long passes, and he could score goals too.

In the Football League Trophy second round against Notts County in October 2012, Harry chased after a clearance. From way out on the right wing, he calmly curled the ball over the goalkeeper's outstretched arm and in off the post.

Goooooooooooooaaaaaaaaaalllllllllllllllllllllllll!!!!!!!!!!!

'Extraordinary!' the TV commentator cried out, as Harry celebrated with his teammates.

'Was it a shot, or was it a cross?' they asked.

'Of course it was a shot!' he told them confidently.

If Ronaldinho could claim that goal against England in the 2002 World Cup, then Harry was definitely claiming this one.

During the 2012–13 League One season, he scored once with his right foot and twice with his powerful head.

'That nearly burst the net!' his teammate Nick Blackman cheered, giving him a big high-five.

As a defender, Harry loved keeping clean sheets and making important tackles, but scoring goals was also really fun. It was an amazing feeling to hear the fans at Bramall Lane cheering his name.

Harry, Harry Harry, Harry, Harry, Harry Harry, HARRY MAGUIRE!!

Harry was always looking for ways to improve – more tackles, more passes, more dribbles, and more goals.

On the first day of the 2013–14 season, Sheffield United were once again playing Notts County, this time at home. They were drawing 1–1, but that really wasn't the result that the Blades wanted – they wanted to win!

Stephen McGinn curled a free-kick all the way to Harry at the back post. He watched the ball carefully as it dropped down towards him. He was unmarked, but it was going to take a brilliant header to beat the keeper from there. BOOM! Like a bullet, the ball flew into the top corner of the net.

Gooooooooooooaaaaaaaaaalllllllllllllllllllllll!!!!!!!!!!!

Harry ran over to the Sheffield United fans with his arms in the air and a massive smile on his face. It was the winning goal and he was the hero.

Two weeks later, the Blades were losing 1–0 to
Colchester United. Febian Brandy passed a quick free
kick to Harry near the halfway line.

'Shoot! Shoot!' the fans urged.

Why not? Harry dribbled forward and hit a
swerving, long-range right foot rocket. It wasn't
his best strike ever but it caught the goalkeeper by
surprise. He spilled the ball into his own net!

Goooooooooooooaaaaaaaaaallllllllllllllllllllllll!!!!!!!!!!!!

Harry pointed up at his family in the stands and
punched the air. Two goals in three games – what a
start to the season!

'What would we do without you?' his manager
asked.

Two months later, Harry was still Sheffield United's
joint top scorer with two goals. The Blades were
bottom of the league. What a disaster! They needed a
hero more than ever.

Against Crewe Alexandra, a cross bounced across
the penalty area, and Harry reacted quicker than any
of the defenders around him. With a clever header,
he steered the ball low into the bottom corner. 1–0!

'Get in!' Harry roared but he wasn't done yet. Ten minutes later, he scored another header to make it 2–0.

Goooooooooooooaaaaaaaaaalllllllllllllllllllllll!!!!!!!!!!!!!

Harry was definitely his team's top scorer now! Those goals gave Sheffield United the confidence to climb back up the table. By the end of 2013, they were out of the relegation zone but Harry was still their top scorer.

'Maybe I should play up front instead!' he joked.

From corners and free kicks, Harry was simply unstoppable in the air.

Step One: He used his strength to outmuscle his marker.

Step Two: He used his height to win the header. *BOOM!*

Step Three: He used his power and technique to find the back of the net. *GOAL!*

Eventually, Chris Porter took over as United's top scorer, but Harry only finished two goals behind him. He was becoming an amazing all-round player – defender *and* attacker.

CHAPTER 14

BATTLING WITH THE BIG BOYS

Sheffield United didn't quite make it to the League One play-offs in 2014, but the season was still a big success.

The Blades hadn't got past the fifth round of the FA Cup in years but suddenly, they were beating everybody: Colchester United, Cambridge United... even Aston Villa!

Against Villa, it was Harry vs Christian Benteke, their big Belgian target man. Some young players would have been nervous but Harry couldn't wait to test himself against one of the Premier League's strongest strikers.

'Let the battle begin!' Harry told Neill.

Wherever Benteke went, Harry was always right behind him. He was a big centre-back but he was also quick and clever, and the Belgian couldn't escape from him.

With every header and block, Harry grew in confidence. He felt ten feet tall! He couldn't get carried away, though. This was top-level football. Everything could change in a second. Harry had to stay focused until the final whistle.

FWEEEEEEEEEEEEEEET!

It was over – Aston Villa 1 Sheffield United 2. The players ran around hugging each other as if they had just won the FA Cup. It was a proud day that Harry would never forget. He had won his biggest battle yet!

'See, you're Premier League quality, big man!' Neill told him, feeling like a proud parent.

Could the Blades pull off another cup upset against Fulham? Yes!

Harry got the ball near the halfway line and dribbled forward at speed.

'Keep going!' the Bramall Lane crowd screamed. They were up on their feet, waiting, hoping...

On the edge of the penalty area, Harry shrugged off a tackle and crossed the ball to Chris. 1–0 to Sheffield United!

Harry punched the air. He was helping his team at both ends of the pitch.

When their captain, Michael Doyle got sent off, it was Harry who took the armband. He was still only twenty years old but he was a born leader.

'Stay strong, we can do this!' he called out to his nine teammates. He was always talking, always organising the defence.

In the seventy-fifth minute, Fulham's Hugo Rodallega got the ball on the edge of the box. Harry threw himself to the floor to try and block the shot but it flew past him and into the bottom corner. 1–1!

'No!' Harry lay on the grass with his head in his hands for a few seconds, but then he got back up and carried on. He had to. Sheffield United needed to hold on for a draw and a replay.

At Craven Cottage, United won a corner in the very last minute. This was their last chance to score, before the match went to penalties.

Harry stood near the back post, waving his arms in the air. 'On my head!' he called out to Jose Baxter. The cross was brilliant and so was Harry's header back across goal to Shaun Miller. 2–1 – they were through to the FA Cup Fifth Round!

Again, the players celebrated like they had just won the whole competition. It was such an exciting time to be a Sheffield United player or supporter. Harry was both, so it was doubly exciting for him.

'United! United!' he cheered.

The Blades were on a roll. They beat Nottingham Forest 3–1 and then Charlton Athletic 2–0 to make it through to the FA Cup semi-finals. It was a fantastic achievement for a team in League One.

'Wembley, here we come!' Harry yelled at the top of his voice. He couldn't wait to return to the Home of Football, and win this time.

The fans couldn't wait either. Thousands of them travelled down to London for the game against Hull City. One more win and Sheffield United would be in the final for the first time since 1936.

At half-time, they were 2–1 up and halfway there.

'Just keep going lads,' their manager encouraged them. 'You're all heroes already but if we win this, you'll be legends!'

In the second half, however, Hull fought back with two quick goals. There was nothing that Harry could do to stop them. Sheffield United were in shock and they fell apart. It was game over, and the end of their incredible cup run.

'What a nightmare!' Harry muttered to himself at the final whistle. In his head, he kept replaying all five of Hull's goals. 'We let in FIVE - what was I doing out there today?'

'Don't be so hard on yourself, you played well,' Neill said, putting an arm around his shoulder. 'Without you, there's no way we would have got this far. No way!'

Once his disappointment faded, Harry looked back happily on his FA Cup adventure. He was particularly proud of his performances against the Premier League clubs, Aston Villa and Fulham. He had battled against the big boys, and won both times. Harry now felt ready to do that week in week out, game after game.

CHAPTER 15

HEADING FOR HULL

By the end of the 2013–14 season, Harry was one of the highest-rated youngsters in English football. If scouts hadn't already known about him, they certainly did after Sheffield United's incredible cup run.

'He's got great feet for a big centre-back!'

'Look at that composure on the ball – he can really play!'

Scouts from Manchester United, Chelsea and Tottenham came and went. Arsenal sent their old defender Martin Keown to Bramall Lane.

'Maguire's very good,' Keown reported back, 'but I'm not sure he's quick enough for the Premier League.'

It was Championship club Wolves who made the first bid of £1 million for Harry.

'No way!' Sheffield United said firmly.

Wolves came back with a second bid: £1.5 million.

'No way!' Sheffield United said firmly again. 'Harry's worth a lot more than that.'

Soon, they received a higher bid from Hull City. Harry couldn't believe it. 'They still want to buy me after the FA Cup semi-final?'

Yes! The Tigers had been watching Harry for years in League One. Eventually, their main scout, Stan Ternent, decided to speak to the manager, Steve Bruce.

'There's a young defender at Sheffield United that I think you should take a look at.'

'Okay, what's his name?'

'Harry Maguire. He's only twenty-one but he's already played 150 games for them! He's tall, he's strong, and he's talented with the ball too. He's been in the League One Team of the Year for the last two years. I think he's ready for the next step but see what you think.'

'Thanks for the recommendation, Stan. I'll go and watch him play.'

Bruce was very impressed by Harry's stats but what about his actual skills? The Hull manager was very impressed by those as well.

At first, he just looked like another big, beefy centre-back, who wrestled with strikers and won lots of headers.

'No, we won't need one of those in the Premier League,' Bruce muttered to himself.

But then Harry got the ball down and started to play. He passed and moved up the pitch, turning defence into attack. He had the confidence to take players on and dribble straight past them.

'Wow!' The Hull manager was blown away by Harry's composure. '*That* is exactly what we need in the Premier League!'

When the Tigers played Sheffield United in the FA Cup semi-final in April 2014, Bruce got another chance to see Harry in action. Harry didn't have his best game in defence but he still created lots of chances in attack when he brought the ball forward. The Hull midfielders couldn't cope with his confident, powerful runs.

'He looks like he's been playing at this level for years,' Bruce told his assistant, Steve Agnew. 'We *have* to sign him, before someone else does!'

Sheffield United rejected Hull's first offer of £2 million but the second was too good to turn down: £2.5 million was a lot of money for a League One club.

'We really want you to stay here,' the Blades manager, Nigel Clough, told his star player, 'but it's your choice now. Have a think about it.'

The more Harry thought about it, the more excited he became. If he signed for Hull City, he would finally get to play in the Premier League, and the Europa League too! That had been his dream for years. He would get to play alongside experienced stars like Curtis Davies, Michael Dawson and Tom Huddlestone. Harry knew that he could learn so much from Hull's players, and also from Hull's manager.

Bruce had been a brilliant centre-back for

Manchester United in the 1990s, winning three Premier League titles alongside legends like Ryan Giggs, David Beckham and Eric Cantona. Harry was sure that he would have lots of great advice for a young defender with big ambition.

'It's time for a new challenge,' he told his parents. 'I'm ready!'

'Of course you are,' they reassured him. 'We believe in you!'

It would be sad to say goodbye to Sheffield United after so many happy years, but what if Harry never got another opportunity like this? If he didn't take it, he might regret it forever.

It also helped that Hull was only an hour's drive away from Sheffield. Harry wasn't yet ready to leave his family, and Yorkshire, behind.

'I'm sorry but I can't stay another season,' he told Clough. 'This is my chance to play in the Premier League.'

His manager understood. 'Good luck, you're going to be great!'

After passing the medical and signing the contract,

it was photo time. Harry was a Hull player now!
He stood in the stands of the KC Stadium, wearing
the orange-and-black-striped shirt and holding up an
orange-and-black-striped scarf. There was a big smile
stretched across his face.

'I can't wait to get started!' Harry told the club's
website.

At least he wasn't starting his scary new adventure
alone. On the very same day, Hull also signed a
Scottish left-back. His name was Andrew Robertson
and they quickly became good friends.

'Dundee United? Never heard of them!' Harry
liked to tease Andrew about his former club. 'I
thought there was only one decent team these days –
Celtic.'

'Hey, the Scottish Premier League is still a lot
better than English League One, Big Man!'

Harry was a year older than Andrew but they got
on really well. They were both young players who
had just made the big move to the best league in the
world. Together, they coped with the challenges of
being the new kids at the club. Before the opening

match of the season, they each had to sing a song in front of the entire Hull squad. Andrew went first.

'Excellent, Andy!' the audience cheered and sang along.

'Right, your turn, H!'

Harry was as calm as ever as he stood up on a chair in the middle of the dressing room. The pressure was on. It was time to get the party started:

'Come on, let's twist again!' he sang, shaking his hips from side to side.

The other players were soon rolling on the floor with laughter. What a performance! Somehow, Harry managed to keep his balance and not fall off the chair. When he finished, he got a standing ovation.

'With moves like that, you're going to be a big hit here at Hull!' Curtis predicted.

CHAPTER 16

SLOW START AT HULL

Harry played for Hull in the Europa League and the League Cup, but he had to wait a long time for his Premier League debut. Often, he wasn't even on the bench.

'I don't get it. What am I doing wrong?' Harry asked his family.

'Just keep working hard and be patient,' they replied.

Harry wasn't used to being patient. He wanted to keep playing game after game, just like he had at Sheffield United. The Hull coaches, however, didn't think he was ready for that.

'We need to get you fitter first,' they told him.

That was one of the biggest differences between League One and the Premier League. In order to compete against teams like Chelsea and Manchester City, Harry needed to be a lean, mean running machine! Otherwise, strikers like Diego Costa and Sergio Agüero would destroy him again and again.

'They'll turn you inside out if you're not careful!' Curtis and Michael warned him.

Harry was a big, strong centre-back but he needed to be agile too. In the top division, teams attacked with so much skill and speed. How would he cope with that? It was time for Harry to get serious about his lifestyle. He needed to start eating better and sleeping better.

'I'll do anything to play in the Premier League!' he told his coaches at Hull.

With that positive, can-do attitude, Harry got fitter and fitter. Andrew was playing week in week out at left wing-back, and that spurred him on. Soon, that would be him! Curtis and Michael were playing brilliantly, and so was James Chester. Harry was the fourth-choice centre-back but at some point, he would get his chance to shine.

In the meantime, he kept smiling and joined in with all the dressing room jokes. Many of them were about the size of Harry's head.

'Is it hard to find hats that fit?' Tom teased.

He always had a comeback ready. 'Is it hard to find clothes that awful?'

In December 2014, Harry's big moment finally arrived. With fifteen minutes to go against Swansea City, Hull were losing 1–0 and Curtis was injured. Bruce looked at his bench and decided to give Harry an early Christmas present.

'Get forward as much as you can!' the manager told him.

Sure thing! Harry ran onto the pitch, proudly wearing the Number 12 shirt. He could now call himself a Premier League player.

'Go on, Big Man!' Andrew called to him.

Harry was desperate to become Hull's new hero. This was it – his chance to shine. Unfortunately, there was no time for him to attack. Instead, Harry had defending to do. He batted bravely in the air against Wilfried Bony and Marvin Emnes.

Before Harry knew it, the match was over. His Premier League debut had ended in defeat. Hull were now deep in the relegation zone. If only he could help...

But no, Harry was back on the bench in the Hull games against Sunderland and Leicester City. Had that been his one and only chance?

Against Everton, Harry came on with thirty minutes to go. Hull were winning 2–0.

'Just keep things tight,' Bruce told him.

Sure thing! Harry stayed focused until the final whistle. There was no way he was going to let Romelu Lukaku or Arouna Koné score.

'Well played, H!' Curtis cheered as they celebrated a very important victory.

Was this Harry's big breakthrough? He hoped so but no, he was back on the bench again for the next game.

Against West Ham, Harry came on at half-time. The score was still 0–0 – what a chance for him to shine! He couldn't wait to play a whole forty-five minutes of football.

Oh dear! Thirty minutes later, Hull were losing badly. When Alex Song played a defence-splitting pass, Harry couldn't keep up with Stewart Downing. 3–0! That horrible sinking feeling was back.

'I just need more game-time!' he groaned.

The only answer was to go out on loan. Harry joined Wigan Athletic and stayed until the end of the season. It felt weird wearing blue and white, like United's Sheffield rivals, Wednesday, but he was willing to do anything for game-time.

Playing in the Championship, Harry's confidence came back quickly. In his first game against Reading, in February 2015, Wigan kept a cleansheet and won for the first time in months.

'Thank goodness you're here!' his new manager Malky Mackay said.

Harry was just happy to be playing game after game again. He was Mr Consistent at the heart of the Wigan defence, winning headers and crunching tackles.

And he got forward to attack too. Away at Blackpool, a corner-kick came in and he won the header at the back post.

Goooooooooooooooooooooaaaaaaaaaaaaaaaaallllllllllll llllllllllllllll!!!!!!!!!!!!!!!!!!!

The old Harry was back! He ran over to the fans, shaking his fists in the air. 'Get in!' he roared, with joy rushing through his veins.

Harry did his best to rescue Wigan from relegation. He really didn't want to go back down to League One again. Unfortunately, his efforts were too little, too late.

'I've played every game since I've been here, and I've enjoyed my time here,' Harry told the local newspapers. 'The lads and the staff have been brilliant, it's a great club.'

He was sad to leave Wigan in such a bad state but things weren't much better back at Hull either. They had just been relegated from the Premier League to the Championship.

'Wherever I go, I bring bad luck!' Harry told his brothers, and he was only half-joking.

The news wasn't all negative, though. During the summer of 2015, James Chester joined West Brom for £8 million. When Bristol City then tried to sign Harry, Bruce said no.

Hopefully, that meant that Harry would now get lots more game-time at Hull. After a slow start, it was time for Sheffield's star to shine.

PROMOTION AT LAST!

Again, however, Harry had to be patient. Michael and Curtis started the Championship season as Hull's first-choice centre-backs.

'Don't worry, your time will come,' Bruce promised.

But when? Sometimes, Harry forgot that he was still only twenty-two. While he waited, he tried to learn as much as he could from his experienced teammates. Michael and Curtis were always happy to help whenever he had any questions.

'Communication is key,' Michael told him. 'I know I talk a lot out on the pitch but that's a big part of my job! It keeps the defence alert and organised.'

Of course, Harry really didn't want either of his

teammates to get injured, but how else was he going to get into the team? He was desperate to get back to playing game after game.

'Maybe one of them will get a red card instead!' his mum suggested.

Sometimes, Andrew kept Harry company on the Hull bench. It was nice to have supportive friends by his side.

'One day, we'll be Premier League stars and we'll look back on these bad days and laugh. Trust me!'

Slowly but surely, Harry fought his way into the team. First, he played ten minutes, then twenty, then seventy against Brentford. In a back three with Michael and Curtis, he had the freedom to attack, as well as defend.

'Up you go, Big Man!' Curtis called out whenever Hull won a corner-kick.

Harry was causing all kinds of trouble in the Brentford penalty area. He headed the ball into the danger zone and when it bounced back to him, he pulled his right leg back and BANG! The goalkeeper saved his shot but Sam Clucas was there for the rebound. 2–0! Harry and Sam celebrated by sliding across the grass on their knees.

'Premier League, here we come!' they cheered together.

The Tigers were top of the table and full of confidence. How could Bruce put Harry back on the bench after that? He couldn't!

Harry played instead of Curtis, and Hull beat their promotion rivals Middlesbrough 3–0. It was the best team performance of the season.

'Keep up the good work!' his manager told Harry with a big thumbs-up.

Harry played instead of Michael, and Hull beat Reading 2–1. The more games he played, the better he became. Sometimes, Harry took a few risks but he worked and worked to help his team to win. The fans loved his all-action style.

Against QPR, he beat two opponents to the ball and sent them both flying!

'That's it, Harry!'

Against Cardiff, he went up for a corner and a defender wrestled him to the floor. Penalty!

'They just can't handle him!'

Hull were on a roll. Their deadly defence kept cleansheets against Cardiff City, Charlton Athletic, Fulham, Blackburn Rovers... The list went on and on.

'I told you everything would work out for us!' Andrew reminded Harry.

But just when he was feeling on top of the world, Michael returned from injury – and Harry was back on the bench again.

'But I was playing really well!' he moaned.

It seemed so cruel to just drop him like that. Without Harry, Hull slipped from first place down to fourth.

'Bring back Maguire!' the supporters cried out.

Harry came back with a bang against Brentford. In the thirtieth minute, the Hull goalkeeper rolled the ball out to him in defence. After a few sideways passes, Harry saw the space ahead of him and galloped forward.

As usual, Andrew was making a brilliant run down the left wing. Harry spotted it and his long, diagonal ball was an absolute beauty. It floated just over the right-back's head and dropped down in front of Andrew. His cross was so dangerous that the Brentford centre-back could only kick it into his own net. 1–0!

'Keep Maguire in the team!' the supporters cried out.

Sadly, it was too late for Hull to win the Championship title now. The Tigers would have to win promotion through the play-offs instead.

'Not again!' Harry thought to himself.

Twice, he had got to the League One Play-offs with Sheffield United and twice, they had lost. Was it bad luck or bad mistakes? Harry had been relegated twice, and how many times had he been promoted? Zero!

In the play-offs, Bruce selected Michael and Curtis at the back, and Harry on the bench. Hull beat Derby County 3–2 to reach the final at Wembley.

'Well done, lads!' Harry cheered. Even though he wasn't playing in the team, he was still a great team player. 'We're nearly there!'

The final was one of the tightest and nerviest matches that Harry had ever seen. After all, Hull and Sheffield Wednesday were battling each other for a place in the Premier League. What a prize for the winner!

On the bench, Harry looked up at the 70,000 fans and listened to their non-stop noise. How he wished that he could be out there, playing on the pitch against United's Sheffield rivals. Hull needed a hero…

That hero turned out to be midfielder Mohamed Diamé. With twenty minutes to go, he hit a thirty-yard screamer into the top corner. 1–0!

At that moment, Harry was warming up along the touchline. He stopped to watch the ball fly past the goalkeeper and then raced over to join the big team hug.

'Mo, what a beauty!' he yelled.

In the end, Harry did get to play a part in Hull's big day at Wembley. With five minutes to go, he came on to replace Mohamed. The manager's instructions were simple:

'Just don't let them score!'

Those five minutes were the longest of Harry's life. Wednesday had shot after shot but Hull held on.

'Yes, yes, YES!' Harry screamed at the final whistle. 'We're back in the Premier League!'

He had won promotion at last. Harry was the third player up the stadium steps to shake hands and collect his winners' medal. Once it was placed around his neck, suddenly it all felt real. He turned to his captain, Michael, and grabbed him by the face.

'We did it, Daws!' he grinned. 'We did it!'

The players were bouncing up and down before Michael even lifted the trophy. He passed the big silver cup down the line until, eventually, Harry had it in his hands. He kissed the trophy twice and lifted it above his head. What a feeling, in front of all his friends and family at Wembley!

Back down on the pitch, the Hull players posed for team photos together. Harry was right at the centre, dancing, smiling, and shielding his eyes from the spraying champagne.

'Curtis, stop aiming for me!'

'Sorry, your big head's an easy target!'

The celebrations carried on all afternoon and all night too. Harry couldn't wait to be back in the Premier League. This time, he was going to prove himself at the highest level.

CHAPTER 18

AGAINST THE ODDS

As the 2016–17 Premier League season kicked-off, fans disagreed about which team would finish top:

'I reckon Tottenham can do it. They came so close last season and they've got more experience this time around.'

'No, it's going to be Manchester City's year. They've got Pep Guardiola in charge now, and the guy's a genius!'

'What about José Mourinho at Manchester United? He sure knows how to win the Premier League!'

At the other end of the table, most fans agreed about which team would finish bottom:

'Hull City.'

'Yeah, they're going to get hammered every week!'

'They could be relegated by Christmas!'

It had been a very hard summer for Hull. First, their right-back Moses Odubajo picked up a really bad injury in preseason. Then, their manager Steve Bruce resigned and their captain Michael hurt his knee. Finally, their play-off hero Mohamed signed for Newcastle United. Bit by bit, the club's Premier League excitement was fading away.

'Oh no, this is going to be a disaster!' the Hull fans feared.

The opening game against Leicester City was only weeks away, and the Tigers still only had twelve fit players in their first-team squad.

'Come on, lads, we've got to stick together here!' their new manager, Mike Phelan, told them.

Thankfully, there was a strong team spirit amongst the players. They didn't mind battling against the odds.

Harry certainly wasn't giving up on his Premier League dream. He had spent the summer working really hard on every aspect of his game.

On the training pitch, he focused on his fitness. Thanks to the new sports technology, he could look at lots of running stats every day: distance, average speed, and number of sprints. He challenged himself to get faster and faster.

'Look at that acceleration!' Andrew joked. 'Agüero better watch out!'

Off the training pitch, Harry sat through hours and hours of his own performances on video. He found it really embarrassing to watch, but it was a great way to learn from his mistakes.

'No! What were you doing there?' he shouted at himself on the screen. 'Concentrate!'

Harry preferred watching videos of other defenders in action. Premier League legends like John Terry and Rio Ferdinand hardly ever made wrong decisions. They read the game so well that they saw the danger coming and dealt with it every time. They made it look so simple.

'One day, I'll reach that level,' Harry told himself.

Sometimes, Phelan watched videos with him and gave him extra advice. He had been Sir Alex

Ferguson's assistant at Manchester United and so he had worked closely with Ferdinand. Harry eagerly asked him question after question.

'What do you think Rio would have done there?'

'How did Rio know that the striker was going to do that?'

'Who do you think Rio preferred playing against – Fernando Torres or Didier Drogba?'

Each answer added to Harry's football education. He had to learn from the best in order to compete with the best.

Harry played the last ten minutes against Manchester United and then the last forty-five minutes against Arsenal and Liverpool. Hull lost all three matches but he didn't let that get him down. It was all good experience. By the time Phelan gave Harry his first-ever Premier League start against Bournemouth, he felt 100 per cent ready.

'Let's do this!' Harry cheered, high-fiving Curtis, his centre-back partner.

Unfortunately, those high hopes only lasted five minutes. Junior Stanislas' free kick hit the post and

Charlie Daniels scored the rebound, despite Harry's brave dive to stop it. 1–0! After that, Hull just collapsed.

Steve Cook jumped highest to win a header against Harry. 2–1!

Robert Snodgrass gave away a penalty. 3–1!

Adam Smith crossed and Stanislas scored. 4–1!

Joshua King's cross landed on Callum Wilson's head. 5–1!

Daniels passed to Dan Gosling and he curled the ball into corner of the net. 6–1!

Hull had been absolutely hammered. As he trudged off the pitch, Harry felt so many negative emotions at once – humiliation, disappointment, guilt, frustration, anger. It was the worst defeat of his entire career. The horrible sinking feeling stayed in his stomach for days.

'What if I never get to play Premier League football again?' he groaned. He was dreading his post-match video session. Phelan had every right to be furious with him for his poor performance.

'Look, that defeat wasn't your fault,' his manager told him. 'We win as a team and we lose as a team. Every player has to take responsibility. The important thing is how you recover. Rio had bad games too but he always bounced straight back. Now, you've got to do the same!'

Phelan was right; Harry was a strong character and it was time to show it.

Ten days later, he was playing for Hull in the FA Cup against Bristol City. In the last minute of the first half, Ryan Mason curled a high corner into the box. Harry timed his run perfectly and headed home at the back-post. 1–0!

Goooooooooooaaaaaaaaaalllllllllllllllllllllll!!!!!!!!!!!!!!

Harry punched the air proudly. He had finally scored his first goal for Hull! Michael ran over and gave him a massive hug.

'Nice one, H!' his captain shouted, patting his big head.

Soon, Harry was playing in the Premier League again too. Against Crystal Palace, he chested the ball down near the halfway line and looked up. Andrew was making a great run down the left but it would take an incredible long pass to reach him. Instead, Harry calmly dribbled past one player and then played it to Hull's striker, Adama Diomande, who turned and scored. 2–2!

'Great work, H!' Michael shouted.

Against Everton, Harry did it again. He collected the ball at the back and bravely brought it forward.

'Keep going!' the fans urged him on.

Why not? Harry had put his Bournemouth disaster behind him. He now felt really comfortable playing Premier League football. It was his time to shine.

The Everton midfielders backed away in fear as Harry galloped through the middle like a race horse. Eventually, one of them tried to stop him. Foul – free kick!

'Brilliant run, H!' Curtis called out.

Robert fired the free-kick straight into the top corner. 2–1 to Hull!

Against the odds, the Tigers were no longer bottom of the table. Harry was loving every minute of his Premier League adventure, despite all the ups and downs.

'It's a good thing I love rollercoaster rides!' he said with a big smile on his face.

CHAPTER 19

ATTACK FROM THE BACK

Unfortunately, the chaos continued. In January 2017, Hull sacked Mike Phelan and replaced him with a young Portuguese manager called Marco Silva.

'I know we don't have a lot of time,' he admitted in his first interview, 'but I want the fans to believe, like I believe.'

Could the Tigers really stay up? It was going to take a miracle, especially when the club sold two of their best players, Jake Livermore and Robert Snodgrass.

'Come on, lads, we've got to stick together here!' Harry told his teammates.

He didn't know much about Silva but they got

on really well straight away. The new manager
had big plans for the defence, and for Harry in
particular.

'I want you to be the one who brings the ball
forward,' Silva told him. 'We're going to attack from
the back!'

'No problem!' Harry thought to himself. It was the
role that he was born to play.

Silva's first game was the rematch against
Bournemouth. Harry had been looking forward to it
for months. He was desperate to get revenge for that
awful 6–1 thrashing in his first Premier League start.
the Tigers were a much better team now, and Harry
was a much better player.

It didn't look that way, however, when he gave
away a penalty with a clumsy tackle. Hull were 1–0
down after only three minutes.

'No, no, NO!' he screamed.

Harry didn't panic and give up, though. 'That's
not what Rio would do,' he thought to himself. He
had to stay strong and make things right. He pushed
his team up the pitch with his clever dribbling and

passing, and Hull fought back to win 3–1. Silva was impressed.

'You showed real character today,' he told Harry. 'Keep it up – you've got some big battles ahead of you!'

At Stamford Bridge, Harry fought ferociously against Chelsea's star striker, Diego Costa. Hull lost 2–0 but Harry picked up the man of the match award for his all-action performance. At the back, he made eight tackles, seven clearances and eight interceptions. In attack, he took more shots than any of his teammates.

'Great game,' Cesc Fàbregas said, shaking his hand at the final whistle. 'I love the way you play!'

At Old Trafford, Harry frustrated Manchester United's legendary striker Zlatan Ibrahimović all game long. And when Harry got the ball at the back, he wasn't afraid to take a few risks in attack. He even dribbled past his old FA Youth Cup opponent, Paul Pogba. The fans loved Harry's confidence and character.

Ohhhh, Harry Maguire!

Ohhhh, Harry Maguire!

0–0 – an important point for Hull!

At the KC Stadium, Harry and his new centre-back partner, Andrea Ranocchia, kept out Liverpool's ace attackers Roberto Firmino and Sadio Mané. Then just before half-time, Harry headed a corner towards goal and Alfred N'Diaye bundled it in. 1–0!

'Thanks, H!' Alfred cheered, putting an arm around his broad shoulders.

Silva's coaching was working wonders. The team looked fitter than ever and they were passing the ball around beautifully.

Harry was keeping Hull's survival hopes alive, at both ends of the field. Once the defending was done, he loved to attack from the back. It really helped that Harry had one of the best friends by his side. He was now the left centre-back, with Andrew next to him at left-back. Together, they formed a perfect partnership – strength *and* speed, great passes *and* great crosses.

With eight games to go, Hull were just one point away from safety.

'Come on lads, we can do this!' Harry kept telling his teammates.

Now that Michael and Curtis weren't playing so often, he was their heroic leader at the back. Wearing the captain's armband, Harry was improving game after game.

At the start of April 2017, Hull faced Middlesbrough in an epic relegation battle. After an awful start, the Tigers really came back roaring.

Lazar Marković poked the ball in after a goalmouth scramble. 1–1!

Abel Hernández set up Oumar Niasse. 2–1!

'That's more like it!' Harry shouted, punching the air with joy and relief.

The game, however, was far from over. There were still sixty minutes left to play. Could Hull hold on for that long?

No, Harry had a better idea. He got the ball deep in his own half and decided to attack from the back. As he looked up, he saw Sam Clucas making a great run down the right wing. Harry found him with the perfect pass. He curled the ball just past a

Middlesbrough midfielder's outstretched foot, and then in between two defenders. Sam crossed it first-time to Abel. 3–1!

Abel pointed at Sam to thank him for the assist but Sam pointed to his centre-back. 'H, what a ball that was!' he screamed above the deafening crowd.

Middlesbrough scored again just before half-time but luckily, Harry wasn't finished yet. With twenty anxious minutes ahead, Hull won a free kick. Andrew whipped the ball into the box, knowing exactly where his big friend would be: the back post! Harry was unmarked but he still had plenty of work to do. He headed the ball over the goalkeeper's arms and it looped down into the far corner of the net. 4–2 – game over!

Gooooooooooooooooooooaaaaaaaaaaaaaaaallllllllllll llllllllllllll!!!!!!!!!!!!!!!!!!!

What a time for Harry to score his first Premier League goal! The Hull fans went wild as he ran over and jumped into Michael's arms.

Ohhhh, Harry Maguire!
Ohhhh, Harry Maguire!

There was no stopping him now. Away at Southampton a few weeks later, Harry was Hull's hero yet again.

Sofiane Boufal dribbled into the penalty area, past two flying challenges, but he couldn't get past Harry. *TACKLE!*

Nathan Redmond crossed to Dušan Tadić but he couldn't score past Harry. *BLOCK!*

0–0 – another important point for Hull!

He was really making a name for himself now. Every Premier League club wanted a 'Harry Maguire' at the heart of their defence.

'He has very good skills,' Silva praised his captain. 'It's clear to me that he will have a big career in the future.'

That future, however, would not be at Hull. Despite his best efforts, they lost their big battles against Sunderland and Crystal Palace. The rollercoaster ride had come to an end. Harry was relegated for the third time in his career.

This time, however, he was going down with his big head held high. In his first full season in the

Premier League, Harry had been Hull's hero, captain, and Player of the Year.

After the last home game of the season, he walked slowly around the pitch, clapping to the tearful fans. Harry had given 100 per cent to help his team, and they loved him for that.

Ohhhh, Harry Maguire!

Ohhhh, Harry Maguire!

Harry would always be grateful for their support, especially during his difficult early days on the bench. Wow, he had come a long way since then! What was next for Harry?

CHAPTER 20

LEICESTER CITY

Harry was trying to relax on his family summer holiday in Majorca, but he had a difficult decision to make. As he lay there by the pool, soaking up the sun, he asked himself,

'Who do I want to play for next season?'

After his big breakthrough year with Hull, lots of top clubs were queuing up to sign him: Tottenham, Leicester City, Stoke City, Everton, Newcastle United, Southampton, West Ham... The list went on and on.

When his agent told him, Harry's first thought was, 'Great, I'll get to stay in the Premier League!'

Now, however, he had to pick which team to play for. What a hard choice!

Tottenham were the Premier League runners-
up for two years in a row. They had an amazing
manager, Mauricio Pochettino, and amazing players
like Harry Kane, Christian Eriksen and Dele Alli.

'Plus, you'd be playing Champions League
football next season!' Laurence argued.

The only problem was that they already had
a deadly defence. Toby Alderweireld and Jan
Vertonghen were two of the best centre-backs in
the world, and they had Eric Dier as well!

'No, there's no way that I'm going to play week
in week out at Spurs,' Harry decided.

No matter what, he wasn't going back to the
bench again. He was twenty-four years old now.
Wherever he went, he needed guaranteed game-
time.

Harry moved on to his next option, 'Okay, well
how about Leicester City, then?'

The Foxes were the 2015–16 Premier League
Champions and they still had their world-class
forwards, Jamie Vardy and Riyad Mahrez. Harry
could start the attacks from the back and they

would finish them off. Easy!

'They've got some other promising young English players too,' Joe argued. 'Ben Chilwell's good, and Demarai Gray's rapid!'

But, most importantly, what about their defence? Did they have space for a new centre-back? Yes, they had a big, Harry-shaped gap to fill!

Robert Huth and Wes Morgan were both coming towards the end of their careers and Leicester City didn't really have a back-up option.

'Maguire is our man!' their manager, Craig Shakespeare, decided.

He was so desperate to sign Harry that he flew all the way out to Majorca to meet him.

'I hope you're having a nice summer holiday,' Shakespeare began. 'This shouldn't take long. I'm rebuilding the Leicester defence and I want to rebuild it around you!'

That sounded awesome but Harry didn't want to rush into things. This was the biggest decision of his life, and he had to get it right. He had lots of questions for the Leicester manager:

What formation would the team be playing – 4–4–
2 or 3–5–2?

What style of football did he want his team to
play?

And what were the club's expectations for the
season ahead – Top Four, Top Six or Top Ten?

As he answered each question, Shakespeare grew
more and more impressed. Harry was clearly a very
clever young man, who studied football closely.
It only made the Leicester manager even more
determined to sign him.

Harry grew more and more impressed too. Not
only had Shakespeare come all the way to a Spanish
island to speak to him, but he had big, bold plans for
the football club.

'And I want you to be a key part of it!' the
manager told him passionately.

Leicester were building towards a brighter future.
They were improving their academy, their training
ground, and, of course, their squad. The Foxes
were on the up and they were aiming for European
qualification.

'Perfect, where do I sign?' Harry thought to himself.

He didn't want to join a global giant like Manchester United or Chelsea. That wasn't his style. Leicester was a family club that cared about its local community, just like his home team, Sheffield United. He knew that he would be very happy there.

'I've made up my mind,' Harry told his family at dinner one night. 'I'm going to Leicester!'

It was a sad day when Harry went back to say goodbye to all his friends at Hull. They felt like family.

'Good luck, Big H!' Michael cheered.

'Cheers for everything, Daws. I couldn't have done it without you!'

'I'm going to miss playing with you!' Andrew said as they hugged.

'Me too, mate! Why don't you just come with me?'

Back in 2014, Hull had paid £2.5 million to sign Harry from Sheffield United. Three years later, Leicester were writing a much, much larger cheque.

'£17million for someone who just got relegated?' people on Twitter reacted. 'The world's gone crazy!'

'That Hull defence let in eighty goals last season. Leicester are having a laugh!'

Yes, it was an awful lot of money, but there was only one way that Harry could prove his value – by performing well out on the pitch.

First, however, Leicester's new Number 15 needed to settle in. It didn't take him long to make new friends in the squad. There were lots of big, fun characters at the club.

'Alright mate, is it true that you're an Owls fan like me?' Jamie teased. He was from Sheffield too, and had started out in the Wednesday youth team.

Harry rolled his eyes. 'Stop winding me up, you know I'm a Blade through and through!'

Harry quickly became a popular member of the Leicester dressing room, and a key member of the team. He scored his first goal for his new club in August 2017 against Burton Albion and, for once, it wasn't even a header. As the ball bounced down in the box, he smashed it home with his right foot.

Goooooooooooooooooooooaaaaaaaaaaaaaaaalllllllllllll llllllllllllllll!!!!!!!!!!!!!!!!!!!!

It was only a preseason friendly, but Harry meant business. He had new targets for the new year.

'Every player wants to play for their country,' he told the journalists afterwards. 'I felt like this was the club that could help me progress into the England squad.'

Some people laughed at Harry's ambition, but he was being deadly serious. This was going to be *his* season.

With Robert Huth out injured, Harry started alongside Wes Morgan against Arsenal. It wasn't the solid defensive debut that he was hoping for, but he played his part in attack.

In the fifth minute, Harry crept in at the back post, as usual, to head the ball back for Shinji Okazaki. 1–1!

'Thanks, H!' Shinji cheered, giving him a big hug.

A week later against Brighton and Hove Albion, Harry got a cleansheet and a goal. It was a trademark towering header at the back post.

Goooooooooooooooooooooaaaaaaaaaaaaaaaaalllllllllllll llllllllllllllll!!!!!!!!!!!!!!!!!!!!!

As Harry celebrated in front of the fans, Wilfred Ndidi and Wes jumped up on his back. He was so strong that he could carry them both!

'£17million, eh?' Jamie laughed. 'What a bargain for that big head of yours!'

Suddenly, Harry's dreams of a first England call-up didn't seem so silly at all.

CHAPTER 21

ENGLAND CALLING – PART TWO

Even though he was a Premier League star now, Harry was still England's biggest fan. When his brothers and friends went to France to watch Euro 2016, he decided to join them.

'Three Lions on a shirt!' he sang along with the rest of the supporters in Saint-Étienne. As long as he didn't sing too loudly, or badly, he could blend into the crowd.

The match finished Slovakia 0 England 0. It wasn't the most exciting game of football that Harry had ever seen, but the trip was worth it for the amazing atmosphere alone. The fans showed so much passion, even when their team wasn't playing very well.

'You should be out there playing, H!' his brothers told him.

Harry looked down at the white shirt he was wearing, and the blue Three Lions over his heart. Then he looked up at the players on the pitch. Nathaniel Clyne, Jordan Henderson – he had played with both of them for the Under-21s. In that moment, anything seemed possible.

A year later, after a sensational season at Hull and a big-money move to Leicester, Harry's England dream seemed more than possible. The national team manager Gareth Southgate was watching him closely.

'Every kid wants to play for their country,' Harry told the media. 'I want to play in the World Cup.'

Dele Alli, Raheem Sterling, Harry Kane – Harry Maguire was competing against the best players every week in the Premier League. And then there was Jamie, Harry's Leicester teammate.

'If Vards can play for England, then so can I!' he told himself.

In August 2017, nearly five years after his only cap for the Under-21s, Harry finally got the call-up he was hoping for. He was named in Southgate's squad for the World Cup qualifiers against Malta and Slovakia.

'I did it!' he told his family on the phone. 'I'm in!'

It was yet another proud moment for all the Maguires.

When Harry joined the squad at St George's Park, he made a bigger entrance than he had expected. While the other England players arrived with their designer clothes and fancy suitcases, he turned up in his Leicester tracksuit, with his boots and shin pads in a black bin bag. The photos were trending on social media in seconds.

'Harry Maguire looks like he's moving into student halls in freshers' week,' someone wrote on Twitter.

When the news reached Harry's mum, she wasn't happy.

'A bin bag?' she told him off via text message. 'What were you thinking? So embarrassing!'

'Sorry, Mum!' Harry replied quickly.

'If I get called up again, I'll treat myself to some proper luggage!' he joked with the journalists.

Out on the training pitch, however, Harry was 100 per cent focused on football. This was his big chance to impress Southgate. In the squad of twenty-eight players, there were at least other four centre-backs ahead of him: Chelsea's Gary Cahill, Manchester City's John Stones, and Manchester United's Phil Jones and Chris Smalling.

All four were top defenders at Champions League clubs, but Harry was as fearless as ever.

'Let the battles begin!' he told himself.

It was a sharp learning curve for Harry. He was playing at the very highest level now. He listened carefully to all the advice he received, especially from his manager. Southgate had played fifty-seven times for England as a centre-back. He knew what he was talking about when it came to international defending!

In the end, Harry didn't make his debut against Malta or Slovakia. Instead, he watched from the bench as Gary and Phil led England to victory. He wasn't too disappointed, though – he returned to Leicester feeling more motivated than ever. He was nearly there! One month later, he was called up again.

'Nice new suitcase, H!' Jordan teased. 'They must be paying you well at Leicester!'

Harry Kane's late winner against Slovenia meant that England were through to the World Cup with one game to spare! That was especially good news for Harry because Southgate now had the chance to try something new.

'We're going to play a back three against Lithuania,' his manager explained, 'and I want you to play on the left.'

Harry couldn't believe it – he was in the England starting line-up!

Once he had recovered from the shock, he thanked his three Hull managers: Bruce, Phelan and Silva. They were the ones who had spotted his potential as the ball player in a back three. And, of course, his friend Andrew. Without him at left-back, Harry's job would have been so much harder.

'Good luck, mate!' Andrew messaged back, followed by a Scottish flag emoji.

The LFF Stadium in Vilnius wasn't exactly Wembley, but Harry didn't care. He would have happily made his England senior debut in front of one man and his dog!

As the match against Lithuania kicked off, he was more excited than nervous. He tried to treat it like any other of the hundreds of games that he had played.

In the fourth minute, he had the perfect chance to make it a dream debut. Aaron Cresswell's cross was perfect, right on his big head. Somehow, however, he missed the ball completely.

'Noooo!' Harry groaned. He was usually so good in the air.

But instead of dwelling on his mistake, he kept going. England were dominating the game, so Harry did what he did best – attack from the back!

In the twenty-sixth minute, he chipped a clever ball through to Jordan, who headed it back into Dele's path. As Dele ran onto it, a defender fouled him. Penalty!

'Great ball, H!' Jordan called out, giving him a big

thumbs-up.

Phew! He had made up for his earlier error.
England's other Harry – Harry Kane – scored from
the spot. 1–0!

That turned out to be the final score. As he shook
hands with the Lithuania players, Harry felt happy
with his first England performance. One game, one
cleansheet! Apart from that missed header, he had
looked comfortable and composed throughout.
But had he done enough to keep his place against
tougher opponents?

Harry would have to wait and see. In the
meantime, he enjoyed his big moment. After years of
being England's biggest fan, he was now an England
player! Once his teammates had signed his shirt, he
framed it and hung it proudly on his wall at home.

'You never know – that might be my only cap!' he
told his girlfriend, Fern.

It wasn't, though. In November 2017, Harry
played ninety minutes against Germany and then
ninety minutes against Brazil. Battling with the best
attackers in the world, he was as solid as a rock

in England's back three. Three games, three clean sheets!

'I just stopped Neymar from scoring!' Harry laughed.

Sometimes, he had to pinch himself to make sure that he wasn't dreaming. With the 2018 World Cup only months away, Harry was now one of England's first-choice centre-backs. He just had to keep playing well, and keep believing.

CHAPTER 22

LEICESTER'S NEW LEADER

It was turning into a whirlwind season for Harry. Four days after keeping Neymar quiet at Wembley, he was back in the Premier League, with Leicester, taking on Pep Guardiola's awesome Manchester City attack. For forty-five minutes, Leicester's defence held on.

'Keep concentrating!' Harry shouted to his teammates. He was one of their leaders already.

Raheem Sterling played a one-two with Kevin De Bruyne, and then slipped a pass through to David Silva, who quickly crossed to Gabriel Jesus. 1–0!

As the ball rolled past Kasper Schmeichel, Harry kicked the air in frustration. Leicester had been beaten by a magical City move but it was still disappointing. These days, Harry felt every goal he conceded like a punch in the gut. He wanted to be the best defender in the world!

'Next time,' Harry muttered to himself. That was the good thing about playing game after game. He always had the chance to learn from his mistakes. Ten days later, Leicester beat Tottenham 2–1. In the battle of England's 'Harrys', Maguire defeated Kane.

Leicester changed their manager – Claude Puel replaced Craig Shakespeare – but the team tactics stayed the same. With two defensive midfielders protecting him, Harry had the freedom to attack from the back.

'Go!' Claude Puel told him, pointing towards the opposition half.

Against Southampton, Harry chested the ball down in the penalty area, turned and then fired a dangerous ball across goal. Andy King was there for a tap-in at the back post. 3–1 to Leicester!

'Cheers, H!'

Against Manchester United, Leicester were losing

2–1 with seconds to go. As Marc Albrighton curled one last ball into the box, Harry made his trademark dash towards the back post. His England teammates Phil Jones and Chris Smalling watched the cross sail over their heads and thought it was going out for a goal kick.

How wrong they were! Harry stretched out his long right leg and coolly volleyed the ball past the goalkeeper.

Goooooooooooooooooooaaaaaaaaaaaaaaaallllllllllll lllllllllllll!!!!!!!!!!!!!!!!!!!

Harry was Leicester's last-minute hero! He ran past the club mascot, Filbert Fox, and slid on his knees in front of the delighted fans. There was no better feeling in the whole of football.

Harry Maguire! Harry Maguire!

'What a finish!' Shinji shouted.

Harry was dominating in defence too. Training against Jamie every week was tough, but it made him a better player. As a defender, he faced lots of different challenges. With his height and strength, he could battle with the big boys like Lukaku and Costa all game long.

It was the smaller, speedier strikers that caused him more problems. Jamie was one of the quickest players Harry had ever seen. In order to stop him, Harry had to be alert all the time, looking out for signs of danger. Their battles were fierce and full of banter.

'How many have you scored today, Vards?' he asked.

'Shut up, Slabhead! How many Premier League titles have you won?'

Harry was loving life at Leicester. Robert still wasn't back from injury, so he played game after game, in the Premier League, the League Cup *and* the FA Cup. Harry even played twice against his old club, Sheffield United. It was a nice reminder of how far he had come.

'Don't overdo it!' his mum warned him. 'Remember, you've got the World Cup coming up this summer.'

'I know, I can rest when I've retired!' Harry replied.

He had to keep playing. Every header, block, tackle

and interception was taking him one step closer to Southgate's final squad for the tournament in Russia.

Harry started on the bench in England's next friendly against the Netherlands but he didn't stay there long. Joe Gomez got injured in the tenth minute and Harry ran on to replace him.

England had an all-Yorkshire back three now: Kyle Walker on the right, John Stones in the middle and Harry on the left. Kyle was from Sheffield, and he had been a couple of years ahead of Harry at United.

'The Maguire Boys!' he remembered with a grin. 'Yeah, I used to hear lots of good things about you guys!'

John, meanwhile, was born just up the road in Barnsley.

'I started out in the Tykes academy,' Harry explained excitedly. 'Maybe we met when we were younger, Stonesy!'

'I doubt it, mate. I wouldn't forget a big head like yours!'

Between the three of them, Kyle, John and Harry had so much strength, skill and speed. The poor

Dutch attackers had no chance.

The match finished England 1 Netherlands 0. Four games, four clean sheets!

Fingers crossed, Harry had done enough to earn a World Cup place. There was no time to worry, though. Four days after returning to Leicester, Harry was too busy beating Brighton.

In the end, the Foxes finished ninth in the Premier League and reached the quarter-finals of both cups. It had been an acceptable campaign for Leicester but an exceptional one for their new young leader at the back.

At the club's end of season ceremony, Harry won both the Players' Player and Player of the Year awards. He'd achieved this at three clubs – first Sheffield United, then Hull City, and now Leicester City!

The audience clapped and cheered as Harry walked onto the stage, dressed in a smart navy suit. It made a change from his usual club tracksuit! Everyone agreed that he was a worthy winner. He had been Leicester's Mr Consistent, playing every single minute of every single Premier League match.

'I'm really honoured to collect these awards,' he said humbly. 'I've been really lucky to come to this club. There's a great bunch of lads here and a great team spirit. The supporters have been brilliant with me ever since I joined. So thank you, and let's hope we can win a few trophies next season!'

Before that, however, Harry was hoping to win a trophy for his country. On 16 May, Southgate announced his England squad for the 2018 World Cup.

The FA released a video where each player's name was revealed one by one. Raheem Sterling was first, then John Stones, then Trent Alexander-Arnold. Eventually, the camera zoomed in on a tall grey tower block where a girl and a boy were holding up a big white banner. They yelled the two words written there at the tops of their voices:

'HARRY MAGUIRE!'

'Yes, Big Man!' Jamie messaged. He was in the squad too. 'Russia, here we come!'

CHAPTER 23

WORLD CUP 2018

Being selected for England's 2018 World Cup squad was a huge achievement for Harry. However, his ambition didn't stop there. He wanted to start every single match for his country, just like he did for his club. Kyle Walker and John Stones were guaranteed to play but Harry was battling with Gary Cahill for that final place in the back three.

'Cahill's won two Premier League titles *and* the Champions League!' his brothers told him, hoping to fire Harry up. The whole Maguire family was heading out to Russia to cheer him on.

Yes, Gary was certainly the more experienced option. He had fifty-nine England caps, whereas

Harry only had four. However, if Southgate wanted someone who could bring the ball out of defence, Harry was his man!

In England's last two warm-up matches, Gary played against Nigeria and then Harry played against Costa Rica. Gary scored in a 2–1 win, and then Harry kept a clean sheet in a 2–0 win. Before the first group game against Tunisia, Southgate had a big decision to make.

In the meantime, the England players settled into their World Cup base camp in Repino. They were miles away from the capital city, Moscow, and Harry was expecting to be really bored. But instead, he had loads of fun!

When training ended, there were lots of different activities for the players to do together: Fortnite, basketball, pool. When Jamie wanted to play table tennis, he knew who to ask.

'Fancy a game, Big H?'

'Sure, Vards, as long as you're ready for another thrashing!'

It all helped to build a really strong team spirit.

During the Premier League season, they competed against each other for their clubs but this was different. For the World Cup, they were united, competing together for their country.

After weeks of watching and thinking, Southgate picked Harry to play in England's first match against Tunisia. When he heard the great news, he wanted to slide across the grass on his knees. Harry couldn't wait!

The Three Lions started brilliantly. They could have been 2–0 up after ten minutes! Instead, however, it was still 0–0 as Harry went forward for the corner. Ashley Young delivered a deep cross towards England's big men and John headed it goalwards. The Tunisia keeper made a super save but Harry Kane was in the right place for the rebound. 1–0!

All the players piled on top of each other in a happy team bundle. As a big centre-back, Harry had to be careful not to hurt anyone.

'Sorry!' he shouted sheepishly to Raheem.

England were in total control until the thirty-fifth minute. Suddenly, a cross came in and Kyle fouled the Tunisia striker. Penalty – 1–1!

It was a cruel blow but the England players didn't panic. There was plenty of time left to grab another goal.

Harry did what he did best – attack from the back! In the second half, he played like an extra midfielder. He dribbled forward into space, looking for a killer pass. Harry had more touches on the ball than any of his teammates, but with seconds to go, the score was still 1–1.

Corner-kick! Harry rushed forward to attack Kieran Trippier's cross. It was now or never. *BOOM!* He jumped high to win the header. Harry Kane was in the right place again to steer the ball home. 2–1!

The two Harrys were the England heroes! It was an amazing moment that neither of them would ever forget. In their first-ever World Cup match, with the hopes of a nation resting on their shoulders, they had saved the day.

'Nice one, Slabhead!' Jamie shouted as the whole squad celebrated in front of the relieved and jubilant fans.

It was the start of an exciting new era for England. After years of misery and frustration, the nation had finally found another team of fearless footballers.

Back home, the hope was building but at the England base camp, it was all fun and games. The players relaxed by racing inflatable unicorns in the swimming pool.

'Where's the VAR when you need it?' Kyle joked.

A few days later, Harry was answering questions from the media, when a familiar face snuck into the room.

'It's Jamie Vardy here from Vardy News,' he said, pretending that his fist was a microphone. 'Just how big is the diameter of your head?'

'Good one, Vards!' Harry thought to himself. Now his big head was all anyone wanted to talk about.

England's next match against Panama was a whole lot easier. Thanks to goals from John, Jesse Lingard and Harry Kane, they were 5–0 up by half-time! The Three Lions were through to the Round of 16.

Even a 1–0 loss to Belgium couldn't dampen their spirits. England hadn't won a World Cup knock-out match since 2006, but that was all about to change against Colombia. The whole country believed.

'Three Lions on a shirt!' Joe and Laurence Maguire sang along with the rest of the supporters in Moscow. This time, their brother wasn't with them; Harry was out there playing on the pitch instead!

And what a game he was having. At the heart of the England defence, Harry won header after header. It was an angry, competitive match but there was nothing he liked more than a battle.

When Harry Kane scored a penalty, it looked like they were through to the quarter-finals. In the last minute, however, Yerry Mina equalised for Colombia.

The England fans fell silent. Could their warriors keep fighting, or was it game over? Harry certainly wasn't giving up.

'Come on, lads!' he clapped and cheered. 'We can do this!'

Together, the team held on through the thirty minutes of extra-time. Penalties!

'Oh no!' the fans groaned.

England had never won a World Cup shoot-out. They had lost against West Germany in 1990, against Argentina in 1998, and against Portugal in 2006. On top of all that, there were the losses against Germany in Euro 96, against Portugal in Euro 2004, and against Italy in Euro 2012.

As England's biggest fan, Harry had seen a lot of failure. It was time for them to write a new story of success.

Even when Jordan Henderson's penalty was saved, Harry didn't give up hope.

Mateus Uribe stepped up and... hit the crossbar!

Carlos Bacca ran up and... Jordan Pickford made a super save!

Now, Eric Dier just needed to keep cool and...

Goooooooooooooooooooooaaaaaaaaaaaaaaaaaalllllllllll llllllllllllllllll!!!!!!!!!!!!!!!!!!!!

What a moment – England were through to the World Cup quarter-finals after WINNING ON PENALTIES! Harry was ecstatic as he raced over to join the big team bundle.

In the stands in Russia, and back in England, everyone was singing the same old tune:

It's coming home, it's coming home,
It's coming, FOOTBALL'S COMING HOME!

Was football really coming home? Suddenly, the impossible seemed possible.

'Good luck, Big H!' Andrew messaged him before the quarter-final, followed by a Scottish flag emoji.

His friend had just played in the Champions League final with Liverpool. Hull's two young signings had turned into superstars!

Sweden were the next team standing in England's way. It wouldn't be easy but Harry wasn't leaving the World Cup without an almighty fight.

In the thirtieth minute, Harry's thumping header gave England the lead.

Goooooooooooooooooooooaaaaaaaaaaaaaaaalllllllllllll llllllllllllll!!!!!!!!!!!!!!!!!!!

What a time to score his first international goal! Harry raced towards the fans, pumping his fists and roaring like a lion. His country meant so much to him.

Sixty long minutes later, England were through to the World Cup semi-finals! It was an incredible achievement for such a young, inexperienced group of players. Of all the new national heroes, Harry was now the biggest of them all.

First, there was the song:

Harry Maguire, your defence is terrified!
Harry Maguire, na na na na na na na na na na!

Then, there were the memes. A funny photo of Harry talking to Fern after the Colombia match exploded on to the Internet. Everyone was adding their own comedy captions, including Harry himself:

'Can you ask the neighbours to put the bins out on Monday?' he wrote after the Sweden win. 'We're not going home just yet!'

That was one of the many things that the England fans loved about Harry; he was just so normal and down to earth. Despite becoming a World Cup hero, he was keeping his feet firmly on the ground. Ahead of the semi-final, he took part in a fun darts challenge.

'Good luck, Harry!' the fans cheered for their favourite.

He won, of course! Harry was a natural, all-round sportsman. After shaking hands, he went back to focusing on football.

Against Croatia in the semi-final, England got off to an amazing start. In the fifth minute, Kieran curled a free-kick into the top corner. 1–0!

It's coming home, it's coming home,
It's coming, FOOTBALL'S COMING HOME!

No, Harry knew that England weren't in the final yet. There was lots of defending left to do. The back three battled hard, winning headers, tackles and interceptions.

Kyle, John and Harry – they were a brave band of superheroes.

'Nothing's getting past us!'

In the second half, however, Croatia fought back
fiercely. They attacked again and again until finally
they scored. 1–1!

Could England hold strong? Harry did his best but
the whole team was so tired. Deep in extra-time,
Mario Mandžuki grabbed the winning goal. As
Harry watched the ball cross the line, he had that
horrible sinking feeling once again. England were out
of the World Cup.

Harry was very disappointed but it wasn't all
doom and gloom. No-one had expected them to
get so far in the tournament. The players had made
their country very proud. Harry and his England
teammates stood together on the pitch, thanking the
fans with their heads held high.

'This is just the beginning, boys!' Gareth Southgate
promised.

Harry hoped so. He really didn't want his amazing
football adventure to end. It was hard to believe how
far he had come already.

After starting out with Sheffield United, Harry
had risen higher and higher, step by step, game after

game, through ups and downs, highs and lows. League One, then the Championship, then the Premier League – and now the World Cup.

Through hard work, belief and dedication, Harry and his big head had conquered them all.

Turn the page for a sneak preview of
another brilliant football story by
Matt and Tom Oldfield. . .

SALAH

Available now!

CHAPTER 1

EUROPEAN SUPERSTAR

Anfield, 24 April 2018

The atmosphere at Anfield was always amazing but on big European nights, it was extra special. The chorus of the Kop started hours before kick-off and, if Liverpool were to beat Roma, it would go on for days afterwards. The fans sang the old favourites like 'You'll Never Walk Alone', and they sang the new favourites too:

Mo Salah, Mo Salah
Running down the wing,
Salah la la la la la la
Egyptian King!

The eyes of the world were on Liverpool's 'Egyptian King'. Mohamed was in the best form of his life, with forty goals and counting. He had already scored thirty-one in the Premier League and nine in the Champions League. Could he keep shooting his team all the way to the final?

For Mohamed, it was going to be an emotional night, no matter what. First of all, he was playing in his first-ever Champions League semi-final, a moment that he had dreamed about ever since he was an eight-year-old boy. He was following in the footsteps of his heroes like Zinedine Zidane and Francesco Totti.

Mohamed was also playing against his old club. When his big move to Chelsea hadn't worked out, it was Italian football that saved him. At Fiorentina, and then Roma, he had rediscovered his passion, his confidence, and the path to superstardom. He would always be grateful for that.

Mohamed's old manager, Luciano Spalletti, had moved on, but lots of his old teammates were still there – Radja Nainggolan, Stephan El Shaarawy, and his old strike partner, Edin Džeko. In the tunnel, Mohamed hugged each and every one of them.

'Good luck,' he said with a smile, 'may the best team win!'

Liverpool were far from a one-man team. Mohamed was one part of 'The Big Three', the hottest strikeforce in the world. With Sadio Mané on the left, Roberto Firmino in the middle, and Mohamed on the right, the Reds looked unstoppable. Even Philippe Coutinho's move to Barcelona hadn't slowed them down. They had scored five against Porto in the Round of 16 and then five against Manchester City in the quarter-finals too. If the Roma defenders weren't careful, 'The Big Three' would run riot again.

'Come on lads, let's win this!' the Liverpool captain Jordan Henderson shouted as the players took up their positions for kick-off.

Even during his days at Roma, Mohamed had been more of a winger than a striker. With his amazing sprint speed, he would race past defenders and set up chances for Edin. At Liverpool, however, manager Jürgen Klopp had helped turn Mohamed into a proper forward and a goalscoring machine. He still worked hard for his team but he did it higher up the pitch. That way, if a defender made a mistake, he was always ready to pounce.

Liverpool created their first good opening after

twenty-seven minutes. One clever flick from Roberto
was all it took to set speedy Sadio away. He had
Mohamed to his right but Sadio wanted the glory for
himself. In the penalty area, he pulled back his left
foot and... blazed it over the crossbar!

The Liverpool fans buried their heads in their
hands – what a missed opportunity! Two minutes
later, another one arrived. Mohamed played a great
pass to Roberto, who squared it to Sadio. He hit it
first time... high and wide!

Groans rang out around Anfield. They couldn't
keep wasting these opportunities! Liverpool needed
more composure in front of goal. What they needed
was a cool head...

Sadio passed to Roberto, who passed to Mohamed
on the right side of the box. With a quick tap of the
boot, he shifted the ball onto his lethal left foot. Time
to shoot? No, not quite yet. Mohamed took one
more touch to get a better angle, and then curled a
fierce strike into the top corner. The technique was
astonishing and he made it look so easy.

Goooooooooooooaaaaaaaaaalllllllllllllllllllllll!!!!!!!!!!!!
Mohamed put his arms up straight away – he

wasn't going to celebrate a goal against his old team. That didn't stop the Liverpool fans, though, or his new teammates.

'Get in!' Jordan screamed, punching the air.

In the last minute of the first half, Mohamed passed to Roberto near the halfway line and sprinted forward for the one-two. The Roma defenders had no chance of catching him. Instead, their goalkeeper rushed out to the edge of his area to block the shot but Mohamed lifted the ball delicately over him. So calm and so classy! As it rolled into the back of the net, he lifted his arms up again.

Gooooooooooooaaaaaaaaaalllllllllllllllllllllll!!!!!!!!!!!

There was just no stopping Mohamed. In the second half, he beat Roma's offside trap again and crossed to Sadio for a simple tap-in. *3–0!*

They pointed over at Roberto. 'Bobby, it's your turn to score now!'

Mohamed picked the ball up on the right wing and attacked the poor Roma left-back, who backed away in fear. Hadn't Mohamed done enough damage for one day? No! He danced his way through and crossed to Roberto at the back post. *4–0!*

Liverpool's 'Big Three' were all on the scoresheet yet again. It was party time at Anfield:

We've got Salah, do do do do do do!
Mané Mané, do do do do do,
And Bobby Firmino,
And we sold Coutinho!

After seventy-five brilliant minutes, Klopp gave his superstar a well-deserved rest. As Mohamed left the pitch, both sets of fans stood up to clap his world-class performance, and the humble hero clapped right back.

At Basel, Mohamed had become a European star; at Liverpool, he had become a European *super*star. With two great goals and two amazing assists, Mohamed had led Liverpool towards the Champions League final, just as he had led his country, Egypt, to the 2018 World Cup.

'So, just how good *is* Mohamed Salah?' the TV presenter asked.

Liverpool legend Steven Gerrard smiled and replied: 'He's the best player on the planet right now!'

That had always been Mohamed's dream, ever since he first kicked a football on his local pitch in Nagrig.

Hull City

🏆 Football League Championship Play-Offs: 2015–16

Individual

🏆 PFA League One Team of the Year: 2011–12,
2012–13, 2013–14

🏆 Sheffield United Player of the Year: 2011–12,
2012–13, 2013–14

🏆 Hull City Fans' Player of the Year: 2016–17

🏆 Hull City Players' Player of the Year: 2016–17

🏆 Leicester City Player of the Season: 2017–18

🏆 Leicester City Players' Player of the Season:
2017–18

MAGUIRE

15 & 6

THE FACTS

NAME: JACOB HARRY MAGUIRE

DATE OF BIRTH: 5 March 1993

AGE: 25

PLACE OF BIRTH: Sheffield

NATIONALITY: England

BEST FRIEND: Jamie Vardy

CURRENT CLUB: Leicester City

POSITION: CB

THE STATS

Height (cm):	194
Club appearances:	301
Club goals:	18
Club trophies:	1
International appearances:	12
International goals:	0
International trophies:	0
Ballon d'Ors:	0

★ ★ ★ **HERO RATING: 82** ★ ★ ★

GREATEST MOMENTS

Type and search the web links to see the magic for yourself!

4 JANUARY 2014, ASTON VILLA 1–2 SHEFFIELD UNITED

https://www.youtube.com/watch?v=clGWwAvkiSI
Harry was already playing game after game in League One but this FA Cup run gave him the chance to battle with the big boys. At Villa Park, he took on Christian Benteke, one of the strongest strikers in the Premier League, and won! After that, Harry knew that he could play at the highest level.

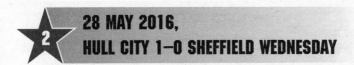

28 MAY 2016, HULL CITY 1–0 SHEFFIELD WEDNESDAY

https://www.youtube.com/watch?v=qBcqlQ9-TzM

Harry was only on the pitch for the final five minutes of this play-off final but it was still a massive moment for him. After two relegations and two play-off failures, he won promotion at last! Best of all, it gave Harry his second shot at playing in the Premier League.

5 APRIL 2017, HULL CITY 4–2 MIDDLESBROUGH

https://www.youtube.com/watch?v=FA7n5TRqHwA

Marco Silva almost pulled off the miracle of keeping Hull in the Premier League. Harry was Silva's leader on the pitch and he saved his best performance for this epic relegation battle. First, Harry set up Abel Hernández with a perfect pass and then he scored a goal of his own.

4 23 DECEMBER 2017, LEICESTER CITY 2–2 MANCHESTER UNITED

https://www.youtube.com/watch?v=1BwcWeNdnJ4
It didn't take Harry long to become a Leicester leader
after his big-money move. The Foxes were losing 2–1
to Manchester United with seconds to go, when up
popped Harry, at the back post as usual. He stretched
out his long right leg and coolly volleyed the ball past
the goalkeeper.

5 9 JULY 2018, SWEDEN 0–2 ENGLAND

https://www.youtube.com/watch?v=yMloUtQRHos
Harry was already an England World Cup hero but,
in the quarter-final, he became a superhero! In the
30th minute, he muscled his way past the Sweden
defenders and powered a thumping header into the
bottom corner. 1–0! And England were on their way
to the semi-finals!

PLAY LIKE YOUR HEROES

THE HARRY MAGUIRE THUMPING HEADER

SEE IT HERE You Tube

https://www.youtube.com/watch?v=L7qSFd6YyYo

STEP 1: When your team wins a corner, make your way forward. This is your big moment!

Step 2: Stop on the edge of the penalty area. You can have a little chat with your teammates if you like because…

Step 3: …You want to leave it as late as possible before making your run. That way, you catch your marker by surprise!

Step 4: Muscle your way through the defence. Don't let anything stop you.

Step 5: Aim for a corner. Top or bottom, left or right – just make your header impossible to save! GOAL!

Step 6: Run towards your fans, roaring like the lion you are.

TEST YOUR KNOWLEDGE

QUESTIONS

1. What was the name of Harry's first football club?

2. What was Harry's first position on the football pitch?

3. Who did Harry's Sheffield United face in the 2011 FA Youth Cup Final?

4. Harry played for the England Under-21s – true or false?

5. How old was Harry when he made his 100th start for Sheffield United?

6. Which other young star joined Hull City on the same day as Harry?

070780890778866669666

MATT AND TOM OLDFIELD

7. Which club did Harry join on loan in 2015?

8. Who did Harry replace in the Leicester City defence?

9. How many games did Harry miss during the 2017-18 Premier League season?

10. Who were England's opponents when Harry made his senior international debut?

11. Who gave Harry the nickname 'Slabhead'?

Answers below. . . No cheating!

1. *Brunsmeer Athletic* 2. *Centre Midfield* 3. *Manchester United* 4. *True - but he only played one match!* 5. *Only 19!* 6. *Andrew Robertson* 7. *Wigan Athletic* 8. *Robert Huth* 9. *Zero!* 10. *Lithuania* 11. *Jamie Vardy*

345

TRIPPIER

TABLE OF CONTENTS

ENGLAND'S FREE-KICK KING

Luzhniki Stadium, Moscow, 11 July 2018

With the sound of 78,000 football fans ringing in their ears, the England players walked out onto the pitch in Russia. Their captain and top scorer Harry Kane led the way, followed by their super saver Jordan Pickford, their big centre-back Harry Maguire, and then Kieran.

It was hard to believe what was happening. Three years earlier, Kieran had been relegated from the Premier League with Burnley. Six years earlier, he had left his childhood club Manchester City to challenge himself in the Championship. Now, at the age of twenty-seven, he was an England hero and he was about to play in a World Cup semi-final.

'Come on, Kieran!' voices shouted from the crowd.

The whole Trippier family was there supporting Kieran in Moscow: his dad Chris – England's biggest fan – his mum Eleanor, and his three brothers, Chris Jr, Curtis and Kelvin. Without them, Kieran could never have made his football dreams come true. And next to them stood his beautiful wife Charlotte and their amazing son, Jacob. Kieran was desperate to win the World Cup, for them and for the whole nation.

Gareth Southgate's inexperienced England team was making the country proud again. They had beaten Tunisia, Panama, Colombia and Sweden. Now, only Croatia stood between the Three Lions and the World Cup final. Whatever the result, it would go down as England's most successful tournament since the summer of 1990, before Kieran was even born! After years of disappointment, the fans finally had something to cheer about:

'It's coming home, it's coming home,
It's coming, FOOTBALL'S COMING HOME!'

As the English national anthem played in the stadium, Kieran sang along loudly with his teammates. Many of them felt like family to him. He set up goals for Harry Kane and Dele Alli week in, week out at Tottenham, and he had known Kyle Walker since the age of seventeen.

For most of those ten years, Kieran and Kyle had battled each other to be the best right-back around – in the England youth teams, and then at Spurs. At last, however, they were playing together in the same team – Kyle in the back three, and Kieran as the wing-back.

'Are you ready, Walks?'

'Yeah, let's do this, Tripps!'

Southgate's tactics were working brilliantly, especially for Kieran. This would only be his twelfth international cap but he was loving life with the Three Lions on his shirt. So far, he had been one of England's star performers. His incredible crosses had set up goals against Tunisia and Panama, and he had also scored from the spot in the penalty shoot-out against Colombia. What could Kieran do now in the semi-final against Croatia?

In the fifth minute, Dele dribbled towards goal but he was fouled by Luka Modrić. *Free kick!*

It was in a good position for shooting, but who would take it – Kieran or Ashley Young? They had both been practising and they both stood over the ball, waiting for the referee's whistle. So, who was feeling more confident about scoring?

'I've got it, Youngie!' Kieran decided. He was fearless and he had a good feeling about this one. He was in the best form of his career.

At Tottenham, it was Christian Eriksen who took the free kicks, but Kieran wasn't called 'The Bury Beckham' for nothing. This was his chance to show off his perfect technique on the world stage, just like he used to do at Manchester City, Barnsley and Burnley. All those years of practice had led to this one big moment. He was ready.

Kieran ran up and curled the ball over the wall and into the top corner. He made it look so easy. 1–0!

Goooooooooooaaaaaaaaaallllllllllllllllllllllll!!!!!!!!!!!!!

Kieran felt like his chest was about to burst with pride and joy. The World Cup semi-final – what a time to get his first-ever England goal! He slid across the grass on his knees, with his arms out wide as if to say, 'Look what I've just done'. Scoring for his country was simply the best feeling ever.

'Tripps, you legend!' Harry cried out as he jumped on his teammate.

'I'm still taking the next one!' Ashley laughed.

Soon, Kieran was at the bottom of a big team bundle. Thanks to him, England were winning. They were on their way to the World Cup final!

But after a mind-blowing few moments, he managed to calm himself down. There were still eighty-five minutes left, and England had plenty of work to do. Just like in their first game against Tunisia, they had chances to score a second goal but instead, they conceded one. In the second half, Croatia crossed from the right and Ivan Perišić beat Kyle to the ball. 1–1!

'Heads up, keep going!' Harry shouted out to his tired teammates.

Did the England players have any energy left for extra time? Kieran did his best to move forward and create more chances. He curled a corner-kick to John but his header was cleared off the goal line.

'So close!' Kieran groaned, putting his hands on his head.

He chased back to defend but by then, every single step hurt. They had played five tough games of football in only twenty-three days, and Kieran's body was telling him to stop. Soon, it was all over. Perišić flicked the ball on and Mario Mandžukić pounced. *2–1 to Croatia!*

As the ball hit the back of the net, Kieran's shoulders slumped. He couldn't carry on. Four minutes later, he hobbled off the pitch with the help of two physios. It was a sad way to end his wonderful first World Cup, but the England fans clapped and cheered for their exhausted and tearful hero.

'We love you, Tripps!'

After the final whistle, Kieran returned to the pitch to thank the fans for their support. As he stood there beside Southgate and his teammates, he felt the pain of losing but also an enormous amount of pride. Against the odds, they had achieved so much together.

No, England weren't bringing the World Cup trophy home, but they had brought football home. The excitement was back, and so was the passion. They had seen it in the crazy videos on social media, and they could feel it right there in the stadium.

'Bring on Euro 2020!' Kieran thought to himself.

Nevertheless Russia 2018 was a tournament that he would never ever forget. He had been fantastic, from start to finish. With his incredible crosses, he had created twenty-four goalscoring chances for his teammates. Twenty-four! That made him the most creative player in the whole entire tournament, ahead of Belgium's Kevin De Bruyne and Eden Hazard, and even ahead of Brazil's Neymar.

Not only that but Kieran was also now England's most famous free-kick king since his childhood hero, David Beckham. He had become only the third player to ever score for his country in a World Cup semi-final. The other two? Legends Sir Bobby Charlton and Gary Lineker.

'Not bad for a boy from Bury!' his brother Kelvin joked.

CHAPTER 2

A BACK GARDEN
IN BURY

In a back garden in Bury, two brothers were playing
football together. Or, to be more accurate, one
brother was dribbling with a football and his younger
brother was chasing after him, round and round
in circles. Despite all his brother's tricks and flicks,
the little boy kept going. He wanted the ball and he
wasn't giving up.

'Come on, Kelvin, no-one likes a show-off!' their
dad, Chris Trippier, called out from the back door.
'Stop teasing Kieran, and let him have a touch.'

'Fine, here you go,' Kelvin sighed, passing the ball
to his younger brother.

As it rolled towards him, Kieran's eyes lit up like

he had just discovered gold. Finally, the ball was his! Carefully, he controlled it and then kicked it back with the side of his right foot. Kelvin looked very surprised when it landed at his feet.

'Hey, that was pretty good! For a six-year-old, I mean.'

That was the highest praise that Kieran had ever heard from his brother. He tried to act cool but inside, he was beaming with pride.

Kelvin was four years older, and Kieran was desperate to copy everything he did, especially when it came to playing football. All those hours of following his brother's fancy footwork around the back garden had been worth it, and all of those hours of practising on his own too. He was now 'pretty good'!

This time, rather than trying another trick on his own, Kelvin passed the ball back to Kieran. He had passed the test. How exciting – now, the two brothers were really playing football together! After a few simple passes, Kelvin decided to make it more of a challenge.

'Nice, now let's try to do it faster!' he said, pinging

the ball across the grass at top speed.

Woah! At first, Kieran couldn't quite control his brother's powerful passes. The ball kept bouncing off his foot or flying straight past it. However, by keeping his eye on the ball, he soon got the hang of it.

'Nice, now let's try one touch!' Kelvin said.

Woah! At first, Kieran's passes went all over the place – high, low, left, right, anywhere except the spot where Kelvin was standing. It was a good thing that the back garden had a high fence. However, by keeping his eye on the ball, he soon got the hang of it.

'Nice, now let's try longer balls!' his brother added, moving further away.

Woah! This was a totally different challenge for Kieran. The side-foot was good for short, accurate passes but now he needed to really *boot* the ball. It was time to try kicking with the front of his foot instead.

Again, at first, Kieran's passes went all over the place – high, low, left, right, anywhere except the spot where Kelvin was standing. However, by keeping his eye on the ball, he soon got the hang of it.

'Nice!'

When their dad came outside to watch, the brothers were fizzing long, first-time passes across the back garden to each other. As a football coach himself, Chris was very impressed, especially with his youngest son. Where had he learned to strike the ball so cleanly?

'Wow, you're a natural, Kieran!' he said.

First his brother, and now his dad – everyone was praising his football skills today! Kieran was delighted. With every pass, he was getting better and better.

'The Neville brothers better watch out for you two!' their dad joked.

Gary and Phil Neville were the new star full-backs for Chris's favourite football club, Manchester United. Together with Ryan Giggs, David Beckham, Paul Scholes and Eric Cantona, they were taking the Premier League by storm. And best of all, the Neville brothers were from Bury too.

'No thanks,' Kieran replied, without taking his eyes off the ball. 'I want to be a winger like Becks!'

'Come and join in, Dad!' Kelvin suggested.

'Oh, go on then!'

When it came to football, Chris never needed much persuading. Kieran and Kelvin's two-person passing game was now a three-person passing game, and it soon became a five-person game when their brothers, Chris Jr and Curtis, arrived.

Kieran was having the best time ever but five footballers in one small back garden? It was a recipe for disaster!

'What on earth is going on?'

Eleanor had just got home from work, and she didn't know whether to laugh or cry. Why couldn't her family play football somewhere else? There was a park just down the road but instead, her husband and sons had turned the back garden into a bombsite. There were plant-pots and paint cans lying everywhere.

'Uh-oh!' Kieran thought to himself, looking down at the ground guiltily. They were in big trouble.

'Watch out!' Kelvin called out suddenly.

Eleanor ducked just in time. The football sailed over her head, bounced off the fence and landed right in the middle of her favourite flowers.

'Sorry, Mum!'

CHAPTER 3

CITY OVER UNITED

That back-garden ball game was just the start of the family football coaching. Soon, Kieran was the star of his dad's local youth team, Seedfield. Playing on the right wing, he set up goal after goal with his dangerous deliveries.

'Close that boy down!' opposition coaches shouted whenever he got the ball. 'Don't let him cross it!'

Kieran loved playing for Seedfield. Football was even more fun when he had teammates to play with, and opponents to play against. It also helped that Seedfield won almost every match.

However, it wasn't long before bigger clubs were watching him. At the age of eight, Kieran was scouted by Manchester United. Manchester United! When they offered him a trial, Chris was the proudest parent in the whole entire world.

'My boy's going to be the new David Beckham!' he boasted to all of his mates.

'No pressure, eh?' Eleanor said to her husband with a smile. 'At least wait until he actually signs a contract or something!'

Training at 'The Cliff' was both an exciting and nerve-wracking experience for Kieran. After all, he was following in some very famous footsteps.

'This is where Becks and Giggsy started out,' he kept thinking to himself as he raced around the pitch. 'And who knows, maybe Sir Alex Ferguson is watching me from his office window right now!'

United weren't, however, the only top club watching Kieran. Their local rivals, Manchester City, also scouted him and invited him for a trial.

'Don't you dare become a Blue!' his United-mad family teased. 'Why would you want to go there anyway? They're rubbish!'

While the Red Devils were flying high, winning

trophy after trophy, the Sky Blues had been relegated from the Premier League all the way down to League One. Despite that, Kieran was determined to give it a go. A couple of his friends already played for the City academy and they loved it there.

'Good luck!' Chris called out as he dropped Kieran off at Platt Lane. Yes, he loved United, but he loved his son even more! All he wanted was for him to be happy, even if that meant playing for the enemies.

'So, how did it go?' Chris asked when he picked him up.

After sessions at United, Kieran was usually pretty quiet on the drive home. He just sat there in the passenger seat, worrying about every little mistake – a poor pass, a missed tackle, a shot off target.

After that first session at City, however, he couldn't stop talking.

'It was so much fun! I was on the same team as Danny and Sam. Remember them?'

'Yes, I—'

'Anyway, so we're about to kick off and the other boys are walking around as if they've already won the game. No chance, we played them off the park. You should have seen their faces!'

'Did you sco—?'

'A couple, but mainly I was setting them up for Sam and our striker, Billy. By the end, the coach was calling me "Becks" because my crossing was so good!'

'Well done, son!' his dad replied. 'So, what happens n—'

'They want me to come back next week!' he cheered, nearly jumping out of his car seat.

If Kieran was happy, then his dad was happy. It was as simple as that. Chris would just have to get used to the idea of having a son who played for City.

At least, Platt Lane was nearer to Bury. Chris often spent long weeks working far from home in order to earn enough money to feed his four growing sons. If Eleanor was ever too busy to drive Kieran to City training, he could always take the bus.

Kieran quickly settled into his new home at City. He felt comfortable there, playing with his friends and working with the youth coaches. Jim Cassell and Steve Eyre loved working with Kieran too. He was a fast learner and a real talent. In all their years of experience, they had rarely seen a nine-year-old kid who could strike the ball so cleanly, accurately and powerfully.

'He's got great vision, even in an eight-a-side game,' they discussed. 'Imagine how good he'll be once he moves up to a full-size pitch!'

Even at the age of nine, Kieran had big plans for his football future.

First, he would become City's wing wizard, racing down the right at Maine Road with 30,000 fans chanting his name.

Then, he would become England's wing wizard, and help his country to win the World Cup! He had watched the 1998 tournament on TV with his dad, and it had made a big impression on him.

Chris was England's biggest fan and so every match of the tournament was an emotional rollercoaster with lots of highs and lows.

'No!' he groaned as Dan Petrescu scored a last-minute winner to make it Romania 2 England 1. He banged his fists against the arms of the sofa.

'Are you okay, Dad?' Kieran asked. He looked like he was in real pain.

'You'll get used to this, son,' he muttered grumpily. 'Our national team always let us down.'

But four days later, his mood had changed.

'Yes!' Chris cried out as David Beckham scored a fantastic free kick to make it England 2 Colombia 0. 'We could go on and win this tournament!'

Kieran watched that free kick over and over again, as many times as he could. He couldn't help it; it was one of the best goals that he'd ever seen. The power, the curl, the dip, and then the celebration! Beckham raced over to the fans, pumping his fists and roaring.

'What a hero!' Kieran thought to himself.

England's second-round match against Argentina had even more ups and downs. There was no chance of his dad sitting still through all the drama. His right leg kept kicking the air as if he was out there playing on the pitch.

'Come on, England!'

Gabriel Batistuta scored a penalty, but then so did Alan Shearer. 1–1!

'Yes!' Chris cried out as Michael Owen scored a wondergoal. 2–1!

'No!' he groaned as Javier Zanetti equalised just before half-time. 2–2!

'NO!' father and son shouted at the screen together as the referee sent Beckham off for kicking out at Diego Simeone.

When the match went to penalties, Kieran could hardly bear to watch.

'We've got no chance here, son,' Chris declared miserably.

His dad was right. First Paul Ince missed and then David Batty. England were knocked out.

For a few minutes, both father and son sat there on the sofa in silence. Then Chris got up and switched off the TV.

'What did I tell you?' he said as he left the room. 'They always let us down in the end.'

'No, not always!' Kieran thought to himself. One day, he was going to prove his dad wrong. He would be Beckham without the red card, and lead England to World Cup glory.

CHAPTER 4

THE HOLCOMBE BROOK HERO

When Kieran wasn't starring for the Manchester City academy, he was starring for his primary school team instead. His life was already football, football, football – all day every day! There was some important education in between, of course. His parents made sure of that.

'If we hear that you've been misbehaving in class,' Eleanor warned him, 'there'll be no football for you, okay?'

'Okay, Mum. I'll be good, I promise!' Kieran replied with a panicked look on his face. The fear of no football was more than enough to keep him out of trouble.

Kieran loved playing with his school friends. It was like being back at Seedfield, with lots of laughs at training, and at the back of the team bus on away trips. They always wanted to win, but it wasn't as serious as it was at the City academy.

Still, with Kieran flying down the wing, Holcombe Brook flew all the way to the Bury Schools' Cup Final. There were other good players in the team, but Kieran was head and shoulders above the rest. He might be joking around with his mates in the warm-up but once the whistle blew, his smile disappeared. It was game-time, and Kieran had to win, no matter what.

Losing just wasn't an option. If he didn't score the goal, he almost always set it up with one of his incredible free kicks or crosses. Could he now lead his school to one last, important victory?

'Best of luck today, Kieran!' the headmaster called out to him as he jogged onto the field to warm up. 'How are you feeling?'

'I'm feeling good thanks, Mr Howarth!' he replied, sounding as calm as ever.

For some of the Holcombe Brook players, the final would be the biggest game of their lives. That was a lot of pressure for ten-year-olds to deal with.

For Kieran, however, it was just the latest in a long line of big games. After all, he had been on trial with Manchester United at The Cliff, playing on the same pitch as Becks and Giggsy, and now he played for Manchester City. So, the Bury Schools' Cup Final? No, there was no reason to feel nervous about that. Kieran was just going to go out there, enjoy himself, and win.

'Come on, boys!' he cheered confidently before kick-off. 'We can do this!'

The Holcombe Brook players pulled up their socks and got stuck in. If Kieran said they could win it, then they could win it. He was their leader, as well as their superstar.

'Go on, son!' Kieran's parents shouted out on the sidelines. Kelvin was there too, to cheer his younger brother on towards the trophy.

Every time Kieran got the ball, the crowd held their breath. Holcombe Brook hoped for a goal, and their opponents feared the worst. Kieran was dominating the game in midfield, using his right foot like a dangerous weapon. What would he do next – a killer cross, a deadly dribble, a perfect pass, a stunning strike? He was capable of anything.

'Keep going, Kieran!' his coach encouraged him.

It was a very exciting final, full of fast, end-to-end football. There could only be one winner, though, and who would it be? What Holcombe Brook needed was a calm head, someone who could produce a real moment of magic...

Kieran got the ball in his own half and dribbled forward. As he looked up for a teammate to pass to, he spotted that the opposition goalkeeper was off his line. Should he? Why not?! It was definitely worth a try. If Becks could do it for Manchester United against Wimbledon, then why couldn't he score from the halfway line too? If it worked, Kieran would go down in Bury Schools' history...

In a flash, he pulled back his right foot and aimed for goal. BANG! As the ball sailed through the air, everyone held their breath and watched. Surely not?!

The keeper turned and sprinted back towards his goal but he was too late to stop it from landing in the back of the net.

Gooooooooooooooooooooaaaaaaaaaaaaaaaaalllllllllllll llllllllllllllll!!!!!!!!!!!!!!!!!!!!!

What a strike, what a feeling! Kieran was the Holcombe Brook hero yet again. With the pressure on, he had scored an absolute worldie! He ran around punching the air, until his teammates piled on top of him.

'Yes, mate!'

'You legend!'

'We're the Champions!'

On the sidelines, his family swapped big hugs and big grins. They were so proud of their little match-winner.

'Well done, Kieran!' they cried out.

After the trophy presentation, his teammates lifted their hero up into the air and carried him around the pitch. With a winners' medal around his neck and the Bury Schools' Cup in his hands, Kieran felt on top of the world.

If only he could score the winning goal in cup finals every day! He could never get bored of the buzz. Oh well, there would just have to be many more triumphs ahead; Kieran would make sure of that.

Eventually, the celebrations had to end, and everyone walked back to their cars to drive home. They might not have said it out loud but they were all thinking the same thing – his teammates, his opponents, his family, the Holcombe Brook headmaster:

'That boy has a very bright football future ahead of him!'

CHAPTER 5

SET PIECES AT CITY

At Manchester City, youth coaches Jim Cassell and Steve Eyre were thinking exactly the same thing. Kieran was well on his way to becoming a top professional footballer. He ticked all the right boxes:

✓ **He had a fantastic family around him.**

Chris and Eleanor were there cheering Kieran on at every academy match, and so were his grandparents. The City coaches knew just how important that love and support was for a promising young player. There would be plenty of times ahead when Kieran would need a hug, or some words of advice. Plus, his grandma was always there to keep his feet on the ground.

'What's wrong with you, lad? Get stuck in!' she often shouted on the sidelines. If Kieran had a bad game, she was never shy to tell him so.

✓ **He had terrific talent.**

Kieran's touch and technique were excellent, week in, week out. It was rare to see such a consistent young player. He wasn't a typical tricky winger, amazing one minute, and awful the next. Instead, he worked hard for his team and kept things simple.

'That's it – one touch to control it, then look up and CROSS!'

Kieran's remarkable right foot was deadlier than ever now that he was playing on bigger pitches. Defenders just couldn't deal with his lovely long balls and crosses. He could find the danger zone every time.

✓ **He had amazing ambition.**

Kieran wasn't content with just becoming a professional footballer. Of course, that would be a great achievement, but he was aiming a lot higher than that. He wanted to be a superstar for Manchester City *and* England!

By 2002, City were back in the Premier League, and their manager Kevin Keegan was giving lots of his young players a chance to shine. Shaun Wright-Phillips, Joey Barton, Stephen Jordan... the list went on and on.

'That will be me soon!' Kieran declared. He would do whatever it took to make his dream come true.

✓ **He was a confident character.**

Yes, Kieran liked to practise the same pass again and again until it was perfect, but he certainly wasn't a right-foot robot! He was competitive and mischievous, and that's what Jim and Steve liked most about him.

'Confidence,' the City youth coach called it. 'You don't get anywhere in this sport without it!'

Jim lived near the Trippiers and he knew their neighbourhood well. It wasn't an easy place to grow up and, without the right guidance, good kids could lose their way and get into trouble. The City youth coach was determined to make sure that didn't happen to Kieran.

'If you live right, you'll make it!' Jim kept telling him.

He often dropped Kieran home at the end of training, but only after he had completed his favourite football challenge.

'Right, first to twenty?' Steve said, grabbing a big bag of balls.

'You don't give up, do you, Coach?' Kieran replied cheekily. 'Fine, if you're ready to get beaten again…'

Steve was left-footed and Kieran was right-footed, so they took it in turns to shoot from either side of the D. The challenge was simple – the first person to score twenty free kicks was the winner. They could usually find a young goalkeeper who was up for some extra shot-stopping.

'Go!'

Kieran took five steps backwards in a diagonal line away from the ball. When he was even younger, he used to copy Beckham's run-up and arm-swing, but now he preferred to do things his own way. He ran forward confidently and kicked the ball with plenty of power, lift and curl.

There wasn't a group of big, brave defenders in front of Kieran but he always pretended that there was. That was the first part of scoring a free kick. Somehow, he had to get the ball past the wall, whether it went over them, around them, or even under them if they jumped!

The second part was getting the ball past the keeper. To do that, Kieran needed power, but above all, he needed accuracy. Most shots near the middle of the goal would be easy to save. Instead, he had to find one of the four corners: top left, bottom left, top right or bottom right.

Becoming a free-kick king took lots of talent and practice. Kieran had the talent and he was always willing to put in the practice.

'Yes!' he cried out, throwing his arms up in the air. 'Sorry, Coach, can I just check the score – am I really winning this *8–1*? This is getting embarrassing for you!'

Steve sent another free kick flying high over the crossbar. 'Hmmm, it's not my day today.'

'It never is, Coach!'

Occasionally, however, Kieran's confident character got him into a bit of trouble.

One day, the groundsman at Platt Lane came storming into Steve's office. He wasn't happy at all.

'It keeps happening and I won't stand for it!' he muttered angrily. 'Whoever it is, needs to stop RIGHT NOW!'

The City youth coach had no idea what the groundsman was talking about. 'Sorry, what keeps happening?'

'When I'm out there on the lawnmower, one of those pesky kids keeps kicking footballs at my head! But by the time I turn around, he's disappeared. He thinks he's clever but when I catch him—'

'Ok, I'm really sorry about that,' Steve said, trying to calm the groundsman down. 'I'm going to find out who's doing it and when I do, they'll be punished, I promise!'

The City youth coach knew exactly who the troublemaker was, but he didn't have the heart to punish him properly. A warning would be enough.

'If you don't find a new way to practise your long passing,' Steve told Kieran with a smile on his face, 'then I'll have to tell that groundsman where you live!'

CHAPTER 6

HERO AT HOME

Kieran wasn't the only successful footballer in his family. He was following in his brother's footsteps once more. Kelvin was working his way up through the ranks at Oldham Athletic. 'The Latics' played in League One and, at the age of seventeen, he was already training with the first team.

'It's so cool – you're going to make your senior debut soon!' Kieran said excitedly.

Years after those first back-garden games, he was still Kelvin's biggest fan. He looked up to his brother for advice about everything. It was pretty cool to have his hero right there at home with him!

When he was bored, Kieran would knock on his

brother's bedroom door with a ball in his hands.

'Fancy a kickabout outside?'

'Oh, go on then!' Kelvin usually said. When it came to football, he never needed much persuading.

Kieran always looked forward to playing with his brother because he gave him lots of great tips. They could talk about the best free kick technique for hours! It was part of Kieran's football education. He wanted to know everything about everything.

'Can I come and watch you train today?' Kieran asked.

'*Again*?' his brother rolled his eyes. 'Ok, but don't embarrass me in front of my new teammates!'

Kieran loved to watch the Oldham sessions. Whenever Kelvin let him, he was there on the sidelines, taking it all in. Kieran went to all of his brother's matches too, but he preferred the practices. For a football-mad thirteen-year-old, it was like a sneak peek into his future. This was what being a professional player was really like.

There were lots of jokes! 'A happy team is a successful team,' Jim often told them at the City academy and that seemed to be true at Oldham. The players loved to mess around, especially when the manager wasn't looking. Sometimes, they tried silly skills, sometimes they took stupid shots, and sometimes, they just kicked balls at each other.

'That's the sort of thing we do at school!' Kieran thought to himself. He couldn't wait to be part of the City first team, training together every day.

There were lots of drills! Kieran loved finding ways to improve. He kept a close eye on each training exercise – running, passing, crossing, shooting, one vs one, three vs three, piggy in the middle. If Kelvin hadn't forced him to leave his kit at home, Kieran would have jumped over the fence and joined in!

There were lots of tactics! That was one of the biggest changes from junior to senior level. Suddenly, it was all so organised. There was a plan for absolutely everything, from defending corners on the left, to attacking free kicks on the right.

'How do you remember all of the manager's instructions?' Kieran asked Kelvin on the way home.

His brother shrugged. 'Practice,' was all he said.

It certainly seemed to be working. Kelvin was getting closer and closer to his Oldham debut. After one game on the bench, he played the last thirty-five minutes away at Brentford in October 2004.

'Congratulations!' Kieran was cheering before Kelvin even got through the front door. 'What did it feel like when you came on?'

His brother shrugged like it was just another football match. 'Good,' was all he said.

Over the next few weeks, Kelvin became a regular in the Oldham defence. He was a speedy right-back, who could also play on the left.

'Just like Phil Neville!' their dad liked to say. Even though his youngest son played for City, Chris was still a massive Manchester United fan.

Kieran never missed a chance to cheer on Kelvin at Oldham's home ground, Boundary Park. He was so proud of his brilliant brother, the professional footballer. He was now playing in a proper stadium in front of thousands of cheering fans. If Kelvin could do it, then so could Kieran! His brother's success made him more determined than ever.

CHAPTER 7

THE WOODHEY HIGH HERO

Kieran's sporting success didn't stop once he got to secondary school. No, it just kept growing and growing! That was largely thanks to Mr Garcka, his cool new PE teacher at Woodhey High.

'I know you love football, but we play lots of different sports here,' he explained when Kieran arrived in Year 7. 'Would you be interested in trying something new?'

More competitions, and more chances of winning? Yes please! Kieran loved that idea. He was willing to give anything a go.

'You're really fast. What about running?' Mr Garcka suggested.

So, Kieran joined the school cross-country team. To this day, over ten years later, he still holds the Woodhey High record for the fastest 400 metres!

'You've got a lovely right foot, but what about a sport where you use your hands instead?' Mr Garcka suggested.

So, Kieran joined the school basketball team! Just like in football, he dribbled forward and set up lots of chances to score.

'You're a great team player, but what about a one vs one sport instead?' Mr Garcka suggested.

So, Kieran joined the school table tennis team! Just like in football, he had to make sure that every single shot was accurate and aimed at the corners.

Between Manchester City and all his new extra activities, Kieran hardly had a spare minute to relax. That was probably for the best, though, his parents, teachers and coaches all agreed. As long as he was busy, he was keeping out of trouble.

'If you live right, you will make it' – that's what Jim always told him.

Kieran enjoyed learning lots of new skills from

all his new sports, but nothing would ever compare to football. It would always be his favourite, no matter what.

'Don't worry, I won't be swapping footie for ping-pong anytime soon!' he joked with Jim.

Kieran was still progressing well at the City academy but Mr Garcka wanted to make sure that his student had a Plan B, just in case things didn't work out. So many fifteen-year-old footballers were released by their clubs, with broken hearts and no career plans. The PE teacher really didn't want Kieran to be one of them.

'If you couldn't be a football player, what would you want to be?' Mr Garcka asked.

Kieran shrugged. He was so sure that he would achieve his dream that he hadn't really thought about it.

'What about being a football coach?'

Like Jim and Steve? Sure, that would be fun! Kieran was always looking to improve himself, so maybe he would be good at helping others to improve too.

'Brilliant, I'll sign you up!' Mr Garcka told him as he walked away.

'Wait a minute, sir. Sign me up for what?'

Mr Garcka had signed Kieran up for his first coaching qualification. The teacher divided a big group of ten-year-olds into teams to compete in a mini-World Cup. Each team would be managed by one of Woodhey High's bright young coaches.

'Yes, we're England!' Kieran cheered patriotically. 'We're definitely going to win the World Cup now.'

He didn't have much time to work with his new team. 'What would Jim and Steve do?' he kept thinking. After a few passing and shooting drills, Kieran gave each player a position that he thought would suit their skills best. His main message, however, was aimed at the whole team – work together and you'll win.

'Good luck!' he shouted as they took to the pitch for their first match. 'Enjoy it!'

By working together, Kieran's team battled all the way to the final, and then all the way to a dreaded penalty shoot-out.

'Now, I really wish we weren't England!' Kieran muttered to himself.

He thought about the defeat to Argentina at the 1998 World Cup, but also the more recent defeat to Portugal at Euro 2004. What was it that his dad had said? 'England always let you down in the end.' No, Kieran was determined to be the manager who ended nearly forty years of hurt.

'Just take your time and try your best,' he encouraged each of his worried young players before they stepped up. He knew what he was talking about. He was his school's penalty taker and he hadn't missed a single one. 'Remember, you've done so well to get this far!'

With their young manager's support, England did it – they lifted the World Cup trophy! Kieran was delighted, and so was his PE teacher.

'You did an excellent job with those kids,' Mr Garcka congratulated him. 'You'll make a great football coach one day!'

For now, though, Kieran was fully focused on being a great football player. The City academy had asked him not to play for his school but he couldn't help himself. Woodhey High needed him! Whenever he could, he raced back from training just in time to catch the school team bus.

Mr Garcka was always relieved to see Kieran. 'Phew, I didn't think you were going to make it today!'

'No chance, I wouldn't miss it for the world, Sir!'

In his final year, Kieran helped Woodhey High to reach the Bury Schools' Cup Final, just like he had with Holcombe Brook Primary. Could he win the double? Yes, and not only that, but he also scored a stunning hat-trick in the final!

From his own half, he dribbled past one defender, then another, then another, then another, before beating the keeper.

Goooooooooooooooooooooaaaaaaaaaaaaaaaaaallllllllllllll llllllllllllllll!!!!!!!!!!!!!!!!!!!!

As a clearance came out to him, he struck the ball sweetly on the volley, straight into the top corner.

Goooooooooooooooooooooaaaaaaaaaaaaaaaaaallllllllllllll llllllllllllllll!!!!!!!!!!!!!!!!!!!!

From the edge of the box, he curled a shot into the back of the net.

Gooooooooooooooooooooaaaaaaaaaaaaaaaaalllllllllllll llllllllllllllll!!!!!!!!!!!!!!!!!!!!!

Kieran punched the air and hugged his teammates. What a way to become the Woodhey High hero! He had yet another winners' medal to add to his collection. Kieran was really living up to his name as 'The Bury Beckham'.

CHAPTER 8

RIGHT WING TO RIGHT-BACK

By the age of 16, Kieran was spending more and more hours on the training field at Platt Lane. The closer he got to the Manchester City first team, the more he needed to up his game. There were so many talented young players at the club, all competing for a small number of professional contracts.

'Don't worry, you're on the right track,' Jim and Steve reassured Kieran.

Michael Johnson and Daniel Sturridge were the latest young stars to come out of the academy. They had just led City all the way to the final of the 2006 FA Youth Cup. Michael was a box-to-box midfielder who loved to pass, while Daniel was a skilful striker who loved to shoot.

What did Kieran have that would help him stand out from the crowd? He was good at taking free kicks but would that be enough?

'No, I need more than just that,' he told his family. 'Even Becks doesn't get in the England team just because of that. I need a special talent that I can use all the time.'

Aha, got it! Kieran would be a hard-working winger who loved to cross. His right foot was already really good and with practice, practice, practice, he would make it even better.

After most training sessions, Kieran would go back out with Steve and a big bag of balls. They still played first-to-twenty free kicks from time to time, but usually, Kieran now preferred practising cross after cross. There were so many different match situations to prepare for.

Steve was always setting him new challenges. It was like being in the back garden in Bury with Kelvin all over again.

'Cross it early! Hit it first time on the run and aim for the six-yard box.'

'This time, take a touch and then curl the ball high to the back post.'

'Next, dribble forward a few yards before fizzing it into the front post area.'

Sometimes, Steve wouldn't say anything at all. He would just make a late run into the box and call for the cross. 'Now!'

Every time he pulled his right foot back to kick the ball, Kieran had so many different things to think about – the timing of the cross, the height, the power, the angle, the curve. It sounded so complicated but Steve was right; it was actually pretty simple:

'If you keep delivering the ball into the danger zone, then eventually, someone's got to score!'

Thanks to all his extra hard work, Kieran's crossing became more and more consistent from every possible angle. Jim and Steve both still believed in 'The Bury Beckham' 100 per cent but they were having second thoughts about what his best position might be.

Was Kieran really a right winger, after all? He didn't have fancy footwork like Aaron Lennon, or Manchester United's new star, Cristiano Ronaldo. Plus, not all teams played with wingers anymore. The classic 4–4–2 was being replaced by new football formations. There was the 3–5–2, the 4–3–3, the 4–2–3–1...

Where else could Kieran play on the pitch? What if they turned him into a right-back instead? Gary Neville played there for Manchester United and he was a great crosser too. From further back, Kieran would have even more time and space to put brilliant balls into the box.

Plus, being a full-back wasn't such a boring job anymore. It was now a fun position, with lots more freedom to get involved in the game. Ashley Cole at Chelsea, for example, used his speed to attack all the time! Kieran could make those overlapping runs too.

'It's worth a go,' Jim and Steve decided after lots of discussion.

Kieran was more than happy to try a different position. If it got him into the City first team, he would try absolutely anything!

'I might be a bit small to be a goalkeeper, though!'
he joked.

Kieran knew exactly who to talk to about
becoming a right-back – his hero at home! Kelvin
couldn't help laughing when he first heard the news.

'You don't have to copy me in every single way,
you know!'

'As if! Don't flatter yourself.'

The brothers began practising in the back garden,
until their mum asked them to play in the park
instead.

Kieran had lots to learn about defending. Marking,
tackling, blocking, heading – they were all things
that he used to do as a winger, but now they were
much more important. He was going to need plenty
of help from his teammates and coaches.

'That's your man, Tripps!' Kieran's friend, Ben
Mee, called out from centre-back. 'Track him!'

'Get tighter!' Steve screamed from the sidelines.
'Stop the cross!'

It was a steep learning curve for Kieran but minute

by minute and mistake by mistake, he was becoming less of a right winger and more of a right-back.

Jim and Steve were delighted with their decision. 'At this rate, it looks like we've found City's Number 2 for the next fifteen years!'

CHAPTER 9

HEROES AT UNITED

Growing up in the Greater Manchester area, Kieran couldn't help supporting Sir Alex Ferguson's United team, especially having a dad like Chris.

'United!' he cheered when they first won the Premier League in 1993,

'United!' he cheered when they won the double in 1996,

'United!' he cheered when they won the treble in 1999,

And 'United!' he was still cheering when they won their tenth Premier League title in 2008.

By then, Kieran's first Manchester United hero had left the club. David Beckham was every boy's idol, with his football skills and boy-band good looks. But for a young right winger like Kieran, he was extra special.

He copied the way Becks struck his fantastic free kicks.

He copied the way Becks curled in his incredible crosses.

He copied the way Becks looked up and picked out a perfect long pass.

Kieran copied Becks' shaved head and he had even copied Becks' Wimbledon wonder-strike when he scored from the halfway line for Holcombe Brook Primary in the Bury Schools' Cup final.

When people gave him the nickname 'The Bury Beckham', it was the proudest moment of his life!

But when Kieran changed his position, he changed his hero too. He was a right-back now and luckily, Manchester United also had a brilliant right-back. Best of all, he was even born in Bury!

'What did I say all those years ago?' Kieran's dad laughed. 'I told you that you and Kelvin would be the new Neville brothers!'

Gary Neville didn't have as much style as his best friend Becks, but he made up for that with his passion and dedication. No-one fought harder than Neville for United. He was always organising his teammates and urging them on until the final whistle.

'Why do you like him?' Kieran's friends always asked. 'He's so boring and all he does is shout!'

'That's not true – you don't win eight Premier League titles and two Champions Leagues for being good at shouting!'

Or all those England caps either. Gary Neville had played for his country eighty-five times, at two World Cups and three European Championships. That was Kieran's biggest dream of all – to play for England at major tournaments. So alongside his brother Kelvin, Neville was a pretty awesome hero to have.

Kieran watched him carefully whenever United were on TV. If he wanted to become City's next right-back, Kieran needed to improve his defending, and Neville was one of the best defenders around. He wasn't the quickest or the strongest, but he was one of the smartest. He never lost his concentration, and he was always in the right place at the right time. Neville battled bravely for every header, block and tackle.

'You'd really hate to play against him, wouldn't you?' his dad said with a smile.

'Yes,' Kieran agreed enthusiastically. 'I hope people say that about me too one day!'

He had a long list of things that he admired about Neville, but the top three were:

1. **His leadership!**
   Neville did spend a lot of time shouting, but that was only because he wanted to win so much. And it worked because he inspired his United teammates to keep winning trophy after trophy. Kieran tried to show that same passion when he was out there on the pitch for City.

2. **His decision-making!**
   Neville always seemed to know when to defend and when to attack. But how did he

know? That was something that Kieran was still working hard on with his coaches at City.

3. **His energy!**

Neville never stopped running up and down the pitch, all game long. When he got the chance to go forward, he kept things simple, just like Kieran did. He looked up to see who was in the box and then delivered a dangerous cross.

'He can't bend it like Beckham but he puts the ball in the right area every time!' Kieran argued.

And how did Neville become so good at crossing? With practice, practice, practice. By spending even longer on the training ground, Kieran hoped to one day reach that highest level. He was determined.

Meanwhile, Jim and Steve were working on new nicknames for him:

'The New Neville?'

'The City Cafu?'

'No, nothing beats The Bury Beckham!'

CHAPTER 10

YOUTH CUP WINNER

Manchester City hadn't won the FA Youth Cup
since 1986, before Kieran was even born! By
the time he joined the club's Under-18s, it was
twenty-two years later, but after signing his first
professional contract, he was feeling even more
confident than usual.

'Come on lads, this is going to be our year!'

'Yeah!' his teammates roared.

City had a very strong side: Kieran, Ben and
Dedryck Boyata at the back, with Vladimír Weiss
on the wing, and Daniel up front. Daniel was now
playing for the first team too but he had unfinished
business in the FA Youth Cup. He had suffered a

painful defeat to Liverpool in the final two years earlier.

'Not this time!' Daniel vowed.

City powered their way past Millwall, Reading, Bristol City and Plymouth Argyle. Kieran raced down the right, curling in incredible cross after incredible cross. The team scored lots of goals, and they didn't concede many either.

'Great work, lads!' Jim clapped and cheered on the sidelines.

The coach was delighted with his young players. They were doing the club proud. With a 2–1 win over Jordan Henderson's Sunderland, City were into the FA Youth Cup final again.

Their last opponents would be the toughest of all – Chelsea! Their owner, Roman Abramovich, was a billionaire and he had invested lots of money in the club's academy. Not only had Chelsea built the best training facilities in England, but they had also spent millions on buying the best young players from all over the world. How were City's local boys supposed to compete with that?

'You've got nothing to fear!' Jim told his players before kick-off at Stamford Bridge. 'You've all worked so hard to get here. Now, you're only two games away from winning the cup. Go out there and get the job done!'

Jim had full faith in his players. His academy was developing one first-team star after another: Shaun Wright-Phillips, Joey Barton, Micah Richards, Daniel... the list went on and on. Jim was constantly telling the manager, Sven-Göran Eriksson, about his next top talents.

City's Number 2 was one of them, and he certainly wasn't worried about playing in a Premier League stadium in front of thousands of fans. No, Kieran was absolutely buzzing ahead of his big day! He wanted to compete at the highest level possible, and that's exactly what he was doing.

From the Bury Schools' Cup final, Kieran had fought his way to the FA Youth Cup final. He had been the Holcombe Brook hero and then the Woodhey High hero. Could he now become the Manchester City hero too?

Kieran calmly dribbled past Gaël Kakuta, the Chelsea winger, and played a brilliant ball down the line to Daniel. He cut inside and tested the goalkeeper with a swerving strike.

'Good stuff, lads!' Jim shouted. 'More of that!'

Kieran, however, had defending to do. Kakuta attacked at speed, weaving one way and then the other. The winger's feet danced but Kieran didn't dive in. He watched and waited until... SLIDE TACKLE!

'Well done, Tripps!' Ben cheered and the City fans roared.

Kieran smiled proudly. All his hard work with Steve was really paying off. He was earning that 'New Neville' nickname. He ran up and down the right, all game long, helping his team out at both ends of the pitch.

In the end, the first leg finished in a 1–1 draw. That result left City in a great position to win the FA Youth Cup in the second leg back home at the Etihad. They would have to do it without their goalscorer, Daniel, however. He was now City's starting striker in the Premier League.

'Good luck – bring it home, boys!' he told his
teammates.

Despite letting in an early own goal, City did
just that. They showed their strong team spirit by
bouncing back brilliantly. First, Ben scored a header
and then City won a free kick within shooting range.
Kieran was desperate to take it, but so was Vladimír.

'Fine, you can have this one,' Kieran muttered
moodily, 'but you better score it!'

No problem! Vladimír stepped up and curled the
ball around the wall and into the top corner. *GOAL!*

'I'm still taking the next one!' Kieran teased as
they celebrated together in front of the fans.

With five minutes to go, David Ball scored a
penalty to seal the victory. City were the 2008 FA
Youth Cup winners!

Chelsea grew more and more frustrated as the
clock ticked down, and in the last minute, one of
their players flew in with a nasty, reckless tackle
on Kieran.

'Argghhhh!' he screamed out in agony.

Kieran had been excited about the after-match party, but sadly, he wouldn't be there to enjoy it; he had to leave the pitch on a stretcher and miss out on all the fun. He missed out on the confetti, the cheering, the dancing, and most importantly of all, the lifting of the trophy.

But he refused to let that bad luck bring him down. At the age of seventeen, he had just played an important role in City's biggest achievement for years. With the winners' medal around his neck, it felt like the future was his to reach out and grab with both hands.

Next step: the first team. Kieran was now ready to become City's new right-back.

When Jim next saw Eriksson walking down the corridor, he called out confidently, 'Don't worry, we've got lots more academy lads coming your way soon!'

CHAPTER 11

A WORLD CUP TO FORGET

City's young right-back was soon England's young right-back too. And after only one cap for the Under-18s, Kieran moved straight up to the next level. He was flying!

The England Under-19s coach Brian Eastick was looking to strengthen his squad for the 2009 European Championship qualifying round, and City was always a good place to look. Daniel and Ben were now playing for the Under-20s but Kieran was a year younger than them. Plus, Eastick needed a new right-back.

'Congratulations!' Kieran's family cheered when he shared his exciting news. 'First the FA Youth Cup, and now this – there's no stopping you. You'll be in the England senior squad in no time!'

For now, though, Kieran was off to Northern Ireland, where the Under-19s had three games in five days. It was a good thing that he was used to playing lots of football! He started the first two games, and England won both of them. Then when Eastick rested him against Serbia, the team got hammered 4–1.

'They're lost without you!' Kieran's family argued.

Despite that defeat, England were through to the 2009 European Championships in the Ukraine. Kieran couldn't wait to play in his first international tournament. It was going to be a challenge and an adventure. His City teammate Andrew Tutte was going with him, and so were Danny Welbeck and Danny Drinkwater from United.

'Manchester's finest!' they joked together. Although they were rivals for their clubs, they were teammates for their country.

England arrived at the tournament with high expectations, so two draws in the first two games was a very disappointing start. In the first match against Switzerland, they were on the verge of a 1–0 victory but they conceded a late equaliser. The second match against Ukraine finished 2–2.

'Come on, we have to win this last group game!' Eastick urged his players.

Unfortunately, Kieran had watched the first two games from the bench. The England manager had picked a speedy kid from Sheffield instead, called Kyle Walker. Against Slovenia, however, Eastick decided to take a risk. He moved Kyle to centre-back and brought Kieran in at right-back.

'No more of those rapid forward runs, okay, Walks?' Kieran teased. 'That's my job now!'

Although they were competing with each other, they got on really well. With Kieran and Kyle playing together, England ran riot.

In the tenth minute against Slovenia, Kieran won the ball on the right and dribbled forward. He passed to Nathan Delfouneso, who passed to Danny Welbeck, who flicked it back for Henri Lansbury to shoot. 1–0!

'It's great to have you back, Tripps!' Danny cheered as they celebrated a great team goal.

It was great to be back and that was only the beginning. They ended up thrashing Slovenia 7–1. After that, Eastick had no choice but to keep Kieran in the team!

England were through to the semi-finals, where they faced their old rivals France. After an awful start, they fought back bravely to win 3–1 in extra-time.

'We're in the final!' Kieran screamed, hugging their man of the match, Nathan.

Was Kieran about to add an Under-19 European Championship winner's medal to his collection? He hoped so.

England were feeling confident, even though they had to play the tournament hosts again. This time, with 25,000 locals cheering them on, Ukraine took an early lead from a corner-kick. Kieran was protecting the back post but the shot flew past the keeper at the front post. There was nothing Kieran could do except pick the ball out of the net and boot it downfield.

'Come on, heads up!' he shouted, doing his best Gary Neville impression. 'We're good enough to beat this lot!'

Kieran couldn't do anything about Dmytro Korkishko's fantastic free kick in the second half either. It was game, and tournament, over for England.

'We should have won that!' Kieran kept thinking, long after the final whistle had blown. They had let the pressure get to them.

'Unlucky lads,' Eastick told his devastated players. 'You've done so well to get this far and don't forget – we've got the Under-20 World Cup coming up in a few months!'

A World Cup! Kieran couldn't wait. He was in the squad that travelled to Egypt in September, but there was no Kyle, no Nathan, no Henri, and there were no Dannys either. Instead, Kieran found himself surrounded by his City youth teammates. Ben was back, Andrew was there, and several others had been called up too.

'It's like a club tour!' they joked.

The laughs didn't last very long, though, once the

tournament kicked off. For Kieran, it turned out to be a first World Cup to forget.

England held on for eighty-four minutes in their first match against Uruguay, until Tabaré Viúdez scored a stunning scissor-kick winner.

'How did we let that happen?' Kieran cried out, but his fellow defenders just slumped their shoulders and stared down at the grass.

Things got even worse in their next match against Ghana. Four of England's key players were too ill to play, but the others did their best to carry on. Kieran curled a lovely free kick into the box and Ben flicked it goal-wards... SMACK! The ball hit the crossbar.

'So close!' they both groaned with their hands on their heads.

After that, however, Ghana stormed forward in attack and England had no way of stopping them.

1–0, 2–0, 3–0, 4–0!

Kieran couldn't believe it. He trudged off the pitch in total despair. It was an absolute disaster! After all his hopes and expectations, his first World Cup was over already.

'Come on, we have to win this last group game!' Eastick urged his players. One victory would at least cheer them up a bit before the long journey home.

That team-talk had worked brilliantly at the Under-19 Euros, but not this time – the best that England could do was draw against Uzbekistan, and they nearly lost again. Not only were they heading home, but they also finished bottom of the group.

'What a nightmare!' Kieran thought to himself. He couldn't wait to get back to Manchester City and move on with his career. Then hopefully, one day, he would get the chance to have a World Cup to remember with England.

CHAPTER 12

STOP-START AT CITY

Back in 2008 when Kieran and his teammates
won the FA Youth Cup, Manchester City were the
underdogs and Chelsea were the rich boys. That was
all about to change, however.

Months later, City had a billionaire owner too, and
Sheikh Mansour was even richer than Abramovich.
He wanted to win the Premier League title as soon as
possible, no matter how much money that cost.

'Uh-oh, we're in trouble,' Kieran told Ben
gloomily.

It was potentially very bad news for the club's
young players. If City suddenly started spending lots
of money on international superstars, would the

homegrown boys every get the chance to play? All they could do was wait and see.

Soon, City had bought themselves a brand-new defence – Wayne Bridge on the left, Vincent Kompany and Tal Ben Haim in the middle, and Pablo Zabaleta on the right.

'Wow, that was quick!' Kieran gasped.

Kieran was still only eighteen but he was already itching to play proper first-team games. That now looked very unlikely at City. In Summer 2009, Kieran didn't go on the South Africa tour, and he didn't play in the Scottish friendlies against Rangers and Celtic either.

However, the City manager Mark Hughes did take him to Spain for the Joan Gamper Trophy game against Barcelona.

'It's now or never,' Kieran told himself. If he got the chance to play, he had to take it.

The atmosphere at the Nou Camp was out of this world. There were over 94,000 people there, just to watch a pre-season game. As he warmed up, Kieran couldn't help looking over at Barcelona's stars: Carles

Puyol, Thierry Henry, Zlatan Ibrahimović and, of course, Lionel Messi. What a team! Was he really about to share a pitch with them? It seemed too good to be true.

Kieran watched from the bench as City took the lead through Martin Petrov. The minutes ticked by, and still he sat there as a sub. Just as he began to give up hope, he got the call he was waiting for:

'Get ready, kid. You're coming on!'

Down on the touchline, Kieran took a long, deep breath. What a place to play your first-senior game! He was wearing Number 54 – was the shirt his now? No, he had to go out there and earn it first.

Before he ran on, Hughes gave him some final instructions. 'I want you to keep things tight in defence. Oh, and enjoy yourself!'

With ten minutes left, City were still 1–0 up. Kieran replaced Shaun Wright-Phillips to help out the right-back, Javier Garrido. He chased up and down the pitch, alert to every Barcelona pass.

Block! Interception! Tackle!

Before he knew it, the final whistle had blown and

Kieran was shaking hands with Messi and Zlatan.

'I'm never washing my hands again!' he laughed with Vladimír.

Kieran hoped that Barcelona game would be the start of something special. However, once the new Premier League season started, he was back playing for the City Under-23s again.

'I guess that's it, then,' he said grumpily.

It was so frustrating to get a brief taste of the big time, and then have it taken away like that. Kieran kept working hard, but he knew that he could learn so much more by playing proper league football. He wasn't getting any closer to the City first team; in fact, he was probably getting further away. Did Hughes even remember who he was anymore?

It didn't really matter because, by December, Hughes was no longer the manager. Kieran tried to impress the new boss, Roberto Mancini, but with City chasing the Premier League title, the young kids didn't stand a chance.

Jim and Steve could both see that Kieran was losing faith in his first team dream. If they didn't do something soon, City might end up losing one of their top young talents.

'What about sending him out on loan?' they suggested to the Under-23s manager, Glyn Hodges. 'The boy needs proper match experience.'

Hodges was happy with the idea, and so was Kieran. Whether at City, or elsewhere, Kieran just wanted to play professional football – week in week out.

CHAPTER 13

BARNSLEY AND BACK

Kieran was raring to go as he arrived at the Barnsley training ground. He was only joining The Tykes for one month, while their two regular right-backs recovered from injuries. However, if he played well, who knew? Maybe manager Mark Robins would want to keep him a bit longer.

'Welcome,' Robins said, shaking his hand. 'I hope you're ready for a challenge!'

Kieran nodded back eagerly. 'You bet, boss. Bring it on!'

First impressions were important. Kieran wanted to look confident, but not *too* confident. He was a young kid coming down from the Premier

League, and he needed to show respect towards
Barnsley's experienced professionals. He wanted
to learn from them; that's why he was there in the
Championship.

However, Kieran also needed to prove himself at
his new club. He didn't want the Barnsley players
to think that he was a boy amongst men. He could
handle himself! So, once the practice session started,
he showed no fear. He wasn't the tallest or the
strongest, but he was tough and he played with
passion and belief.

'That's one way to introduce yourself to your new
teammates!' Robins smiled to himself as Kieran won
the ball with a crunching tackle. He sprinted down
the right wing and delivered an incredible cross onto
Daniel Bogdanović's head. *GOAL!*

The Barnsley manager was impressed, so impressed
that he threw Kieran straight into the starting line-up,
away at Middlesbrough. Within minutes, Kieran saved
the day for his new team.

Boro's striker Chris Killen raced onto a long ball
and flicked it past Barnsley's keeper, Luke Steele.

He looked up, expecting to find an open goal, but no, there was a defender in his way – Kieran! After sprinting back, he bravely blocked Killen's shot with his body.

'Thanks, Tripps!' Luke said, looking very relieved.

Sadly, Barnsley still lost the match, and shortly afterwards they lost at home to Plymouth Argyle too. It really wasn't the strong start that Kieran had hoped for. He was used to winning every week.

'Chin up, kid – you're doing a great job,' Robins reassured him. 'You couldn't have done anything about any of those goals.'

Kieran was desperate to win a game, or even a point, but it wasn't to be. In his third match for Barnsley, against Scunthorpe, he picked up an injury and, after just one month at his new club, that was the end. He returned to Manchester City, feeling a mix of pain and frustration.

'Unlucky, mate. You went to Barnsley and all you got was an injury!' Ben joked.

Kieran laughed it off and focused on getting fit again. After a few games for the Under-23s, he moved up to the City senior squad for their pre-season tour of the USA.

'Maybe Mancini hasn't forgotten about us, after all!' he told Ben, Andrew and Dedryck.

But despite Kieran's excitement, he didn't play a single minute of City's four matches in America. 'Why am I even here?' he wondered to himself. He was a footballer, not a tourist! He needed to get out and play. Surely, there was a club out there who actually wanted him?

Yes, Barnsley! Even in that short time in early 2010, Robins had spotted Kieran's amazing potential. He fought hard to get him back on loan for the whole of the next season, 2010–11.

'Thanks for believing in me, boss,' Kieran said to his manager. 'You won't regret it. This time, there'll be no stopping me!'

Every Championship game was a new and exciting challenge for Kieran. Some weeks, Kieran went toe to toe with tricky wingers like Wilfried Zaha at Crystal Palace and Scott Sinclair at Swansea City. Other weeks, he battled against big powerful forwards, and at other times, he had to close down dangerous crosses.

However, no-one in the league could deliver dangerous crosses quite like Kieran. That was his special talent, after all! In his first four games of the season, he set up three goals.

Against Bristol City, Kieran crossed the ball low and hard for Andy Gray to poke it in. GOAL!

Against Middlesbrough, he curled a corner-kick straight onto Jason Shackell's head. GOAL!

Against Norwich City, he swung in a free kick straight onto Jay McEveley's head. GOAL!

'Tripps, your right foot is ridiculous!' his grateful teammates cheered.

Kieran was delighted. All those hours on the City training ground with Jim and Steve had been totally worth it. He was part of the Barnsley team now.

Two wins and two clean sheets – this was the strong start that he had hoped for during his first loan spell. Second time around, he was playing game after game and really helping his team. Barnsley sat safely in mid-table, and Kieran's incredible crosses were making sure of that.

Against Nottingham Forest, he dribbled all the way to the by-line and then dragged the ball back with a clever Cruyff turn. When the left-back tried to tackle him, Kieran spun cleverly and chipped the ball to Andy at the back post. GOAL!

'Mate, you should be a winger with skills like that!' Jason shouted as they celebrated together.

Kieran shook his head, 'No thanks, it's much more fun to attack from the back!'

A few weeks later, Barnsley were losing 1–0 to Ipswich with seconds to go. Kieran needed to get the ball into the danger zone quickly before the referee blew the final whistle. His perfect pass reached Jacob Mellis just in time, who blasted the ball into the bottom corner. 1–1!

'Cheers, Tripps!' Jacob screamed, hugging him in front of the fans.

Everything was going so well for Kieran at Barnsley. With every game, he was improving. It still wasn't enough to impress Mancini at City, but it was enough to impress the England Under-21s manager,

Stuart Pearce. Kieran was called up for a friendly against Germany.

'Tripps!' his old Under-19 teammates Henri and Nathan cheered happily as the squad met up at the airport.

It was great to see his friends again, but Kieran was focused on football. He wanted to play and he wanted to shine. Unfortunately, it turned out to be a very difficult debut. The German winger Peniel Mlapa was big, strong and quick, and when he dribbled forward, it was so hard to stop him. Kieran lost the battle but he never gave up, and Pearce was pleased with his perseverance.

'Trippier had a solid game at right-back,' he told the media.

On his way back to Barnsley, Kieran beamed with pride. He was now only one step away from the England senior team, and one giant leap closer to his big World Cup dream.

CHAPTER 14

FREE-KICK WIZARD

It wasn't just Kieran's crossing skills that caught the eye at Barnsley; it was also his long-range shooting. When it came to free kicks, he could bend the ball like Beckham.

'You'd need two keepers to stop that!' Luke Steele complained as another strike flew into the top corner in training.

Kieran's homework was paying off. He still spent hours watching YouTube videos of Beckham and Italy's Andrea Pirlo. Their vision and technique were unbelievable! He never got tired of seeing the way they struck their free kicks and long passes. Perfection! Kieran tried to learn as much as he could from them and then put it into practice on the pitch.

Soon, Kieran was taking of all his team's set pieces. It was a big responsibility for a twenty-year-old, but he loved it. After creating lots of chances for others, surely it was only a matter of time before he scored one himself...

In February 2011, Barnsley were losing 3–2 against Leeds United – and there were just ten minutes to go. When Jacob won a free kick just outside the penalty area, Kieran rushed over to grab the ball first. He was determined to be the hero.

As he waited for the referee's whistle, Kieran thought about everything he had worked on with Steve at Manchester City. The run-up, the curl, the dip, the power. It was time to put it all together and score.

Usually, Kieran aimed his free kicks over the wall, or around it, but this time, the ball went *through* the wall. The Leeds keeper Kasper Schmeichel couldn't see a thing until it was too late. 3–3!

Goooooooooooooooooooooaaaaaaaaaaaaaaaaalllllllllllll llllllllllllll!!!!!!!!!!!!!!!!!!!

Kieran had scored his first senior goal, and in a Yorkshire derby too! He raced over to his manager, pumping his fists passionately.

'Get in!' he screamed at the centre of a big team hug.

It was the best feeling of his whole entire life. And after doing it once, Kieran was desperate to do it again.

In another Yorkshire derby – this time against Doncaster – he would get his chance. With five minutes to go, Barnsley were losing 2–1. Free kick! Stephen Foster ran forward to take it, but Kieran had a better idea.

'Trust me, I've got this!' he assured his teammate as he placed the ball down.

The tall wall jumped up but Kieran curled the ball over their heads and into the top corner. 2–2!

Gooooooooooooooooooooaaaaaaaaaaaaaaaalllllllllllll llllllllllllll!!!!!!!!!!!!!!!!!!!

What a strike – Kieran to the rescue again! He ran over to the fans with his arms out wide for a hero's welcome. As a kid in Bury, he had dreamt about

moments like this. Now, it was really happening to
him.

'You're a legend!' his fans and teammates
screamed.

Kieran was loving life at Barnsley but as the games
flew by, his return to Manchester City got closer and
closer. He had learnt so much during his first full
season of senior football. He didn't want it to end.

What a season it had been – forty-one games, eight
clean sheets, six assists, two goals, and the Barnsley
Young Player of the Year award. Kieran was really
going to miss everyone at the club and they were
going to miss him too.

'Come back next year, Tripps!' the supporters
begged.

'How am I meant to score goals without you?'
Andy joked as they said their goodbyes.

'It's been an absolute pleasure working with you,'
Robins told him. 'You're going to be a top, top player
one of these days!'

It was a sad and confusing time for Kieran. When
Barnsley tried to buy him, Manchester City said no.

Okay, so did that mean that they were going to give him a chance?

It didn't seem that way, though, because a few weeks later, he was sent out on loan again!

Burnley really needed a new right-back, and Kieran was top of Eddie Howe's wish-list. The manager wanted his team to play fast, attacking football and that suited his style perfectly.

'Let's do this!' Kieran agreed immediately.

Burnley were still a Championship side, but hopefully not for much longer. They were chasing promotion, rather than battling relegation. Kieran had played with Jay Rodriguez at Barnsley, and he knew that he was a top striker. It also helped that his friend Ben was already there at Burnley. Together, they would get The Clarets back into the Premier League.

'We're going to show City what they're missing!' they cheered.

Against Cardiff City, Kieran dribbled forward and then *ZOOM!* With a clever stepover, he beat the left-back, and kept on running. What next? Even at top speed, he still delivered a perfect cross for Charlie Austin to head home. *GOAL!*

'Nice one, Tripps!' Ben shouted from defence.

Kieran had his first Burnley assist, but what about his first Burnley goal? It was a free kick, of course! In the League Cup against Milton Keynes Dons, he curled the ball up over the wall and it dipped down into the bottom corner.

Goooooooooooooooooooaaaaaaaaaaaaaaaaalllllllllllll lllllllllllll!!!!!!!!!!!!!!!!!!

Kieran lept up and punched the air. He was off the mark at Burnley! New club, same free-kick king.

CHAPTER 15

LEAVING CITY BEHIND

It was 0–0, with thirty minutes gone. As the ball came to Kieran on the edge of the Brighton penalty area, he took a quick touch to control it and then *BANG!* His shot flew through a crowd of defenders, past the goalkeeper, and into the top corner.

Goooooooooooooooooooaaaaaaaaaaaaaaaaalllllllllllll llllllllllllll!!!!!!!!!!!!!!!!!!!

Kieran was having so much fun at Burnley that he almost forgot about Manchester City. He still checked their results every weekend, and messaged Jim and Steve, but he no longer felt part of his childhood club. He was a Claret now.

So, Kieran was delighted when Eddie Howe told

him that he wanted to sign him permanently.

'I know your loan deal lasts until the end of the season but we want to buy you now,' the Burnley manager explained. 'You're a huge part of this team and you're getting better and better. We really don't want to lose you in the summer!'

Kieran was desperate to keep playing week in week out. Howe was right about him; he was improving all the time. Burnley were a big club. They had been in the Premier League before, and they were trying to get back there as quickly as possible.

That fitted perfectly with Kieran's plans. He was determined to work his way back up to the top, but would City let him leave? Yes, they would. After thirteen years at the club, Kieran was finally saying goodbye for good.

'Are you sure this is what you want?' Jim asked him before he signed his contract.

Kieran shrugged, 'City are never going to give me a chance. I'm twenty-one now – it's time for me to move on with my career.'

'I know, I know, but they're making a massive

mistake with you! Good luck, kid. Go and become a superstar and prove them wrong.'

A week later, Ben also signed for Burnley. Together, both friends were leaving City behind.

'No regrets,' they agreed.

Their new club certainly had no regrets. For £400,000, Kieran was an absolute bargain for Burnley. He scored a screamer against Middlesbrough from forty yards out, and then set up two goals for Jay against Nottingham Forest.

'I'm so glad you're staying!' the striker cried out as they celebrated.

However, Kieran's dream of playing in the Premier League would have to wait another year. Burnley finished the 2011–12 season only thirteenth in the Championship. It had been a disappointing season for the team, but not for their right-back – after starring in all forty-six league matches, Kieran won the Burnley Player of the Year award.

'And I'm only just getting started!' he told his teammates happily.

Kieran couldn't wait for the 2012–13 season to

begin. For the first time in years, he felt settled. Burnley was a great club and he believed they were good enough to get back into the Premier League. Yes, Jay had now just signed for Southampton, but they had been joined by Danny Ings, who was up front with Charlie. One day soon, Kieran would return to the Etihad to play *against* Manchester City.

That idea really spurred Kieran on. He raced down the Burnley right, delivering incredible crosses all game long. Against Sheffield Wednesday, he got a hat-trick – a hat-trick of assists!

On the run, Kieran swung a dangerous ball into the six-yard box. Charlie outjumped the centre-back and… *GOAL!*

Despite being a defender, Kieran was now Burnley's danger man. Every time his teammates got the ball, they looked to pass to him.

'Cross it in, Tripps!' the fans encouraged him.

The team relied on his remarkable right foot. Kieran picked out Charlie again, this time at the back post. His diving header flew past the Wednesday keeper. *GOAL!*

Burnley's deadly duo saved their best goal for last. Kieran got the ball in his own half and played a perfect long pass up to Charlie. He beat the defender and fired the ball into the back of the net. *GOAL!*

'You guys are on fire!' Ben cheered.

But Burnley's wonderful hat-trick still wasn't enough to win the game against Wednesday – it ended in a 3–3 draw. What was going on? They were awesome in attack, but really bad at the back.

That had to change. When Sean Dyche became the new Burnley manager, his first task was to tighten up the defence.

'Uh-oh,' Kieran thought to himself. 'Does that mean I won't be able to get forward anymore?'

But instead of asking him to change his style, Dyche just asked him to improve his defending.

'You're the best crosser in the Championship,' Kieran's new manager told him, 'but it's no good setting up one goal, and then giving another goal away. We're going to turn you into the complete right-back.'

The complete right-back? Kieran loved the sound

of that. He was going to work as hard as possible to become 'The New Gary Neville'. That was his dream.

With practice, practice, practice, the Burnley back four became a much stronger unit. Kieran got better at keeping the opposition left wingers quiet. He marked them tightly, he tracked their runs and he blocked their crosses.

'That's it, Tripps!' Dyche clapped and cheered on the sidelines. 'Great defending!'

Then when he got the chance to attack, *ZOOM!* Kieran raced down the right to deliver more of his incredible crosses for Charlie and Danny to score. He finished the season with twelve assists, the third-highest in the whole league.

'Not bad for a defender!' Dyche said with a smile. He was proud of Kieran's progress.

It had been another disappointing year for Burnley, but another amazing year for their star right-back. This time, Kieran was even named in the Championship Team of the Year.

'Next year, we'll all be in there,' he told the other

Burnley players confidently. 'We're going up, lads – I know it!'

Kieran's old England Under-19 teammate, Kyle Walker, had won the Premier League's Young Player of the Year award at Tottenham. Kieran reasoned that if 'Walks' could do it, then so could he! One more season in the Championship, and Kieran would be 100 per cent ready to take on the top division too.

CHAPTER 16

GOING UP!

Thanks to Dyche's help, Kieran was now the most complete and consistent right-back in the whole of the Championship. He was hard to beat at the back, and impossible to stop in attack.

In August 2013, in another game against Sheffield Wednesday, Kieran dribbled past the opposition's defender, and whipped in another brilliant cross to the back post. 2–0 to Burnley!

'What a ball, Tripps!' cheered the goalscorer, Sam Vokes.

With Charlie now at QPR, Sam and Danny were Burnley's new star strikeforce. They were having the time of their lives, thanks to Kieran's incredible crosses.

He wasn't the only one creating chances, though. The Clarets had Junior Stanislas and Ross Wallace on the wings, and new signings David Jones, Dean Marney and Scott Arfield in the middle. It was a real team effort and by November, Burnley were top of the table. Kieran was on track to achieve his Premier League dream.

'Well done, lads. We've got to keep this up now!' Dyche urged his players.

Second-place would be enough to get Burnley back into the Premier League, but Kieran was desperate to win the Championship title. He really wanted his first trophy in senior football. Manchester City's FA Youth Cup triumph felt like a very long time ago, and he had been too injured at the time to even enjoy it properly.

'Come on, this is our year!' he shouted.

Kieran was still only twenty-three, but after playing over 150 matches, he now felt like an experienced pro. He was a strong character and he was one of the team leaders, in the dressing room and out on the pitch. When they needed him most, he always delivered.

Against his old club, Barnsley, in December 2013, Kieran battled his way down the wing before finding Michael Kightly in space. 1–0 to Burnley!

Against their promotion rivals, Leicester City, a week later, he pinged it through the penalty area to Danny. 1–1!

Kieran was having another sensational season. He celebrated the New Year in style by scoring the winner against Huddersfield Town.

With ten minutes to go, Dean chipped a long-ball forward, aiming for one of the Burnley strikers. But instead, it was Kieran who burst into the box and dribbled around the keeper.

'Go on, Tripps!' the supporters shouted out in shock.

Except for another fantastic free kick in the League Cup, Kieran hadn't scored a goal for nearly two years. Was this his big moment? The angle was tight but somehow, he stretched out his right leg and fired the ball in off the crossbar.

Goooooooooooooooooooaaaaaaaaaaaaaaaaallllllllllll llllllllllllll!!!!!!!!!!!!!!!!!!!!

As he ran towards the corner, Kieran blew kisses to all the fans. 'We're going up!' he called out confidently. Hadn't he said that all along?

With each hard-fought victory, The Clarets got closer and closer to promotion. It was Leicester who won the Championship title, but after a 2–0 home win over Wigan Athletic, Burnley joined them in the Premier League.

Hurrrraaaaaaaaaaaaaayyyyy!!

The scenes at the final whistle were unforgettable. Thousands of happy fans stormed onto the Turf Moor pitch to celebrate with their heroes.

'Nice one, Tripps, you legend!'

We love you Burnley, we do,

We love you Burnley, we do,

We love you Burnley, we do,

Oh Burnley we love you!

Later on, in the dressing room, there was champagne flying everywhere as the players hugged and chanted:

We are going up, say we are going up!!

We are going up, say we are going up!!

It was by far the best moment of Kieran's career. He had always believed in himself, and in his teammates. As they stood there, arm in arm, a feeling of pure joy buzzed all the way through his body. What an achievement! Together, they had done it; they had led Burnley back into the Premier League.

'Aren't you glad we left City behind?' Kieran asked Ben.

His friend just laughed. 'What? City who?'

Kieran's season soon got even better. He finished top of the assists chart, with twelve, and made the Championship Team of the Year for a second time in a row. He was proud of himself, but most of all, he was proud of his team. Burnley had only conceded thirty-seven goals all season. That was the lowest in the league! The defence said a big thank you to Dyche.

'We couldn't have done this without you, Boss!'

Kieran couldn't wait for his next big challenge to begin. He was ready to take on the best clubs in England – Manchester United, Chelsea, Liverpool, Arsenal, Tottenham, and of course, his old club

Manchester City. It hadn't been easy, but Kieran had battled his way back to the highest level.

'Bring it on!'

Over the summer of 2014, there were rumours that Arsenal wanted to sign him, but Kieran ignored them and signed a new contract at Burnley. He was happy and settled at Turf Moor. This was the club that had shown faith in him, and so this was the club that he would play for in his first Premier League adventure.

CHAPTER 17

GOING DOWN

Kieran couldn't have asked for a tougher Premier League debut. Burnley were playing Chelsea, and that meant that he was up against their Belgian wing wizard, Eden Hazard.

'Bring it on!' he shouted in the dressing room before kick-off.

Dyche had signed a few new players but mostly, he was sticking with his stars from the Championship. They deserved their chance at the top level.

When Scott scored a great goal to put Burnley 1–0 up, Turf Moor went wild. What a start!

'Get in!' Kieran roared in front of the fans.

Unfortunately, their lead didn't last long. Kieran kept Hazard quiet when he was out on the left, but the playmaker moved all over the pitch. Plus, Chelsea had Diego Costa, Oscar and Cesc Fàbregas too. Twenty minutes later, Burnley were 3–1 down.

'We can't give them free headers like that!' Kieran groaned, throwing his arms up in frustration.

They were playing at the top level now, against awesome attackers who only needed one chance to score. Burnley didn't have time to slowly find their feet in the Premier League. They needed to improve their defending immediately, and so that's exactly what they did.

They drew 0–0 against Manchester United…

Then 0–0 against Crystal Palace…

And then 0–0 against Sunderland too!

The Clarets had won their first points of the season, but they'd only scored one goal in six games! Danny was crying out for Kieran's incredible crosses, but he was too busy at the back.

In the Manchester United game, Ashley Young attacked down the left wing but Kieran won the ball

off him. As Wayne Rooney ran in for the tackle, he
flicked it through his legs. Nutmeg!

'Nice one, Tripps!' the Burnley fans cheered.

Kieran was loving every minute of life in the
Premier League. Game after game, he was battling
against quality wingers, and every single one was
different. Palace's Wilfried Zaha was a deadly
dribbler, whereas West Brom's Chris Brunt liked
to cross the ball with his lethal left-foot. And
Arsenal's Alexis Sánchez? Well, he was amazing at
everything.

After ten games, Burnley languished at the bottom
of the table, with six defeats, four draws, and ZERO
wins. Some people were saying that they were the
worst Premier League team EVER.

'Come on, let's prove them wrong today!' Dyche
told his players before their eleventh game, a big
home match against Hull City.

Kieran was determined to win the three points for
his team. In the fiftieth minute, the ball bounced out
to him on the right wing. He was in lots of space,
so he took his time. He controlled it, looked up,

and then calmly curled it into the box. As soon as it left his boot, Kieran knew that it was one of his incredible crosses.

Power? Perfect!

Direction? The danger zone!

All it needed was a striker's touch to turn it into a goal. The ball flew over Danny's head, then George Boyd's, but Ashley Barnes was there at the back post to flick it over the goalkeeper's arms. 1–0!

Ashley punched the air and ran over to thank Kieran. 'What a ball!' he cried out.

For the next forty minutes, the Burnley defenders stood strong like soldiers. Tackle! Block! Header! Interception! When the final whistle blew, the players celebrated as if they had just won the league.

'We are staying up, say we are staying up!'

It wouldn't be easy but Burnley believed.

At last, it was time for the match that Kieran and Ben had been waiting for – away at Manchester City! It felt very strange returning to the Etihad Stadium to play for another team. There were so many memories and familiar faces.

'Look who it is!' Jim called out when he spotted
Kieran. 'Are you here for revenge?'

'Hopefully!'

The two clubs were at opposite ends of the league.
City were in second place and challenging for the
title, while Burnley were nineteenth and fighting
relegation.

At half-time, City were 2–0 up and cruising.
David Silva and Jesús Navas were making Ben's
life a misery on the left. But after Dyche's team-
talk, Burnley came out battling. The game wasn't
over yet.

George steered Danny's cross past Joe Hart. 2–1!

Then, with ten minutes to go, Ashley fired a shot
into the top corner. 2–2!

'Get in!' Kieran screamed as the players hugged
in front of their fans. He was so proud of all his
teammates. They stuck together and never gave up,
no matter what.

Burnley held on for a famous draw against the
richest club in the world. For Kieran, it was one
of many magical moments in his first Premier

League season. There were no fantastic free kicks, but there was:

A deep, curling corner-kick against Crystal Palace, which Ben headed home at the back post.

A bursting run down the right at Old Trafford, which ended with a teasing cross and Danny's diving header.

And another Kieran and Ben double act at Stamford Bridge. Six years after playing there for Manchester City in the FA Youth Cup Final, they earned a late point for Burnley.

Sadly, not even these high points were enough to keep them up. Despite another 1–0 win over Hull City, they were relegated back to the Championship. A year after going up, Burnley were going down again.

'Well done lads, I'm proud of you all,' Dyche told his disappointed team in the dressing room. 'We've learned a lot this season and we have to keep moving forward. We gave it our best shot and we'll be back.'

Kieran had always known that it would be a difficult season but he couldn't help feeling devastated. It was gutting after all that hard work.

He had played in all thirty-eight Premier League matches, and he believed that he was good enough to stay.

After the final home match at Turf Moor, Kieran walked around the pitch with Danny, clapping their loyal fans.

'Please don't leave!' the supporters shouted back at them.

Kieran and Danny had been Burnley's star players all season, and top clubs like Liverpool and Tottenham now wanted to buy them. They really didn't want to leave the club, but they also really didn't want to leave the Premier League behind.

Over that summer, Kieran would have a difficult decision to make.

CHAPTER 18

TO TOTTENHAM

'I'd like to thank everyone involved at Burnley for four memorable years,' Kieran tweeted. 'A great club with great fans.'

He didn't leave it at that, though. He felt that he owed the fans a proper explanation. 'I was devastated when we got relegated because I didn't want to leave the club. But I want to play in the Premier League and be the best player I can be.'

The Burnley supporters were sad to see Kieran leave but they understood. He wasn't such a young player anymore. He was twenty-four now, and he had to do what was best for his career.

Plus, it was hard to say no to a top club like

Tottenham. Their manager, Mauricio Pochettino, was
building a brilliant team, packed with young England
internationals. They had Harry Kane, Dele Alli, Eric
Dier, Danny Rose and, of course, his old Under-19
teammate, Kyle Walker.

'Won't you and Walks be playing the same
position?' Ben asked Kieran.

Ben was clearly desperate for Kieran to stay at
Burnley, but it was still a good question. Kyle was
a right-back too, and one of the best in the Premier
League. Would Kieran be joining Spurs just to sit on
the bench?

'No, you'll get plenty of opportunities,' Pochettino
promised him. 'We're going to have a lot of matches
next season, in the Premier League, the League Cup,
the FA Cup, *and* the Europa League. We believe that
you can really improve our squad. You'll have to fight
for your place but so will everyone else.'

Kieran nodded eagerly. He was ready to fight for
his place at Spurs, and to learn from Kyle too. After
all, he would be making a big step-up from Burnley.
There would be no more relegation battles. Instead,

Tottenham would be battling against Chelsea, Liverpool, Manchester United and his old club Manchester City for a Champions League spot.

If he signed for Spurs, Kieran could soon be playing against the likes of Barcelona and Real Madrid. And fingers crossed, he could be playing for England too.

'What do you think I should do?' he asked Kelvin. Even now that Kieran was a Premier League player, he still always asked his big brother for advice.

'You've got to go for it, bro!' Kelvin replied. 'They're one of the biggest clubs in Europe!'

Good – that was exactly what Kieran wanted to hear. He was making the right decision by signing for Spurs. He just had to believe in his own ability.

'I can do this!' he told himself.

Firstly, however, he needed to say a sad goodbye to everyone at Burnley. It was an emotional day, full of hugs, laughs and best wishes:

'Good luck, Tripps! Hopefully, we'll get to play you in the cup this season!'

'And then twice next season once we're back in the Premier League!'

Kieran was really going to miss his teammates, especially his best friends Ben and Danny. He was really going to miss his manager too.

'Thanks for everything, boss,' Kieran said. 'Without you, I wouldn't be half the defender that I am now!'

Dyche smiled. 'Yes, I like to think I've taught you a thing or two! But seriously, you've worked really hard for this chance, Tripps. You're a top Premier League player, so go to Tottenham and show it.'

For £3.5 million, Kieran became Spurs' cheapest signing of the summer. He wasn't exactly the big-name buy that some fans were hoping for. 'Kieran who?' some people asked, but he didn't mind that. He would just have to make sure that they remembered his name.

Wearing a smart white shirt, Kieran posed for photos next to the big club badge at White Hart Lane. In his hands, he held up the brand-new Tottenham home kit. What number would he choose? Kyle already had the Number 2 shirt...

'What else is available?' Kieran asked. He was happy to wear whatever he was given.

'9?'

'No sorry, I can't wear 9 – I'm a right-back!'

'What about 16?'

'Yes, that's fine, thanks!' he replied. He had worn that number at Barnsley all those years ago.

Kieran couldn't wait to get started. He had so many talented new teammates to meet! As well as their England stars, Tottenham also had Christian Eriksen, Jan Vertonghen, Mousa Dembélé, Son Heung-min... Their list of stars went on and on.

Kieran had played against most of them for Burnley but playing *with* them was a different and daunting idea. What if he wasn't good enough? What if he couldn't compete? Luckily, when he arrived for his first day of pre-season training, his old friend Kyle was there to greet him with a big hug.

'Mate, it's great to have you here,' he said. 'Tottenham's definitely big enough for the both of us.'

Once the session started, however, Kyle put his game-face on. They weren't friends anymore; they were two rivals, challenging for Spurs' one right-back spot.

'Right, Tripps, let the battle begin!'

CHAPTER 19

FIGHTING FIT

Kieran was on the Tottenham bench for the first match of the 2015–16 Premier League season against Manchester United at Old Trafford. The manager had warned him that Kyle would be starting at right-back instead, but it was still frustrating not to play – at Burnley, Kieran had only missed six league matches in four whole years.

'Just be patient,' he told himself. Pochettino had promised that he would get chances.

Memphis Depay attacked down the right for United and crossed the ball to Wayne Rooney, who had ample space in the penalty area. Where was Kyle? He was sprinting back from the halfway line!

Kyle got there just in time to tackle Rooney but his touch took the ball past Hugo Lloris and into the net. *Own goal!*

Tottenham lost the match 1–0.

'Bring in Trippier!' some fans cried out at the final whistle but Pochettino stuck with Kyle instead. Kieran was disappointed and desperate to make his debut. Why was he still on the bench?

'We need to get you fit first,' his manager explained.

Kieran had arrived at his new club after a relaxing holiday in Mexico. Yes, he was a little heavier and slower than usual, but wasn't that what pre-season training was for? No – not at a top team like Tottenham; Pochettino expected his players to be fighting fit all the time.

'You're an elite athlete,' the manager told Kieran, 'so you have to be dedicated and professional.'

Kieran learnt his lesson. Pochettino expected a really high standard from his players, so he couldn't switch off for a second. If he did, he would be dropped straight away. With extra training and a better diet, Kieran soon felt fitter than ever. All he needed now was a chance to impress.

At first, Kieran's chances all came in the Europa
League. He played every minute of every match
in the competition, and he enjoyed his first taste
of European football. Tottenham finished top of
Group J, after beating big clubs like Anderlecht and
Monaco.

'Come on, we can win the whole tournament!'
Kieran cried out as the team celebrated yet another
goal at White Hart Lane.

The tactics really suited his style. Pochettino
pushed his full-backs really far forward – Kieran on
the right, and Ben Davies on the left. They were a
key part of Spurs' exciting European attack, alongside
Son Heung-min, Nacer Chadli and Érik Lamela.

In the Premier League, however, Kieran was still
waiting for his first Tottenham start. Would it ever
come? Yes, just after Christmas, Pochettino finally
decided to rest Kyle against Watford. Kieran was in!

'Right, I have to make the most of this,' he told
himself.

Tottenham took an early lead at Vicarage Road but

with time running out, the game was tied at 1–1. Spurs were in danger of dropping down to fifth place. Unless…

The ball came out to Kieran on the right. Could he deliver one of his incredible crosses? His first attempt was blocked but he got a second chance. This time, he picked out Son, who flicked the ball cleverly past the keeper. 2–1!

As the Spurs fans danced with joy, Son ran straight over to celebrate with Kieran.

'What a goal!'

'What a cross!'

Kieran was delighted to be one of Tottenham's heroes. Would he get to keep his place after saving the day? No – Pochettino brought Kyle back for the next game against Everton, but he did give Kieran more and more opportunities: a game against Sunderland, then Crystal Palace and then the return match against Watford.

Kieran had really missed playing week in week out in the Premier League. Although the European adventures were fun, the crowds weren't as big and the atmosphere just wasn't the same. But for a three o'clock kick-off on a Saturday, White Hart Lane was full of fans and full of singing.

Come on you Spurs!

We love you Tottenham, we do!

In the first half of that return match against Watford, Ben dribbled into the Watford penalty area twice, but both of his shots were saved by the keeper.

In the second half, it was Kieran's turn to attack. He curled a teasing cross towards Nacer but a Watford defender cleared it just in time.

'So close!' Kieran groaned, looking up at the sky.

Tottenham needed to find a winning goal from somewhere, but where? As Dele attacked down the left wing, Kieran sprinted forward down the right.

'Cross it!' he called out with his arm up in the air.

Dele passed the ball all the way to the back post, to give Kieran a simple tap-in. 1–0!

Goooooooooooooooooooooaaaaaaaaaaaaaaaaaallllllllllllll llllllllllllllll!!!!!!!!!!!!!!!!!!!!

What a moment! It was Kieran's first-ever

Tottenham goal. As he ran towards the corner flag, he jumped up and punched the air.

'Get in!' he cheered.

Now the fans would definitely remember Kieran's name because that goal turned out to be the matchwinner. Spurs stayed in second place in the table, just five points behind Leicester City.

Was Kieran about to become a Premier League champion? He didn't have time to think about that – he had another Europa League match to win. When Nacer got the ball on the right wing, Kieran raced forward on an overlapping run.

'Yes!' he called out for the pass.

Kieran's delivery was so deadly that the Fiorentina defender scored an own goal. 3–0!

His teammates rushed over to congratulate Kieran on his cross.

'That's your goal really!' Nacer told him.

Unfortunately, Spurs ended their excellent season without winning a single trophy. Borussia Dortmund knocked them out of the Europa League, and Leicester held on to clinch the Premier League title.

'Next year, we'll be unstoppable!' Pochettino reassured his players.

Kieran was satisfied with his first season at Tottenham – nineteen games, three assists and one goal. It was a decent start, and there was plenty more to come. The Spurs supporters hadn't seen him at his absolute best yet.

'You better watch out!' he joked with Kyle. Their friendly rivalry was pushing them both to get better and better.

Kieran wasn't getting as much game-time as he had at Burnley, but he didn't even think about leaving. He couldn't give up after one year. He had to stay and fight for his place. During the summer, Southampton tried to sign him, but Pochettino said no.

Phew! Kieran was happy at the club, especially now that Tottenham were playing in the Champions League. They would need their two talented right-backs more than ever.

CHAPTER 30

BREAKING THROUGH

Despite Kieran's positivity, the first half of the next season was almost exactly the same as the last. Again, Kyle was Tottenham's Premier League right-back and again, Kieran only played in Europe and the League Cup.

'Your chance will come,' Pochettino kept promising Kieran, but the player needed to know when. He couldn't wait forever. And who were Spurs' opponents when Kieran finally started another league match? Watford again!

There was one important difference, though – his position. Instead of playing on the right of a back four, he was now playing as the right wing-back, ahead of a back three.

'Great!' Kieran thought to himself. 'Now, I can attack even more!'

This was his big opportunity to shine after weeks on the sidelines. He had hardly played since Tottenham's 2–1 defeat to Monaco in the Champions League. Was Pochettino punishing him for one poor performance? It didn't matter. There was only way for Kieran to prove himself – by assisting Spurs to victory.

Harry Kane was excited to have Kieran back in the team. As a striker, it was so much fun playing with such an incredible crosser. Kieran didn't let him, or his team, down. He looked up and slipped a perfect pass into Harry's path. All Harry had to do was shoot…1–0!

Harry ran towards his teammate with a big smile on his face. 'Cheers Tripps, I knew you'd set me up today!'

Five minutes later, Kieran did it again. He controlled Dele's pass and curled the ball straight into the danger zone. He knew exactly where Harry wanted it. 2–0 – game over!

'What a cross, mate!' he shouted, hugging Kieran tightly. 'I wish we could play you and Walks in the same team. I would never stop scoring!'

Kieran wished that too. When he played, Tottenham almost always won. Why couldn't he play together with Kyle? Surely, it didn't have to be one or the other – it could be both!

'Think of all the double trouble we could cause!' Kieran thought to himself. Still, two assists on 1 January felt like a very good sign.

'2017 is going to be my year!' Kieran told himself confidently.

In fact, his big Tottenham breakthrough was only a few months away. From March until the end of that season, Kieran became a Premier League regular again.

He wasn't surprised when Pochettino picked him to play against his old club Burnley; Kyle needed a rest after two tiring matches for England.

Kieran wasn't surprised when he started against Watford either. It felt like he always playing against them! In the second half, he crossed and Son scored. 4–0!

The shock only came when Kieran kept his place against Arsenal. The North London Derby? Surely, Pochettino would pick Kyle for that! But no, it was definitely Kieran's name written there in the starting line-up – '16 TRIPPIER'. At last, he was breaking through.

'Congratulations, you deserve this,' his dad Chris told him. 'Just make sure you take this opportunity!'

For eighty minutes, Kieran ran up and down the right wing tirelessly for Tottenham. He did his duties brilliantly, both in defence and attack. When he came off for Kyle, they were 2–0 up and the White Hart Lane crowd gave him a loud standing ovation.

'Well played!' Pochettino said, giving him a quick hug on the touchline.

Kieran was buzzing as he sat down on the Spurs bench. What a win it would be, especially against their London rivals! It would leave them only four points behind Chelsea at the top of the table, with four games to go. Could Tottenham win the Premier League title this time?

Despite Kieran's best efforts, though, the answer

was no. He helped his team to beat Manchester United but by then it was too late. In the one match he missed, Spurs lost 1–0 to West Ham.

'Not again!' the fans groaned.

It was the same old story for Spurs, but not for Kieran. He was no longer their second-choice right-back. All that hard work and patience was finally paying off. He had fought his way into the Tottenham team.

Kieran saved his best performance of the season for the final game against Hull City. Harry was desperate to win the Premier League Golden Boot for the second year in a row, and he needed Kieran's help.

'Come on, Tripps,' he shouted in the dressing room. 'With your crosses, I can definitely get a hat-trick today!'

As Eric dribbled the ball forward, Kieran made his move into the penalty area. The pass was perfect, so perfect that Kieran decided to cross it first-time on the volley. He was playing with lots of confidence. As always, Harry was in the right place at the right time to finish things off. 2–0!

Their understanding was unbelievable. It was like they had been playing together forever.

'Thanks, I knew I could rely on you!' Harry said, putting an arm around his teammate.

Kieran smiled. 'Next season, I'll make sure you score even more, H!'

It wasn't just Harry that he was helping, though, in the Hull game. In the second half, he set up Toby Alderweireld to make it 7–1. What a way for Kieran to end his breakthrough season at Spurs.

Soon, the right-back role would be Kieran's to keep, as Kyle moved to Manchester City for £50million.

'Good luck, Walks. Thanks for everything!'

'Good luck, Tripps! That Number 2 shirt is yours now!'

It was far from the end of their rivalry, though. Instead of competing against each other at Tottenham, they would now be competing against each other in the Premier League, and also for England.

CHAPTER 21

ENGLAND CALL-UP

A few days after Spurs' 7–1 thrashing of Hull,
Kieran was told that Pochettino wanted to see him
in his office. His first reaction was panic. Was he in
trouble? Had he done something wrong? He couldn't
think of anything...

As Kieran walked in and shut the door behind
him, his heart was pounding in his chest. He glanced
up at his manager but his face wasn't giving
anything away.

'I know what you did last night,' Pochettino said
at last.

Last night? Kieran tried to think clearly. Where
had he been? He had been at home with his wife,

Charlotte, looking after their baby son, Jacob, all night.

'Boss, I—' he began to say but Pochettino was already on the phone.

'Hi Hugo, could you come to my office please?'

Uh-oh! Hugo Lloris was the Tottenham captain. He looked very serious as he entered the room. Kieran had a horrible feeling in the pit of his stomach. What had he done?

Suddenly, a smile spread across Pochettino's face. 'Congratulations, you've been called up to the England squad!'

'Well done, Tripps!' Hugo added.

Kieran didn't know whether to laugh or cry. He had never given up hope of representing his country at senior level. Even when his last Under-21 cap had become a distant memory, he had refused to believe that his England career was over. He was right all along!

After thanking his manager and captain, Kieran walked out into the corridor. He had a phone call to make.

474

'Mum, Dad,' he said. 'I've been called up to the England squad!'

There was a brief pause on the other end of the line, followed by shrieks of joy.

'Son, that's brilliant news!' Chris shouted.

'We're so proud of you!' Eleanor told him tearfully.

'I really couldn't have done it without you guys,' Kieran replied. He was feeling emotional too. 'Thanks for everything – I owe you!'

'We'll start booking our tickets!'

'No, leave everything to me, Dad. I'll sort it out!'

Kieran thought back to his childhood, and all those hours sat by his dad's side, supporting the national team. Chris was England's biggest fan. During the 2010 World Cup, he had even flown a giant St George's flag outside their home in Bury. The local council asked him to take it down but Chris refused. Now his son was about to play for England! It didn't get any better than that.

Kieran was the only new name in the squad for the matches against Scotland and France. It was a little daunting at first, but at least he was surrounded by familiar faces. He knew the goalkeeper Tom Heaton from Burnley, and four of his Tottenham teammates were there too: Harry, Dele, Eric and Kyle.

'I wish you'd stop following me around, Tripps!' Kyle joked.

Kieran was on the bench for the first match in May 2017 – the World Cup qualifier against Scotland at Hampden Park. England needed to win and so their manager Gareth Southgate picked his strongest team. That meant Harry up front, Dele in midfield and Kyle at right-back.

'Come on, England!' Kieran cheered along with the rest of the fans.

But with seconds to go, they were losing 2–1. What a disaster! On the subs bench, Kieran couldn't sit still. He wanted to be out there so badly, crossing the ball in for Harry to score. Instead, it was Raheem Sterling who set Harry up. 2–2!

'Get in!' Kieran shouted, jumping out of his seat to celebrate.

Three days later, England played their second match – a friendly against France. This time,

Southgate decided to try something new. He went
for a back three with wing-backs, just like Pochettino
at Tottenham. And just like at Tottenham, Kieran
would be playing on the right!

He had a quick phone call to make:

'Dad, I'm starting tonight!'

'That's great, son! We'll be there cheering you on
in the crowd. See you later!'

Kieran had to take lots of deep breaths as he
walked out of the tunnel onto the pitch in Paris. The
atmosphere in the Stade de France was amazing,
as 75,000 people sang Oasis's 'Don't Look Back in
Anger' at the tops of their voices. The England fans
held up pieces of white and red paper to form a giant
St George's flag. It was even bigger than the one his
dad had put up back home in Bury.

As the anthems played, Kieran stood there dressed
in all-white, except for the three blue lions on his
shirt. He was an England international now, and it
was the proudest moment of his entire life.

Five years earlier, Kieran had left Manchester City
behind to battle his way up from the Championship

– and look at him now! But there was no time to stop and enjoy the moment. Kieran had a match to win.

England got off to a dream start. Dele passed to Raheem, who flicked it to Ryan Bertrand. Ryan crossed to Harry. 1–0!

Right, time to focus. On the right, Kieran stayed calm and kept things simple. He didn't want to make any mistakes on his debut. By half-time, however, it was 2–1 to France. Their young stars Kylian Mbappé, Ousmane Dembélé and Paul Pogba were teaching England a tough lesson.

'Welcome to international football!' Kieran thought to himself as he picked himself up and carried on. He still had a lot to learn at the highest level.

After seventy-six minutes, with the score at 2–2, Kieran was substituted. It was a solid start to his international career and as he left the field, he hoped that he had done enough to get another England chance.

'Well done!' Southgate said, patting him on the back.

'Well done!' his mum shouted too when they met up after the match. In the end, England had lost 3–2 but Kieran wasn't letting anything ruin his big day.

'I've never cried so much in my life!' his dad admitted. 'You played really well, son.'

Well enough to get another England call-up? Kieran would have to wait and see. The 2018 World Cup was now only one year away. If he had a strong season as Tottenham's first-choice right-back, who knew what might happen…

CHAPTER 22

FIRST-CHOICE, FINALLY!

Tottenham had a new 'Number 2' for the 2017–18 season: Kieran! He had certainly earned the shirt. After waiting patiently for his chance, he was finally first-choice.

He wasn't Spurs' only option at right-back, though. Pochettino had replaced Kyle with Serge Aurier from PSG. Although Serge cost a lot of money, that didn't worry Kieran. He was focused on his own game and he wasn't giving up his starting spot without a real fight.

'Are you ready, Tripps?' Harry shouted eagerly as the season kicked off. He couldn't wait to carry on their perfect partnership.

Kieran nodded eagerly. 'Let's go out there and score some goals!'

Over the summer, he had been working hard on his attacking play. As a wing-back, Kieran couldn't just cross the ball every time. That was too predictable and too easy for the defenders. He had to find other ways of getting the ball forward to Dele and Harry – short passes, long passes, through-balls.

'I've got a full box of tricks now,' he told his brother, Kelvin. 'Just you wait and see!'

In the Premier League against Everton, Kieran passed to Harry and kept running down the right for the one-two. But Harry decided to whip the ball into the box instead. It flew over everyone's head, including the keeper. *GOAL!*

'Was that a cross or a shot?' Kieran asked as they celebrated together.

Harry smiled and shrugged. 'Does it matter? I scored!'

In the Champions League against APOEL Nicosia, the one-two worked brilliantly. Harry passed it wide to Kieran and then burst into the box, calling for one of his incredible crosses. One touch, a quick look up, and then BANG! Kieran made it look so easy, as he curled the ball straight onto Harry's head. *GOAL!*

'Tripps, what would I do without you?' he screamed, hugging him tightly. With Kieran's help, Harry had his first hat-trick of the season.

Against Huddersfield, Kieran set him up with a header. Tottenham's Number 10 chased after it and fired a shot into the bottom corner. *GOAL!*

'Cheers, mate!' Harry cheered, giving him a high-five.

Fifteen minutes later, Kieran threw the ball to Harry and he turned and scored. *GOAL!*

'Hey, that one was all my own work!' Harry laughed.

Against Liverpool, Kieran chipped the ball cleverly over Dejan Lovren's head and Harry ran in and scored. *GOAL!*

Tottenham were flying but Kieran was about to face his toughest test yet – Real Madrid, the twelve-time Champions League winners. He would be taking on the most lethal left wing in the world: Marcelo and Cristiano Ronaldo.

'Come on, we can beat them!' Kieran shouted in the dressing room before kick-off. He was Tottenham's first-choice now, and he feared no-one.

As the two teams walked out at Wembley, Kieran was hit by a wall of deafening noise. There were over 83,000 fans in the stadium and almost all of them were cheering for Tottenham.

Come on you Spurs!

Kieran didn't look up, though. He kept his eyes fixed on the grass in front of him. He was fully focused on winning this massive football match.

'When Marcelo pushes up, he leaves a big gap behind him,' Pochettino had told Kieran. 'That's your space to run into!'

Midway through the first half, Harry Winks got the ball in central midfield and played a brilliant pass out to the right. Marcelo watched it fly over his head and then turned to find... Kieran! He was doing exactly what his manager had asked him to. Kieran watched the ball carefully onto his right foot and crossed it first-time to Dele. *GOAL!*

Tottenham were beating Real Madrid! Kieran

chased after Dele, pumping his fists at the cheering crowd.

For Kieran, 2017 really had turned out to be his year. Not only had he become Tottenham's first-choice and an England international, but now he had an assist against Real Madrid in the Champions League. It was his thirteenth in all competitions, six more than any other Premier League defender.

'That pass was world-class!' Dele told him.

As Kieran looked over at the bench, Pochettino gave him a big thumbs-up. Their plan had worked but now Spurs had some defending to do.

Kieran kept his eyes on the ball as Ronaldo dribbled into the penalty area. Real Madrid's superstar danced from side to side, with a stepover to the left, and then a stepover to the right, but he didn't make a silly tackle. When Ronaldo eventually decided to shoot, Kieran blocked it.

'Great work, Tripps!' Hugo shouted.

Kieran was having his best game ever. On the edge of the Real Madrid box, he showed off some stepovers of his own. He beat Isco and then nutmegged Marcelo.

Trippier! Trippier!

The Spurs fans loved him. In the second half, Kieran even made a goal line clearance to stop Ronaldo from scoring. Eventually, he did get a goal but it was too little too late. 3–1 – Tottenham had beaten Real Madrid!

'We did it!' Kieran cried out at the final whistle, hugging Dele.

The Spurs players walked around the Wembley pitch, clapping their amazing supporters. They were through to the next round of the Champions League!

Kieran was in dreamland but a few weeks later, there was a horrible wake-up call awaiting him. It was Manchester City vs Tottenham, Kyle vs Kieran.

After months playing as an attacking wing-back, Kieran returned to his old right-back role. It turned out to be a total disaster. City's winger Leroy Sané skipped past him again and again.

'I need some help here!' Kieran called out to his teammates.

He couldn't even get his crosses right. 'Sorry!' Kieran shouted as the ball sailed high over Dele's head. Tottenham were lucky to be losing only 1–0 at half-time, but it wasn't long until things got a whole lot worse.

City were running riot down the left. Kieran was way out of position as Kevin De Bruyne dribbled forward. He sprinted back as fast as he could but it was no use. 2–0 to City!

Ten minutes later, Sané escaped past Kieran and crossed to Raheem. 3–0!

'Offside!' Kieran cried out hopefully but the linesman's flag stayed down.

The match ended in a humiliating 4–1 defeat for Tottenham. It was a painful reminder for Kieran that he wasn't a superstar yet. In the dressing room afterwards, he didn't hide away. He owned up to his errors.

'I let everyone down today,' he told his manager and teammates, 'but it won't happen again, I promise.'

Kieran didn't let one bad game get him down. He soon went back to being Spurs' Mr Consistent on the right:

Tottenham 2–0 Manchester United,

and Tottenham 1–0 Arsenal!

'North London is white, not red!' Kieran cheered at

full-time.

Sadly, 2017–18 had turned out to be yet another trophy-free season for Spurs. They lost to Juventus in the Champions League Round of 16, to Manchester United in the FA Cup semi-final, and to Kyle's Manchester City in the Premier League title race.

'We can't keep getting so close,' Kieran moaned. 'Eventually, we've got to go all the way and win something!'

His strong season wasn't over yet, though. On 16 May 2018, Southgate announced his England squad for the World Cup in Russia. The FA released a video where each player's name was revealed one by one. Raheem was first, then John Stones, then Trent Alexander-Arnold. Eventually, the video zoomed in on a boy in Bury:

'KIERAN TRIPPIER!' he said. 'Go on, lad!'

Kieran, Harry, Dele, Danny and Eric – they were all off to Russia together!

After telling his proud parents, Kieran tweeted his followers: 'It's an honour to be named in the England squad. I can't wait for my first World Cup.'

CHAPTER 23

A WORLD CUP TO REMEMBER

It may have been Kieran's first World Cup, but would he actually get to play? Kyle was off to Russia too, so would Kieran just be England's back-up right-back?

No, because Southgate had found a brilliant way to fit them both into the same starting line-up. In the pre-tournament friendlies, the manager moved Kyle to the back three and brought Kieran in as the wing-back. Problem solved!

Netherlands 0–1 England,

England 1–1 Italy,

England 2–1 Nigeria.

'It's like the Under-19s all over again!' Kieran and Kyle joked.

It was so much fun that the two could play together again in the same team. They formed a perfect partnership down the England right. Kyle provided the speed and Kieran provided the crosses. Against Nigeria, he curled a corner-kick into the six-yard box for Gary Cahill to score. *GOAL!*

Kieran couldn't wait for the World Cup to get started. England had a great group of players and everyone got on really well with each other. At the base camp in Repino, he didn't just hang out with his Tottenham teammates; he hung out with everyone!

One day after training, Kieran played ten-pin bowling with Trent, Gary and Jesse Lingard. Another day, he played with Jack Butland and Jordan Henderson, who was dreadful.

'Maybe you should stick to football, Hendo!'

Ahead of the first match against Tunisia, Southgate sorted out England's set-piece tactics. He gave Kieran and Ashley Young the important task of taking all the corners and free kicks.

'It's a key part of our game-plan,' Southgate told them, 'so we're relying on you guys to get it right!'

'Yes, Boss!'

Kieran would take the corners from the right, and Ashley would take the corners from the left. But when it came to free kicks, they would have to battle it out amongst themselves. They spent hours playing 'first to twenty free kicks' after training. Their contests were a lot closer than the ones Kieran used to have with Steve at Manchester City.

'This one to win it, Youngie… Get in!'

England's game-plan worked straight away. In the tenth minute against Tunisia, Ashley's corner reached John Stones at the back post. The keeper saved his powerful header but Harry was in the right place at the right time for the rebound. 1–0!

'What a start!' Kieran cheered as he jumped on Harry. Soon, they were both at the bottom of a big team bundle.

England were on fire and they should have scored a second goal but instead, they conceded one. A cross came in from the left and Kyle fouled the Tunisia striker. Penalty!

'No way, ref!' Kyle and Kieran protested in unison

but it was no use. 1–1!

England had to stay strong and fight back. Kieran was their star player, creating chance after chance for his team. If he kept delivering incredible crosses, surely Harry or Dele would score eventually. It had worked so many times at Tottenham.

In the last minute of the match, England won a corner on the right. Kieran took a deep breath and aimed for the penalty spot. As usual, the cross was perfect. Harry Maguire won the first header and Harry Kane scored from the second. 2–1!

This time, Kieran was the last player to join the big team bundle because he had to run all the way across the pitch. It was worth it, though. He was an England World Cup hero now!

'I couldn't have done it without you, guys!' Harry Kane said at the final whistle, with one arm around Ashley, and the other around Kieran.

When he checked his phone, Kieran had so many messages.

'Congrats, Tripps, what a performance!' said Ben.

'Very proud of you, kid,' said Jim.

'Bro, you've created the most goalscoring chances in the World Cup so far!' said Kelvin.

It was a night that Kieran would never ever forget. He had come a very long way since that early loan spell at Barnsley.

And he was only just getting started. In the eighth minute against Panama, Kieran curled another corner-kick towards the penalty spot. This time, it was John who headed the ball home. 1–0!

'Come on!' Kieran shouted in front of the fans.

The match finished 6–1 to England. With two wins, they were through to the Round of 16. Back home, the nation began to believe:

It's coming home, it's coming home,
It's coming, FOOTBALL'S COMING HOME!'

The England players, however, were not getting carried away. It was knock-out football from now on. One mistake could really cost them, especially against a top team like Colombia.

'If we play our way, we can win this!' Southgate

assured them before kick-off.

Back at the 1998 World Cup, Beckham had scored that fantastic free kick against Colombia. Kieran remembered watching it on TV with his dad. Twenty years on, could he copy his childhood hero?

Hopefully!

Kieran was a man on a mission. He burst down the right wing and delivered the cross, but Harry Kane's header landed on top of the net.

'Great ball, Tripps!' he called out with a big thumbs-up. 'Keep them coming!'

Early in the second half, Kieran aimed for Harry again from a corner. The England captain ran towards the ball but he was being fouled. Penalty!

Harry wasn't going to miss from the spot. 1–0! As long as they defended well, England were heading into the World Cup quarter-finals.

'Keep your concentration!' Southgate urged.

But right at the end, Colombia's centre-back Yerry Mina won a header in the penalty area. Kieran was there on the goal line but he couldn't keep it out. 1–1!

'No, no, NO!' he screamed, staring down at his feet.

They couldn't give up now. England battled on through extra time to penalties. Uh-oh! They had lost so many shoot-outs in the past, but this time the team was well-prepared. They had practised for this and Southgate knew his top five takers:

Harry Kane... scored!

Marcus Rashford... scored!

Jordan Henderson... missed!

Oh no, were they going to lose on penalties yet again? Colombia missed their third spot-kick, which meant England had the chance to equalise. Kieran walked slowly forward, from the halfway line to the spot.

'Don't rush. Take your time!' his manager had told him.

Kieran didn't get to take penalties for Burnley or Tottenham but he used to take lots when he was younger and he never missed. If he could do it in the FA Youth Cup, then he could surely do it in the World Cup too.

With a deep breath, he ran forward and… scored!
It was a perfect penalty, right in the top corner. The
Colombian keeper had no chance. Kieran calmly
turned to his teammates on the halfway line and
pumped his fist.

'Nice one, Tripps!' Jesse yelled out.

Kieran's spot-kick had given his team the advantage.
Jordan Pickford saved the next Colombian penalty and
then Eric scored. It was over – England had won their
first-ever World Cup shoot-out!

'We did it!' Kieran roared loud and proud as his
country celebrated a famous victory.

'It's coming home, it's coming home,
It's coming, FOOTBALL'S COMING HOME!'

What a wonderful first World Cup it was turning out
to be! In the space of two weeks, Kieran had gone
from unsung wing-back to 'The Bury Beckham'. In
the stadium in Moscow, Charlotte lifted up their
young son, Jacob, so that he could get a better view
of the action.

'Your daddy's a national hero now!'

Could England now go all the way and lift the trophy? Why not? With Kieran crossing the ball to Harry, they could beat anyone. They had a strong team spirit and 53 million people cheering them on.

With a 2–0 win over Sweden, the Three Lions were into the semi-finals. One more win, and Kieran would be playing in a World Cup final.

The last team standing in their way was Croatia. They had top-quality players like Luka Modrić and Mario Mandžukić, but if England could get off to another good start...

When Dele won an early free kick, Kieran got ready to shoot. 'I've got this, Youngie!' he told Ashley confidently. Then he ran up and curled the ball over the wall and into the top corner.

Goooooooooooooooooooooaaaaaaaaaaaaaaaallllllllllll llllllllllllll!!!!!!!!!!!!!!!!!!

What a start, and what a way to score your first-ever England goal! Kieran felt on top of the world as he slid across the grass on his knees.

That fantastic feeling lasted all the way until the

sixty-eighth minute. But after Croatia equalised, England's exhausted players were fighting a losing battle.

'Keep going!' Southgate shouted from the sidelines.

His team struggled on but eventually in extra-time, Mandžukić scored the winning goal for Croatia. England were left devastated and defeated. They had got so close to the World Cup final.

Unfortunately, Kieran couldn't carry on. He limped off the pitch with tears in his eyes, as the fans clapped and cheered. It wasn't how he wanted to end his life-changing tournament. But even so, he had arrived in Russia as an underrated right-back, and was now leaving as a national hero – just like all of the England players.

'Last night hurt and will for a while but we must take positives from the last few weeks and look forward to the future,' he posted on Twitter. 'It's been a journey that we can all be proud of.'

What a journey it had been for Kieran. Like the England team in Russia, he had overcome so many obstacles. From his back garden in Bury, he had battled through rejection at Manchester City and relegation at Burnley to make it all the way to the top. He was now first-choice at Tottenham and only the third England player ever to score in a World Cup semi-final. Even his hero Becks couldn't compete with that.

Turn the page for a sneak preview of another brilliant football story by Matt and Tom Oldfield. . .

PICKFORD

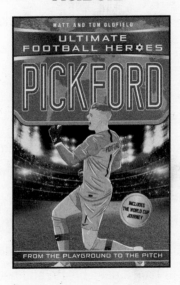

CHAPTER 1

ENGLAND'S PENALTY HERO

Otkritie Arena, Moscow, 3 July 2018

The tired England team assembled on the pitch. After 120 nail-biting minutes, only a penalty shoot-out stood between them and the World Cup quarter-finals. They needed a hero. Could it be their young keeper, playing in only his seventh international match? Jordan took a deep breath and believed.

Colombia's late equaliser had been a crushing blow. After making a super save to deny Mateus Uribe, Jordan just couldn't keep out Yerry Mina's powerful header.

'Now we'll just have to do it the hard way,' Jordan said to himself.

Still, Gareth Southgate looked like the calmest person in the stadium. 'Okay lads, we knew penalties were part of the deal in the knockout rounds,' he said. 'We're ready for this.'

Jordan nodded. They had spent hours practising on the training ground to make sure that they were all as comfortable as possible if it came to this.

He watched Gareth walk from player to player, checking on injuries and last-minute confidence levels.

'All good?' he asked Marcus and Kieran.

Both looked straight at their manager and nodded. No hesitation. While the physios worked quickly to heal players' tired legs, Gareth wrote down five names on a sheet of paper for the referee:

Harry Kane, Marcus Rashford, Jordan Henderson (or Hendo, as everyone called him), Kieran Trippier, Eric Dier.

'Remember everything we've talked about,' Harry shouted over the noise from the crowd. 'Pick your spot and be decisive. Don't feel rushed, and just ignore their keeper.'

'Come on, boys!' Jordan yelled, jumping up and down to release some of the nervous energy.

Jordan had his own plan to follow. After watching hundreds of clips of penalties on his laptop, he had sat down with England's other goalkeepers, Jack Butland and Nick Pope, to decide on the team tactics. Which way should he dive for each of Colombia's takers? He was leaving nothing to chance.

'Here you go,' Jack said, handing him a water bottle, which had notes written on it. 'Good luck!'

'Thanks, mate!' Jordan replied.

He gripped the bottle tightly as he read the words. He felt ready for the biggest moment of his life.

Harry was back from the coin toss. 'We're going second, lads,' he said.

Gareth had a few final words: 'I'm so proud of all of you. So are all the fans. This is just one more test laid out in front of us. Now go and be heroes!' The players all clapped and cheered.

As they walked over to the halfway line, Gareth put his arm around Jordan. 'There isn't any other shot-stopper in the world I'd want protecting our net tonight. Just trust your instincts.'

Jordan felt ten feet tall. He didn't know what to say so he just high-fived Gareth and then jogged over to the far end of the pitch. He was in his zone now, but he took a minute to glance at the England flags behind the goal. Even from a distance, he could see the passion. There was fear too. Penalties had not been kind to England in the past. In fact, they had never won a World Cup shoot-out. Ever!

'You can do this, Jordan!' the supporters shouted. He winked back at them. Yes, he could!

As he walked over to the goal, Jordan tucked his bottle into a red towel so that the Colombia keeper wouldn't spot England's secret plan. What if David Ospina asked to have a sip of water? That would be a disaster!

Luckily, he didn't. Jordan took one last look at his bottle and then stepped onto his line. Radamel Falcao was up first. Jordan waited as long as he could before diving to his right, but Falcao placed it perfectly down the middle. 1–0!

Jordan dragged himself up, shaking his head. 'Forget it and move on,' he told himself. There would be other chances to save the day.

He had a more important job to do first. He grabbed the ball and carried it over to Harry. This was part of Gareth's plan. It gave the Colombian keeper one fewer reason to approach the England penalty takers to put them off.

'You've got this, big man,' he said, patting Harry on the shoulder.

Harry smashed his penalty into the bottom corner. Unstoppable – 1–1!

Jordan guessed the right way on Colombia's second penalty, but Juan Cuadrado picked out the top corner. 2–1!

When Marcus' perfect strike made it 2–2, the pressure went up another level. On his way back to the halfway line, Marcus ran over to Jordan to bump fists. 'We believe in you, man,' he said, pointing at his goalkeeper as he walked away. 'A big save is coming. I know it!'

Colombia made no mistake with their third

penalty either. Jordan tried not to panic. He
was getting a good spring off his line, but the
Colombians had not given him a sniff so far. Still,
he could see that they had put all their best
penalty takers first.

Seconds later, his heart sank. Hendo hit his penalty
well but the Colombian keeper guessed right and
pushed it out… *Saved!*

Now Jordan really had to step up, or England's
World Cup dream would be over.

He went through the same routine again:
bouncing on his line, making himself big, timing his
dive. He correctly guessed left for the fourth penalty
but saw the ball fly high above his dive. He turned to
see it crash off the bar and bounce safely away from
the goal… *Miss!*

'Yeeeeeeees!' he screamed, looking over at his
teammates. The England fans roared. They were
back in it.

Kieran kept his nerve with a beautiful penalty.
3–3! It was basically sudden death now.

Jordan tried to stay calm but his heart was racing

after the Colombia miss. He felt even more confident now.

'One stop, one stop,' he mumbled under his breath. That might be all it took to become England's penalty hero.

As Carlos Bacca stepped up for Colombia's fifth penalty, the crowd fell silent. Jordan watched Bacca run up and then he sprung to his right. His eyes lit up as the ball curled towards him. But he was diving too far. Almost in slow motion, he threw up his left hand desperately. The ball was well hit but his hand stayed strong, clawing the penalty away... *Saved!*

'Come ooooooooooooooon!'

Jordan leapt to his feet and punched the air again and again, screaming as loud as he could. The plan had worked. He had just saved a penalty in a World Cup shoot-out! Now England were one kick away from the quarter-finals.

He looked towards the halfway line and saw the huge smiles on his teammates' faces. They stood with their arms linked, ready to sprint forward if everything went to plan.

Jordan felt like he was shaking as he passed the ball to Eric, but he tried not to show it. 'Just take your time,' he said.

Eric did just that. He paced out his run-up, waited for the whistle and then swept the ball low into the bottom corner. England had done it!

The next few minutes were a blur. Jordan leapt in the air and turned to run towards the halfway line. But he was too late. His teammates were already racing over to *him*, England's penalty hero. Harry and Kieran jumped on his back. Then John Stones and Marcus, followed by the whole team.

'You legend!' Kieran screamed.

'I owe you big time!' Hendo called, ruffling Jordan's hair.

Jordan savoured every second with his teammates, who had become his friends over the past few weeks. They hugged and laughed as it all began to sink in. Happiness, relief and exhaustion – all the emotions mixed together.

Gareth joined in the celebrations, hugging every player and saving the biggest one for Jordan. 'I told

you!' he laughed, jabbing Jordan playfully in the ribs.
'I knew you'd do something special tonight.'

Then they ran over to the fans – or limped over,
in most cases. Tomorrow, they would be sore, but
tonight they were buzzing too much to feel it. The
England players had given their nation something to
really cheer about.

'They've had to wait a long time for this!' Jordan
shouted to Harry.

'Get right at the front, Jordan. You're the hero
tonight!' Harry nudged him forward, so that the fans
could sing his name:

Rhythm is a dancer,
Pickford is the answer,
Saving shots from everywhere!

Jordan couldn't believe what he was hearing. What
a feeling! The players took photo after photo before
finally reaching the section where their families
stood waiting. He spotted his girlfriend, Megan, in
the crowd and blew her a kiss. It meant so much

that she was in the stadium to see it all. He could only imagine the celebrations back in England. He remembered that a lot of his friends had been planning to watch the game together, and that made him even prouder.

Jordan could feel happy tears building up and the hairs on the back of his neck stood on end. He just didn't want the night to end. The England fans were in no hurry to go home either.

When the players finally got back to the dressing room, Gareth called for quiet.

'Lads, take a moment to think about what you've just achieved. I could not be prouder of every single one of you. That took guts. We had to fight for everything. They kicked us all over the pitch, but we kept our cool and never gave up.

'And those were terrific penalties, including yours Hendo. I will remember this moment for a very long time. Let's enjoy it tonight. You deserve that. But we've got more memories to make, starting with either Sweden or Switzerland on Saturday. This is just the beginning for this team!'

The players did not have the energy to stand up, but they clapped and cheered. Jordan was so happy for his manager, who had famously dealt with penalty shoot-out heartbreak as an England player, back at Euro 96.

There was only one song for the players to sing. Eric turned on the music and cranked up the volume:

'It's coming home, it's coming home,
It's coming, FOOTBALL'S COMING HOME!'

'If you'd told me five years ago that I'd be saving a penalty at the 2018 World Cup, I'd have laughed in your face,' Jordan told Kieran, giggling. 'I was playing in League Two! It's been such a crazy journey, but it's all worth it now. It doesn't get any better than this!'

As he took off his socks and grabbed a towel, Jordan thought about his journey again – the highs, the lows, the doubts. He was still only twenty-four, but it had been quite a ride so far!

KIERAN TRIPPIER HONOURS

Manchester City Youth
🏆 FA Youth Cup: 2007–08

Burnley
🏆 Football League Championship runner-up:
2013–14

Individual
🏆 Barnsley Young Player of the Year: 2010–11
🏆 Burnley Player of the Year: 2011–12
🏆 PFA Championship Team of the Year: 2012–13,
2013–14

TRIPPIER

2 & 12

THE FACTS

NAME: KIERAN JOHN TRIPPIER

DATE OF BIRTH: 19 September 1990

AGE: 24

PLACE OF BIRTH: Bury

NATIONALITY: English

BEST FRIEND: Ben Mee

CURRENT CLUB: Tottenham

POSITION: RB/RWB

THE STATS

Height (cm):	**178**
Club appearances:	**309**
Club goals:	**11**
Club trophies:	**0**
International appearances:	**13**
International goals:	**1**
International trophies:	**0**
Ballon d'Ors:	**0**

★ ★ ★ **HERO RATING: 82** ★ ★ ★

GREATEST MOMENTS

Type and search the web links to see the magic for yourself!

16 APRIL 2008,
MANCHESTER CITY 3-1 CHELSEA

https://www.youtube.com/watch?v=JNjcoTbGvBs

In the 2008 FA Youth Cup final, it was City's local lads against Chelsea's international squad of superstars. Even without Daniel Sturridge, City still managed to win! Vladimír Weiss was their free-kick king this time, but Kieran was as solid as ever at right-back. Sadly, he got injured in the last few minutes and missed the trophy celebrations.

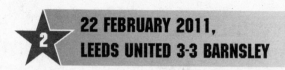

22 FEBRUARY 2011,
LEEDS UNITED 3-3 BARNSLEY

https://www.youtube.com/watch?v=1fO8Zapkmds

During his loan spell at Barnsley, Kieran quickly became the team's set-piece specialist. This free-kick against Leeds wasn't one of his best, but it was his first goal for the club and an important one too. Barnsley were losing the big Yorkshire Derby until Kieran rescued them with his remarkable right foot.

21 APRIL 2014,
BURNLEY 2-0 WIGAN ATHLETIC

https://www.youtube.com/watch?v=lEPUgaVslHg

This was the day when Kieran and Burnley achieved their dream of returning to the Premier League. At the final whistle, the jubilant fans stormed the pitch to celebrate with the players. Two years after leaving Manchester City behind, Kieran was back in the big-time with Burnley.

1 NOVEMBER 2017, TOTTENHAM 3-1 REAL MADRID

https://www.youtube.com/watch?v=VBVAGbm1wBs
Football games don't get much bigger than this – Real
Madrid in the Champions League! But Kieran was
totally fearless and gave one of the best performances
of his life. Not only did he keep Cristiano Ronaldo and
Marcelo quiet, but he also set up Spurs' first goal for
Dele Alli with an incredible cross. At Wembley, Kieran
proved that he was ready to play at the highest level.

11 JULY 2018, CROATIA 2-1 ENGLAND

https://www.youtube.com/watch?v=RbmaLT320hw
The 2018 World Cup semi-final ended in
disappointment for England, but it was still an amazing
moment when he scored his first-ever international
goal with a fantastic free-kick that flew straight into the
top corner. What a perfect way for 'The Bury Beckham'
to complete his wonderful World Cup!

PLAY LIKE YOUR HEROES

'CROSS IT LIKE KIERAN'

SEE IT HERE **You Tube**

https://www.youtube.com/watch?v=QFFseyCoiCE

STEP 1: Keep making runs down the right wing until you receive that perfect pass…

Step 2: Look up. If your attackers are already on the move, then cross the ball early, maybe even first-time if you can.

Step 3: If they're not, take a touch to control the pass and wait until the time is right.

Step 4: BANG! Apply the right power to your cross. Who's your target, and how far away are they?

Step 5: If you're not aiming for a particular player, you want the ball to drop down in the danger zone between the penalty spot and the six-yard line.

Step 6: Put lots of curl on your cross, so that it's even more difficult for the defenders to deal with.

Step 7: GOAL! Make sure that you run over and celebrate. If it wasn't for your killer cross, there would be no goal!

TEST YOUR KNOWLEDGE

1. Who were Kieran's two big Manchester United heroes?

2. How did Kieran annoy the groundsman at the Manchester City academy?

3. Which club did Kieran's brother, Kelvin, play for?

4. Which club did Kieran's Manchester City team beat in the 2008 FA Youth Cup final?

5. Which country did Kieran's England Under-19s lose to in the 2009 European Championship final?

6. Which club was Kieran playing for when he got his first England Under-21 call-up?

7. Which Burnley manager led them to Premier League promotion in 2014?

8. How many games did Kieran miss during the 2014–15 Premier League season?

9. How much money did Tottenham pay to sign Kieran from Burnley?

10. Who was Kieran's big right-back rival for Tottenham and England?

11. How many goals did Kieran score at the 2018 World Cup?

Answers below. . . No cheating!

1. *David Beckham and Gary Neville* 2. *By kicking balls at him and then hiding!* 3. *Oldham Athletic* 4. *Chelsea* 5. *Ukraine* 6. *Barnsley* 7. *Sean Dyche* 8. *Zero!* 9. *£3.5million* 10. *Kyle Walker* 11. *Trick question! The answer is two, if you include his penalty in the shoot-out against Colombia.*

ACKNOWLEDGEMENTS

First of all, I'd like to thank John Blake Publishing –
and particularly my editor James Hodgkinson – for
giving me the opportunity to work on these books
and for supporting me throughout. Writing stories for
the next generation of football fans is both an honour
and a pleasure.

I wouldn't be doing this if it wasn't for my brother,
Tom. I owe him so much and I'm very grateful for
his belief in me as an author. I feel like Robin setting
out on a solo career after a great partnership with
Batman. I hope I do him (Tom, not Batman) justice
with these new books.

Next up, I want to thank my friends for keeping

me sane during long hours in front of the laptop. Pang, Will, Mills, Doug, John, Charlie – the laughs and the cups of coffee are always appreciated.

I've already thanked my brother but I'm also very grateful to the rest of my family, especially Melissa, Noah and of course Mum and Dad. To my parents, I owe my biggest passions: football and books. They're a real inspiration for everything I do.

Finally, I couldn't have done this without Iona's encouragement and understanding during long, work-filled weekends. Much love to you.

The 2018 World Cup saw England's young lions produce their best performance for a generation, and storm to the semi-finals of the World Cup.

Complete your collection with these international edition Ultimate Football Heroes.

AVAILABLE NOW

HAVE YOU GOT THEM ALL?

FOOTBALL HEROES